The Doctrine of
Proprietary Estoppel

AUSTRALIA
LBC Information Services
Sydney

CANADA and USA
Carswell
Toronto, Ontario

NEW ZEALAND
Brooker's
Auckland

SINGAPORE and MALAYSIA
Thomson Information (S.E. Asia)
Singapore

The Doctrine of
Proprietary Estoppel

by

Mark Pawlowski

LL.B.(Hons), B.C.L.(Oxon),
A.C.I.Arb.
of the Middle Temple, Barrister
and Reader in Property Law, University of
Greenwich

London
Sweet & Maxwell
1996

Published in 1996 by Sweet & Maxwell Ltd
100 Avenue Road, London, NW3 3PF
Typeset by Tradespools Ltd, Frome
Printed and bound in Great Britain by Hartnolls Ltd, Bodmin

A catalogue record for this book is available from the British
Library.

ISBN 0 421 56630 2

For my step-son, John

PREFACE

The aim of this book is to provide the reader with a comprehensive survey of the law relating to the doctrine of proprietary estoppel. It is hoped that it will be a useful source of reference not only for practitioners and academics, but also students of equity and land law.

It was Mr Andrew Park Q.C., (sitting as a deputy judge of the High Court) in *Durant v. Heritage* [1994] EGCS 134, who opined that "proprietary estoppel is not an easy area of the law". Apart from the growing number of cases in this area (see, for example, *Matharu v. Matharu* (1994) 68 P. & C.R. 93, C.A.; *Wayling v. Jones* (1995) 69 P. & C.R. 170, C.A. and *Lloyds Bank plc. v. Carrick*, New L.J., March 22, 1996, C.A. (see Addendum)), it is difficult to point to one all-embracing formula which sets out the various constituent elements of the doctrine in clear and precise terms. Many of the cases are not easy to reconcile, adopting different criteria to suit the particular facts of the case. A good example is *Coombes v. Smith* [1986] 1 W.L.R. 808, where Mr Jonathan Parker Q.C. (sitting as a deputy judge of the High Court) rigidly applied the five *probanda* propounded by Fry J. in *Willmott v. Barber* (1880) 15 Ch. D. 96 so as to disentitle the female cohabitee from acquiring any interest in her male partner's house. By contrast, in *Greasley v. Cooke* [1980] 1 W.L.R. 1306, considered by many to be the high-water mark of the doctrine, the Court of Appeal awarded the female claimant an occupational licence in the property for the rest of her life on the basis that, in the circumstances, it would be "unjust and inequitable" for her male partner to resile from his promises.

Despite the modern tendency to seek to rationalise the cases under one unified doctrine of unconscionability, it is evident that the courts require the claimant to prove three essential elements to found a cause of action under the doctrine. These three elements, assurance, reliance and detriment, are discussed sequentially in Chapters 2, 3 and 4 of the book. Once an "equity" has been established, the court must determine its extent and how best to satisfy it in the circumstances of the given case. The full range of remedies available to the court and the principles on which the court exercises its discretion are discussed in Chapter 5.

In Chapter 6, three broad categories of proprietary estoppel are examined in some detail to show that each has a different rationale and set of criteria as their foundation. It is suggested that these categories, (involving imperfect gifts, common expectation and unilateral mistake) remain valid, notwithstanding the modern trend towards applying an underlying concept of unconscionability as the basis for proprietary estoppel claims.

There has been much academic debate as to whether the inchoate equity arising from proprietary estoppel can bind third parties. There is also some controversy as to the effect of the equity on third parties once it has crystallised into a concrete judicial remedy. These questions are discussed in Chapter 7.

It is, perhaps, true to say that the doctrine has played its most important role in the context of resolving property disputes between cohabitees. With the apparent limitations placed on the development of the constructive trust in this field by the House of Lords' decision in *Lloyds Bank plc v. Rosset* [1991] 1 A.C. 107, H.L., several commentators have turned to the doctrine of proprietary estoppel as providing a broader-based foundation for the adjustment of property rights between unmarried couples, in the absence of specific legislation in this country giving the courts power to declare interests in property after an unmarried union has broken down. The development of the estoppel doctrine along the lines of the New Zealand experience provides an interesting comparison with the current English position. The subject of estoppel and cohabitees is discused in Chapter 8.

The interesting question as to whether an estoppel-based right in property can give rise to a possessory title under the Limitation Act 1980 is considered briefly in Chapter 9. Finally, the current judicial trend towards recognising the notion of unconscionability as an overarching foundation for the application of the proprietary estoppel doctrine is reviewed in Chapter 10.

Unfortunately, much of the recent caselaw on proprietary estoppel remains unreported. One of the aims of this book has been to bring these cases to light in either the main text or accompanying footnotes. Reference is also made, where appropriate, to Commonwealth authorities to highlight points of principle. In addition, a small selection of forms are set out in the Appendix as a guide to the drafting of pleadings.

Without doubt, the doctrine of proprietary estoppel has an important role to play in modern land/equity law. It can provide a remedy where resulting and constructive trust principles do not. It may, according to some of the authorities, enable an inchoate right to be binding on a third party. It may provide a replacement for the doctrine of part performance which was abolished, in respect of contracts entered into after September 27, 1989, by the Law of Property (Miscellaneous Provisions) Act 1989. It may permit the grant of informal rights in property and complete an imperfect gift. It may render voluntary services which, generally speaking, are not compensatable, the subject of a successful claim for reimbursement or the acquisition of a proprietary interest in the property improved. How far the doctrine will be extended in future years remains a fascinating question.

I am again very much indebted to Liz Anker of the University of Warwick for her kind permission to use the facilities of the University library, where most of the material for this book was researched. Without her kind assistance, this book would probably not have been written! I would also like to thank Paul Vaughan, Head of the Law School, University of Greenwich, for his kind indulgence in allowing me time "out of school" to complete this project. My thanks also to Sweet & Maxwell for their diligent efforts in bringing this work to print.

Finally, I owe a very special debt to my wife, Lidia, who has, once again, had to suffer my long absences from home "to get that damned thing done"!

I have endeavoured to state the law accurately as at July 1, 1996.

July 1996   Mark Pawlowski
                                                    School of Law
                                          University of Greenwich

ADDENDUM

Lloyds Bank plc v. Carrick, New L.J., March 22, 1996, C.A.

In this case, a widow void her house and gave the proceeds of sale (£19,000) to her brother-in-law on the basis of an oral agreement that it would form the purchase price for a maisonette where she would live, the lease of which was owned by him. He subsequently charged the lease as security for a loan in favour of the plaintiff bank. Title to the maisonette was unregistered and the lease remained in the brother-in-law's name. The Court of Appeal held that the widow had no interest valid against the bank sufficient to raise a defence against its claim for possession when the brother-in-law defaulted on the charge.

The bank's argument was that the widow's interest in the maisonette was an estate contract within the Land Charges Act 1972, which was void for want of registration against the bank, as a purchaser for money or money's worth. As against this, it was argued on behalf of the widow that she had an interest separate and distinct from that which arose under the unregistered estate contract by virtue of (1) a bare trust; (2) a constructive trust; and (3) proprietary estoppel.

On the first point, Morritt L.J., who gave the leading judgment of the Court[1], concluded that, whilst the brother-in-law had no beneficial interest in the maisonette and could properly be described as a bare trustee, nevertheless, the source of the trust was the contract which, by virtue of section 4 (6) of the Land Charges Act 1972, was void against the bank as a purchaser for money or money's worth, in the absence of registration prior to completion.

The second contention (based on constructive trust principles) was that the widow was entitled to the whole beneficial interest in the property and that that interest was not registrable so that the bank, having had constructive notice of it, took subject to it. This too was rejected by Morritt L.J. who held that, where there was a specifically enforceable contract, the court was not entitled to superimpose a further constructive trust on the vendor other than that which already existed in consequence of the contractual relationship.

The third contention was based on proprietary estoppel. It was submitted that such an estoppel arose in the widow's favour because she had paid the purchase price and carried out improvements[2] to the maisonette in the belief common to both her and her brother-in-law (and to that extent encouraged by him) that she either did own it or would own it free of all incumbrances. In this connection,

---

[1] Sir Ralph Gibson and Beldam L.J. agreed.
[2] She had an extension built on to the property at a cost of about £5,000.

reliance was placed on *Inwards v. Baker*[3] and *E.R. Ives Investments Ltd v. High*[4] as establishing that such an estoppel gives rise to an interest in land capable of binding a successor in title with notice. It was submitted by the bank *inter alia* that the facts did not warrant such an estoppel as they did not cover all the elements referred to as *probanda* in Fry J.'s judgment in *Willmott v. Barber*.[5] On this point, Morritt L.J., agreeing with the observations made by Oliver J. in *Taylor Fashions Ltd v. Liverpool Victoria Trustees Co Ltd*,[6] concluded that it was not now necessary to establish all the five *probanda* referred to by Fry J. in the *Willmott* case to establish a proprietary estoppel. His Lordship also observed that it was a matter of "some doubt" whether the principles of proprietary estoppel differed from those of that species of constructive trust which was referred to by Lord Bridge in *Lloyds Bank plc v. Rosset*.[7]

In Morritt L.J.'s view, however, the widow's claim based on proprietary estoppel also failed on a number of grounds. First, as in the case of a constructive trust, there was no room for the application of proprietary estoppel when, at the time of the relevant expenditure, there was already a trust arising in consequence of an enforceable contract to the same effect as the interest sought pursuant to the estoppel. At the time that she paid the purchase price and committed herself to expenditure on improvements to the maisonette, she believed (rightly) that she was spending the money in respect of her *own* property albeit under an uncompleted contract. In this respect, the case was no different from that in *Western Fish Products Ltd v. Penwith District Council*,[8] where it was held by the Court of Appeal that the doctrine could not be applied to cases in which there was no belief or expectation of having or aquiring an interest in *someone else's* land. Secondly, this was not a case in which the widow's expectations had been defeated by the brother-in-law seeking to resile from the position he had encouraged her to expect. On the contrary, the widow's expectations had been defeated because the contract was not registered at any time before the charge was granted to the bank. Third, it was common ground that the right arising from a proprietary estoppel cannot exceed that which the party sought to be estopped encouraged the other to believe that she had or would aquire.[9] In the instant case, in so far as the brother-in-law encouraged the widow to believe that she was (or would become) the beneficial owner of the maisonette, there was no further right to be obtained for she was and, subject to the legal charge, still would retain a beneficial interest in the property. It could not be unconscionable for the bank to rely on the non-registration of the contract in these circumstances. It was plainly unsound to confer on the widow indirectly and by means of a proprietary estoppel binding on the bank that which the statute prevented her from obtaining directly by the contract it had declared to be void.

In the circumstances, it was unnecessary for the court to consider the bank's

---

[3] [1965] 2 Q.B. 29, C.A.
[4] [1967] 2 Q.B. 379, C.A.
[5] (1880) 15 Ch. D. 96 at 105-106.
[6] [1982] Q.B. 133.
[7] [1991] 1 A.C. 107, H.L. It is significant that Lord Bridge treated the two labels as interchangeable. See also *Austin v. Keele* [1987] A.L.J.R. 605, P.C. See, Ch. 1, pp. 10–16.
[8] [1981] 2 All E.R. 204, C.A. See, Ch. 1, pp. 18-19.
[9] See Ch. 5, pp. 81–82.

further submission to the effect that a proprietary estoppel could not give rise to an interest in land capable of binding successors in title.[10] Accordingly, this "interesting argument" was left open "to await another day", although, according to Morritt L.J., it was "hard to see how in this court it can surmount the hurdle constituted by the decision of this court in *E.R. Ives Investments Ltd v. High*".[11]

Price v. Hartwell, [1996] EGCS, CA.

The defendant was the daughter of the plaintiff and her husband. In 1971, they moved to a house purchased in the sole name of the defendant. The plaintiff's husband paid the deposit and the defendant took out a mortgage for the balance. In 1972, they moved to a house purchased in the names of the defendant and her parents using the net proceeds of sale of their former house and a mortgage taken out for the balance.

Between 1972 and 1975, the defendant was the only one in regular employment and paid all effective outgoings including mortgage repayments and rates.

In 1975, they moved to 798, Walsall Road, Birmingham, purchased in their joint names for £8,975, of which £3,475 was provided out of the net proceeds of sale of their home and the balance by mortgage. The defendant paid the mortgage instalments, rates, water rates, ground rent and other outgoings, except for food. In 1981, the defendant married and left her parents' home to live in rented accommodation. The defendant continued to pay the mortgage on Walsall Road so that her parents would have a roof over their heads.

In 1983, the plaintiff's husband was injured and asked the defendant and her husband to move into Walsall Road on the basis that the house would be theirs after the deaths of himself and the plaintiff. The defendant and her husband paid one-third of the mortgage and the parents paid two-thirds. In addition, the defendant and her husband paid the cost of repaying moneys raised to build a garage. In 1989, the plaintiff's husband died.

Following a dispute between the parties, the plaintiff gave notice severing the joint tenancy of the property. The plaintiff then left the property and lived elsewhere but continued to pay two-thirds of the mortgage repayments.

The plaintiff later brought proceedings for an order for sale of the property and division of the net proceeds of sale. The trial judge held that the defendant was permitted to reside in the property so long as she made the mortgage repayments and ordered her to refund to the plaintiff the amount of the mortgage repayments paid by the latter since the notice of severance of the joint tenancy.

The Court of Appeal, agreeing with the trial judge, held that all the elements of proprietary estoppel had been established to make good the expectation of the defendant which the plaintiff had encouraged. The estoppel which bound the plaintiff was based on statements made to the defendant that the house would be hers on the death of her parents. The trial judge was also correct to order reimbursement of all payments made by the plaintiff. The court had a wide discretion to do what was best in the interests of the parties generally.

---

[10] See further on this point, Ch. 7, pp. 132–141.
[11] [1967] 2 Q.B. 379, C.A. See further, Ch. 7, particularly pp. 132–135.

CONTENTS

TABLE OF CASES

TABLE OF STATUTES

1. NATURE OF THE DOCTRINE

(A) Introduction

The essence of proprietary estoppel[1] is that if a legal owner of land has so conducted himself, either by encouragement or representations, that the claimant believes that he has or will acquire some right or interest in the land and has so acted to his detriment on that basis, it would be unconscionable for the legal owner to assert his strict legal rights.[2] The basic requirements of the doctrine are that the legal owner makes a representation to the claimant that the latter either has or will be granted an interest in the land, and the claimant relies on this representation by acting to his detriment or otherwise by changing his position. In *Re Basham (dec'd)*, Mr Edward Nugee Q.C. (sitting as a High Court judge) set out the principle of proprietary estoppel, in its broadest form, in the following terms:

> "Where one person, A, has acted to his detriment on the faith of a belief, which was known to and encouraged by another person, B, that he either has or is going to be given a right in or over B's property, B cannot insist on his strict legal rights if to do so would be inconsistent with A's belief".

The above-cited passage was accepted recently by the Court of Appeal in *Wayling v. Jones*[3] as an accurate statement of the general principle, the basis of which is to prevent a legal owner from insisting on his strict legal rights "when it would be inequitable for him to do so having regard to the dealings which have taken place between the parties".[4] The foundation of the doctrine is "the interposition of equity" which comes in to "mitigate the rigours of strict law".[5] In this respect, it is similar to the parallel doctrine of promissory estoppel, since the court's jurisdiction to grant relief is based on the inequity that would result

---

[1] See generally, Spencer Bower & Turner, *The Law Relating to Estoppel by Representation*, (3rd ed., 1977), Chap. 12 and P.D. Finn, Chap. 4, "Equitable Estoppel", in P.D. Finn, *Essays in Equity*, (Sydney, 1985).
[2] Snell, *Principles of Equity*, (29th ed.) at pp. 573–574. See also, *Bennett v. Bennett*, May 18, 1990, C.A., unreported, available on Lexis, where this formulation was adopted by Slade L.J.
[3] (1995) 69 P. & C.R. 170, 172, C.A.
[4] *Crabb v. Arun District Council* [1976] Ch. 179 at 188, C.A., *per* Lord Denning M.R. See also, *Hughes v. Metropolitan Railway Co.* (1877) 2 App. Cas. 439 at 448, P.C., *per* Lord Cairns L.C.
[5] *ibid.*, 187, *per* Lord Denning M.R.

from the strict assertion of legal rights.[6] Grey[7] has identified this as a "principle of inhibition", although recognising also that "the doctrine has the indirect effect of creating rights on behalf of the claimant who successfully asserts an 'equity' founded upon estoppel".[8]

Thus, proprietary estoppel is viewed both as a method of preventing unconscientious dealing in relation to land and as a means of creating informal proprietary interests in land whenever a party has acted to his detriment in reliance upon an oral assurance that he has such an interest. As such, the doctrine forms an exception to the principle that equity will not perfect an imperfect gift. Estoppel is used to get round this difficulty—an oral grant of an interest in land is invalid but, when coupled with an assurance and detrimental reliance, the imperfect gift becomes duly completed. The origins of the doctrine date back to the seventeenth century, although the early cases do not refer to it as a form of "estoppel" but rather as "raising an equity".[9] The modern law is often said to stem from the House of Lords' decision in *Ramsden v. Dyson*,[10] which is considered in some detail in Chapter 6. The growing judicial trend, however, is the recognition that the governing principle underlying proprietary estoppel cases is the notion of unconscionability,[11] although it is accepted that the precise circumstances in which this "new equity" may arise is still largely "ill-defined"[12] and not "fully explored".[13]

(B) Essential Elements

It is difficult to point to one all-embracing judicial formula which sets out the various constituent elements of the doctrine in clear and precise terms. Although the principle of proprietary estoppel has been propounded on numerous occasions in the courts, judicial statements tend to vary in detail as to the precise basis and scope of the doctrine. This inconsistency was alluded to by Ungoed-Thomas J. in *Ward v. Kirkland*[14] who said[15]:

> "The equity has been differently expressed from time to time. In *Dillwyn v. Llewelyn*, it was expressed as operating through providing valuable consideration which in the circumstances established a contract. In

---

[6] See, *e.g. Layton v. Martin* [1986] 2 FLR 227, where Scott J. said that "the proprietary estoppel line of cases are concerned with the question whether an owner of property can, by insisting on his strict legal rights therein, defeat an expectation of an interest in that property, it being an expectation which he has raised by his conduct and which has been relied on by the claimant": *ibid.* 238.

[7] Grey, *Elements of Land Law*, (2nd ed.).

[8] *ibid.* 313.

[9] *i.e.* "raising an issue whether equity ought to intervene in the application of the strict common law to avert a serious injustice to the applicant or to prevent an unconscionable act by the other party": *Stevens v. Stevens*, March 3, 1989, unreported, C.A., available on Lexis.

[10] (1866) L.R. 1 H.L. 129. For earlier cases, see Chap. 6, p. 116, n. 92.

[11] This aspect is explored fully in Chapter 10.

[12] *Walker v. Walker*, April 12, 1984, C.A., unreported, available on Lexis, *per* Browne-Wilkinson L.J.

[13] *Re Sharpe, (A Bankrupt)* [1980] 1 W.L.R. 219 at 223, *per* Browne-Wilkinson J., who went on to say that "it seems that such rights are found to exist simply on the ground that to hold otherwise would be a hardship to the plaintiff": *ibid.* 223.

[14] [1967] Ch. 194.

[15] *ibid.* 235.

Plimmer v. Wellington Corporation, it was expressed as making a revocable licence irrevocable. It has also been expressed from time to time as operating by a form of estoppel. The foundation of it, however, in all these instances, is the recognition by the court that it would be unconscionable in the circumstances for a legal owner fully to exercise his legal rights".

The courts invariably embark upon a two-stage process in determining whether a claimant is entitled to a remedy based on proprietary estoppel. In the first place, it is necessary for the claimant to establish an estoppel equity on the facts. Although the modern approach is to explain the doctrine of proprietary estoppel in terms of a general concept of "unconscionability",[16] the courts[17] require the claimant to prove three essential elements to found a cause of action on the grounds of this type of estoppel. The three essential ingredients are : (1) an assurance, (2) reliance, and (3) detriment or change of position. They are discussed fully in Chapters 2, 3, and 4, respectively. In essence, if a legal owner of land gives some *assurance* involving present or future rights in it, he will be estopped or prevented from going back on that assurance if the person to whom it has been given has *relied* on it to his *detriment*.

According to *Snell's Principles of Equity*,[18] there are four ingredients to establish a proprietary estoppel. First, the claimant must show that he has incurred expenditure or otherwise acted to his detriment (*i.e.* the element of detriment). Secondly, the expenditure or detriment must have taken place in the belief either that the claimant owned a sufficient interest in the property to justify the expenditure, or that he would obtain such an interest (*i.e.* mistaken belief). Thirdly, the claimant's belief must have been encouraged by the owner of the land or others acting on his behalf (*i.e.* the element of assurance). Fourthly, there should be no bar to the equity (*e.g.* misconduct or delay on the part of the claimant[19]). This particular formulation of the doctrine was applied by the Court of Appeal in *Brinnard v. Ewens*.[20] The element of mistaken belief or reliance on the representation made is considered in detail in Chapter 3.

Once an equity has been established, the second stage of the process is for the court to determine how best to *satisfy* that equity in the circumstances of the given case. The court has a very wide discretion in the exercise of its remedial powers and may select a form of relief from a broad range of remedies. At one extreme, it may simply deny the legal owner's claim to possession of the property without conferring on the estoppel claimant any proprietary interest in the subject land. At the other end of the scale, it may feel it appropriate to order the legal owner to convey the fee simple (with or without compensation) to the claimant in satisfaction of the latter's equity. The full range of remedies available to the court and the principles on which the court exercises its discretion are examined in Chapter 5.

---

[16] See Chap. 10.
[17] See, *e.g. Stevens v. Stevens*, March 3, 1989, C.A., unreported, available on Lexis, *per* Slade L.J.
[18] (29th ed.), at pp. 573 *et seq.*
[19] See further, Chap. 5, pp. 99–102.
[20] (1987) 19 H.L.R. 415 at 416, *per* Nourse L.J., discussed in Chap. 3, p. 52. See also, *Ezekiel v. Orakpo*, February 20, 1980, C.A., unreported, available on Lexis; *Denny v. Jensen* [1977] 1 N.Z.L.R. 635 at 638, Supreme Court of Dunedin, *per* White J.

(C) Categories of Proprietary Estoppel

Although, as mentioned earlier, the modern tendency is to seek to rationalise the estoppel cases under one unified doctrine of unconscionability,[21] it is evident that three broad categories emerge from the caselaw on proprietary estoppel, each having a different rationale and set of criteria as their foundation: (1) imperfect gift cases, (2) common expectation cases and (3) unilateral mistake cases. In the first category, the doctrine of proprietary estoppel may be invoked, in appropriate cases, to complete an imperfect gift. In this context, the device of estoppel is used as a mechanism by which equity sanctions the informal creation of proprietary rights in land. In all the cases in this category, it is the lack of legal formality that creates the problem and proprietary estoppel is used simply to make up for its absence. The emphasis is on the form of the donor's assurance—the court endeavours to award the claimant what was intended to be gifted to him. In the second category, referred to frequently as "estoppel by encouragement", emphasis is placed by the courts on the claimant's reliance on a *shared expectation* with the legal owner that he will acquire rights in the latter's property. Unlike the imperfect gift cases, the situation is not that A has attempted to make a gift of land to B (without complying with the requisite legal formalities), but rather that the parties have dealt with each other on a common expectation that B would acquire some interest in A's land. In these cases, the correct approach is to look at all the circumstances in each case in order to determine how best to satisfy the estoppel equity. In the third category of case, namely, unilateral mistake, often referred to as "estoppel by acquiescence", one party is mistaken as to the nature of his rights in the land. Here, equity intervenes so as to prevent the other party (the legal owner) from fraudulently taking advantage of the other party's error. In this category of case, however, the criteria for establishing the equity appear to be more strict, stemming from the formulation promulgated by Fry J. in *Willmott v. Barber*.[22]

These three orthodox categories of proprietary estoppel are discussed in Chapter 6.

(D) Comparison with Other Concepts

It is important to distinguish proprietary estoppel from other similar concepts.

(i) Promissory Estoppel

The question has often been raised judicially as to whether it is still useful or, indeed, correct, to divide possible forms of estoppel into distinct categories.

---

[21] See M. Lunney, [1992] Conv. 239. See also, Chap. 10.
[22] (1880) 15 Ch. D. 96 at 105–106, discussed in Chapter 6, pp. 117–118.

Thus, in *Crabb v. Arun District Council*,[23] Scarman L.J. said[24] that he did not find helpful the distinction between promissory[25] and proprietary estoppel.

One obvious distinction, however, between promissory estoppel (or estoppel by representation) and proprietary estoppel, which has been clearly established, is that a promissory estoppel cannot create any new cause of action where none existed before.[26] The point is considered further elsewhere.[27] There are other important distinctions. Historically, proprietary estoppel has its origins in the seventeenth century[28]—promissory estoppel is much younger.[29] The former is permanent in its effect whereas the latter may operate temporarily since the promisor may resile from his position by giving the promisee notice so that he has a reasonable opportunity of resuming his former position—only if this is not possible does the representation become final and irrevocable.[30] A proprietary estoppel may give rise to an award in land capable of binding third parties. Moreover, it can arise outside the scope of a contractual relationship.[31] In the Australian case of *Beaton v. McDivitt*,[32] Young J. observed[33]:

> "It is quite clear that it is an inadequate explanation of the line of cases which I have been discussing to say that unless one can find a contract express or implied, the principles known as proprietary estoppel cannot be applied: clearly the principle is wider than this. For instance, the principle

---

[23] [1976] Ch. 179, C.A.

[24] *ibid.* 193. He opined that "the distinction may indeed be valuable to those who have to teach or expound the law; but I do not think that, in solving the particular problem raised by a particular case, putting the law into categories is of the slightest assistance". See also the remarks of Robert Goff J. in *Amalgamated Investment & Property Co. Ltd v. Texas Commerce International Bank Ltd* [1982] Q.B. 84 at 103.

[25] The doctrine of promissory estoppel came into prominence with the decision of Denning J. in *Central London Property Trust Ltd v. High Trees House Ltd* [1947] K.B. 130. It has become firmly established in subsequent cases: See, *e.g. Combe v. Combe* [1951] 2 K.B. 215, C.A.; *Ajayi v. R.T. Briscoe (Nigeria) Ltd* [1964] 1 W.L.R. 1326, P.C.; *W.J. Alan & Co. Ltd v. El Nasr Export and Import Co.* [1972] 2 Q.B. 189, C.A. The doctrine emerged in *Hughes v. Metropolitan Railway Co.* (1877) 2 App. Cas. 439, P.C.

[26] See, *e.g. Coombe v. Coombe* [1951] 2 K.B. 215 at 224, C.A., *per* Birkett L.J.; *Syros Shipping Co. SA v. Elaghill Trading Co.* [1980] 2 Lloyd's Rep. 390. See generally, M.P. Thompson, (1983) 42 C.L.J. 257.

[27] See below, pp. 16–17.

[28] See, *e.g. Edlin v. Battaly* (1668) 2 Lev. 152; 83 E.R. 494, *Hobbs v. Norton* (1682) 1 Vern. 136; 23 E.R. 370, *Bath and Mountague's Case* (1693) 3 Chan. Cas. 55 at 104; 22 E.R. 963, *Huning v. Ferrers* (1711) Gilb Eq. 85; 25 E.R. 59, *Savage v. Foster* (1723) 9 Mod. 35; 88 E.R. 299, *East India Co. v. Vincent* (1740) 2 Atk. 83; 26 E.R. 451, *Att.-Gen. v. Balliol College Oxford* (1744) 9 Mod. 407, 88 E.R. 538, *Stiles v. Cowper* (1748) 3 Atk. 692; 26 E.R. 1198, *Hardcastle v. Shafto* (1794) 1 Anst. 184; 145 E.R. 802 at 805, 839, *Jackson v. Cator* (1800) 5 Ves. 688; 31 E.R. 806, *Gregory v. Mighell* (1811) 18 Ves. 328; 34 E.R. 341. For a full survey of the older authorities, see Spencer Bower and Turner, *The Law Relating to Estoppel by Representation*, (3rd ed., 1977), Ch. 12 at pp. 289–295.

[29] See Spencer Bower and Turner, *The Law Relating to Estoppel by Representation*, (3rd ed., 1977), Ch. 12 at p. 307, where it is stated: "The new promissory estoppel, on the other hand, had never been heard of until 1946, when Denning J.'s judgment in *Central London Property Trust Limited v. High Trees House Limited* was delivered ... "

[30] See, *e.g. Tool Metal Manufacturing Co. Ltd v. Tungsten Electric Co. Ltd* [1955] 1 W.L.R. 761, H.L.; *Ajayi v. R.T. Briscoe (Nigeria) Ltd* [1964] 1 W.L.R. 1326 at 1330, P.C., *per* Lord Hodson.

[31] See, *e.g. Holiday Inns Inc. v. Broadhead* (1974) 232 EG 951, where Goff J. said: "The authorities also establish, in my judgment, that this relief can be granted although the arrangement or understanding between the parties was not sufficiently certain to be enforceable as a contract": *ibid.* 1087.

[32] (1985) 13 N.S.W.L.R. 134, Supreme Court of New South Wales.

[33] *ibid.* 150–151.

applies in cases where there is a contract, in cases where there is a contract which is unenforceable because of the Statute of Frauds and in cases where there is no contract but the parties have supposed there is a contract through not realising that one of the contracting parties is incompetent to contract: see, *e.g. Ward v. Kirkland*. However, some parts of the principle now called proprietary estoppel are simply contract, it being realised that parts of the old rules as to consideration that, detrimental reliance have remained are so that *ex post facto* consideration is nonetheless consideration notwithstanding that it does not conform to the normal rules for consideration which are applicable to contracts under the modern doctrine of consideration."

It is submitted that proprietary estoppel remains a distinct and separate category of estoppel.[34] It was treated as a separate category in *Att.-Gen. of Hong Kong v. Humphreys Estate (Queen's Gardens) Ltd*[35] and *J.T. Developments Ltd v. Quinn*.[36] Unlike other catgeories of estoppel which come into play where the parties are already in some form of legal relationship (*e.g.* a contract), proprietary estoppel may be used to ground a cause of action[37] seeking the grant of an interest in or right over land.[38] Thus, according to Snell's *Equity*[39]:

"The two main forms in which the doctrine of equitable estoppel exists may be called 'promissory estoppel' and 'proprietary estoppel', respectively; for in the first form E is precluded from resiling from his representation or promise, whereas in the second form E is precluded from denying C's supposed rights in E's property".

---

[34] This is the view put forward by Spencer Bower and Turner, *The Law Relating to Estoppel by Representation*, (3rd ed., 1977) at pp. 306–307, where the learned authors conclude that "it is already possible, in the estoppel cases, to find traces of a distinct tendency loosely to 'lump together' the doctrines of acquiescence, or 'proprietary estoppel', and of promissory estoppel, as if they were one, or took their origin from the same source, or were regulated by the same principles. It is for this reason that the term has not been adopted in this treatise; by keeping to the old terms this book has been able, it is hoped, to adhere more clearly to the presentation of these two doctrines as two, and not one". Snell's *Equity*, (29th ed.) is of the same view: " ... the distinction between promissory and proprietary estoppel is a valid one", *ibid.* p. 570. See further, P.T. Evans, [1988] Conv. 346; (1981) 97 L.Q.R. 513.

[35] [1987] A.C. 114 at 121, P.C., *per* Lord Templeman.

[36] (1991) 62 P. & C.R. 33 at 45, C.A., *per* Ralph Gibson L.J.. See also *Kammins Ballrooms Co. Ltd v. Zenith Investments (Torquay) Ltd* [1971] A.C. 850, H.L., where the two doctrines of promissory estoppel and acquiescence are recognised as being quite separate. See further, Spencer Bower & Turner, *The Law Relating to Estoppel by Representation*, (3rd ed., 1977), Chap. 12, pp. 308–309.

[37] *Bennett v. Bennett*, May 18, 1990, C.A., unreported, available on Lexis, where Slade L.J. observed: "Unlike other forms of estoppel it is, in appropriate circumstances, capable of operating positively so as to give rise to a cause of action".

[38] See, *Western Fish Products Ltd v. Penwith District Council* [1981] 2 All E.R. 204, C.A., which holds that proprietary estoppel can only operate where the claimant acts to his detriment in the expectation of acquiring a right or interest over the defendant's land, and not where he has incurred expenditure on his own land in the expectation, encouraged by an officer of a planning authority, that he would acquire planning permission.

[39] (29th ed.) at p. 570.

(ii) Resulting Trust

It is evident that a clear distinction exists between the doctrine of proprietary estoppel and the operation of a resulting trust, as illustrated in the unreported case of *Walker v. Walker*.[40] Here, a father had contributed £5,067 towards the purchase of a house, which was placed in the name of his son and daughter-in-law. The rest of the purchase money was obtained by way of mortgage. The father's claim to an equitable share in the house on the basis of a resulting trust failed since it was held, on the facts, that the money was intended as a gift by the father to the son. In the course of his judgment, Browne-Wilkinson L.J. alluded to the possibility of applying the principle of proprietary estoppel to the facts before him in so far as the father might have been able to make a case that he was entitled to such an estoppel equity on the basis that he had made, not an outright gift of the money to the son, but a gift on the understanding that he would have a room in the house and be provided with his keep, which understanding was encouraged by the words or actions of the son. If such a case had been made out, the court could have enforced the equity arising under the proprietary estoppel in such manner as was just (*e.g.* by requiring repayment of the whole or part of the money and by imposing a charge on the house to secure such repayment[41]). The difficulty, however, in the instant case was that no such case was raised by the pleadings. On the pleadings, the claim was based on a resulting trust (*i.e.* a claim to a beneficial interest in the house itself arising simply from a contribution by the father to the purchase money). A claim based on proprietary estoppel was quite different. The pleadings would have had to allege that the son had represented to the father that he would be provided with a home in the house, that the father advanced the money in reliance on such representation and that the father had been evicted from the house in breach of the representations so made. Moreover, the relief claimed would not have been for a beneficial interest in the house or the proceeds of sale thereof but, at most, for some security for repayment of the gift or part of it. It was argued on behalf of the father that a proprietary estoppel claim was open on the pleadings since there was no real distinction between a resulting trust and a constructive trust arising from proprietary estoppel. On this point, Browne-Wilkinson L.J. observed:

> "Broadly, a resulting trust arises where the facts alleged and proved consist of the payment of money by A to or for the benefit of B (otherwise than for the sole benefit of B) without a declaration of express trusts which fully exhaust the beneficial interest: in such a case the beneficial interest results to A to the extent that it is not exhausted by the express trust. But, where a constructive trust is alleged to arise from a kind of proprietray estoppel, the crucial factor is not the payment of the money by itself but the representation made by the defendant as to his future conduct and the reliance placed by the plaintiff on such representation."

---

[40] Unreported, April 12, 1984, C.A., available on Lexis.
[41] See, *e.g. Hussey v. Palmer* [1972] 1 W.L.R. 1286, C.A.

(iii) Relief against Forfeiture

It has already been noted earlier that proprietary estoppel operates so as to temper or "mitigate the rigours of strict law".[42] In essence, the doctrine acts as a restraint upon the legal owner, preventing him from exercising his strict legal rights in circumstances where it would be unconscionable for him so to do. In this sense, therefore, a close analogy exists between proprietary estoppel and the grant of relief against forfeiture of proprietary interests in land.[43] As Gray[44] puts it, "the owner of land is effectively restrained from obtaining arbitrary eviction of the estoppel claimant or from otherwise causing him prejudice".

(iv) Contractual Licence

There are conflicting views as to whether a contractual licence and proprietary estoppel can overlap. In *Tanner v. Tanner*,[45] Lord Denning M.R. described a contractual licence in terms resembling a proprietary estoppel. In this case, the defendant, a spinster, gave birth to twin daughters of whom the plaintiff was the father. The plaintiff and defendant subsequently decided that a house should be purchased to provide a home for the defendant and her baby daughters. The plaintiff bought a house on mortgage, and the defendant left her rent-controlled flat and moved with the children into the house. Three years later, the plaintiff offered the defendant £4,000 to move out of the house. The Court of Appeal held that the inference to be drawn from the circumstances was that the defendant had a contractual licence to have accommodation in the house for herself and the children so long as the children were of school age and reasonably required the accommodation. It was held that she had provided consideration for the licence by giving up her rent-controlled flat and looking after the children. Since the defendant had moved out, the court awarded her compensation of £2,000 for the loss of the licence.

It has been argued[46] that a clear distinction should be drawn between contractual licences and estoppel or equitable licences. In the former category, the acceptor provides consideration to support his acceptance. For a breach by the offeror, the acceptor may sue for damages or specific performance.[47] No question of any estoppel arises—the plaintiff does not ask that the defendant be estopped from asserting his strict legal rights but instead avers that the defendant has breached his promise under the contract. By contrast, in the estoppel type of licence, the representor induces a belief in the plaintiff that, if the plaintiff will expend his money on the land, the plaintiff will acquire some right or interest in the land. Here, the plaintiff's remedy is to seek the court's assistance to estop the defendant from insisting on his strict legal rights in so far as such insistence would be unconscionable having regard to the dealings between the parties. Other commentators[48] have challenged the proposition that

---

[42] *Crabb v. Arun District Council* [1976] Ch. 179 at 187, C.A., *per* Lord Denning M.R.

[43] See generally, Pawlowski, *The Forfeiture of Leases*, (1993), Chap. 1.

[44] Gray, *Elements of Land Law*, (2nd ed.) at p. 356.

[45] [1975] 1 W.L.R. 1346, C.A. See also, *Horrocks v. Forray* [1976] 1 W.L.R. 230, C.A., where it was held that no contractual licence existed.

[46] See, *e.g.* A. Briggs, [1981] Conv. 212 and [1983] Conv. 285.

[47] See, *e.g. Verrall v. Great Yarmouth Borough Council* [1981] Q.B. 202, C.A.

[48] See, *e.g.* M.P. Thompson, [1983] Conv. 50. See also, J. Dewar, (1986) 49 M.L.R. 741.

there is always a clear difference between contractual licences and licences protected by estoppel. It is possible for a licence to display features common to both contract and estoppel.

It now seems settled that a contractual licence gives rise to a personal right in favour of the licensee and does not bind third parties. Thus, if the legal owner sells the property, the purchaser will not be bound by a contractual licence even if he has notice of it because the licence does not create a proprietary interest in land.[49] A third party will be bound by such a license only in exceptional circumstances where the court is prepared to impose a constructive trust on the ground that the third party's conscience is affected.[50]

With regard to a licence arising by estoppel, the position of third parties is less certain.[51] Whilst there is authority supporting the view that an inchoate equity arising from a proprietary estoppel can bind successors in title,[52] it is submitted that, in view of the current position regarding contractual licences, it would be a strange result if a claimant relying on estoppel were in a stronger position than one relying on a contractual agreement. This is the conclusion put forward in Chapter 7.

(v) Equitable Licence

If the legal owner induces the claimant to believe that he or she has a right to occupy the house and the latter acts in reliance on that assurance, equity may impose an equitable licence in favour of the claimant. In this type of case, there is no express (or implied) contract—the court imputes a licence from the circumstances of the case. Thus, in *Hardwick v. Johnson*,[53] a case involving occupation under an informal family arrangement, Lord Denning M.R. was able to impute to the parties a grant by the mother as owner of the house to her son and his wife a joint equitable licence to live in the house on payment of £28 per month.[54] This licence could not be revoked or determined by the mother until some event occurred which would justify bringing it to an end. In relation to an equitable licence, it is necessary for the court to spell out its terms.[55]

Another example is *Re Sharpe, (A Bankrupt)*,[56] where an aunt lent £12,000 to her nephew to purchase a maisonette on the understanding that she would be able to stay in the premises for as long as she liked. Browne-Wilkinson J. implied an irrevocable contractual/equitable licence to occupy the property until the loan was repaid which was held to arise under a constructive trust.

---

[49] *Ashburn Anstalt v. Arnold* [1989] Ch. 1, C.A.
[50] *Ashburn Anstalt v. Arnold* [1989] Ch. 1, 25 at 27, C.A., *per* Fox L.J., who considered it undesirable that "constructive trusts of land should be imposed in reliance on inferences from slender materials": *ibid.* 26.
[51] See G. Battersby, [1991] Conv. 36 and (1995) 58 M.L.R. 637; J. Hill, (1988) 51 M.L.R. 226; S. Moriarty, (1984) 100 L.Q.R. 376; P.N. Todd, (1981) Conv. 347; A. Briggs, [1983] Conv. 285 and [1981] Conv. 212.
[52] See in particular, *E.R. Ives Investment Ltd v. High* [1967] 2 Q.B. 379, C.A. and *Re Sharpe, (A Bankrupt)* [1980] 1 W.L.R. 219. See further, Chap. 7, pp. 132–138.
[53] [1978] 1 W.L.R. 683, C.A.
[54] Roskill and Browne L.JJ. preferred to decide the case on the basis of a joint contractual licence.
[55] *ibid.* 688, *per* Lord Denning M.R.
[56] [1980] 1 W.L.R. 219.

In *Chandler v. Kerley*,[57] it was not possible, on the arrangement envisaged between the parties, to imply a licence for the defendant to occupy the house for life and, therefore, she could not establish an equity. However, it was held that she had a contractual licence which was terminable upon reasonable notice (*i.e.* 12 calendar months so as to give her ample opportunity to rehouse herself and her children without disruption).

(vi) Constructive Trust

It has been strongly argued by Hayton[58] that any distinction between proprietary estoppel and constructive trusts is "illusory" and that the basic principle of "unconscionability" underlies both concepts.

In his view, the criterion for equity's intervention in both cases is unconscionable conduct on the part of the legal owner. This criterion, he suggests, should regulate both when and how the court intervenes in a given case. The remedy is at the court's discretion and should be only what is necessary to remedy the legal owner's unconscionable conduct. Moreover, it should be prospective so as not to bind a third party unless his conscience is affected. Thus, according to Hayton, the underlying rationale of estoppel and constructive trust claims is "the discretionary prevention of unconscionable conduct".[59]

There are, indeed, judicial pronouncements which favour the view that constructive trusts and proprietary estoppel are largely indistinguishable. Thus, for example, in *Grant v. Edwards*,[60] Sir Nicholas Browne-Wilkinson V.-C. opined that the principles underlying the law of proprietray estoppel were "closely akin"[61] to those laid down for the establishment of a constructive trust. He said[62]:

> "In both, the claimant must to the knowledge of the legal owner have acted in the belief that the claimant has or will obtain an interest in the property. In both, the claimant must have acted to his or her detriment in reliance on such belief. In both, equity acts on the conscience of the legal owner to prevent him from acting in an unconscionable manner by defeating the common intention. The two principles have been developed separately

---

[57] [1978] 1 W.L.R. 693, C.A.
[58] D. Hayton, [1990] Conv. 370 at p. 380.
[59] *ibid.* 380.
[60] [1986] Ch. 638, C.A. See also, *Christian v. Christian* (1981) 131 New L.J. 43, C.A., *per* Brightman L.J.; *Savva v. Costa and Harymode Investments Ltd* (1981) 131 New L.J. 1114, C.A., *per* Oliver L.J.
[61] *ibid.* 656.
[62] *ibid.* 656.

without cross-fertilisation between them: but they rest on the same foundation and have on all other matters reached the same conclusions".

Similarly, in *Lloyds Bank plc v. Rosset*,[63] Lord Bridge set out the requisite criteria for the establishment by a non-owning cohabitee of a beneficial interest in property (which is in the sole legal ownership of his or her partner) as applying to both a common intention constructive trust and proprietary estoppel, without drawing any difference between the two concepts.[64] His Lordship said[65]:

"... it will only be necessary ... to show that [the claimant] has acted to his or her detriment ... in reliance on the agreement in order to give rise to a constructive trust *or a proprietary estoppel*". (emphasis supplied).

Again, in *Austin v. Keele*,[66] Lord Oliver of Aylmerton (delivering the judgment of the Privy Council) concluded[67] that, in essence, a common intention constructive trust was an application of the doctrine of proprietary estoppel and, in *Re Basham (dec'd)*,[68] Mr Edward Nugee Q.C. (sitting as a High Court judge) suggested that the principle of proprietary estoppel, at least where the claimant's belief is that he is going to be given a right in the future, was properly to be regarded as giving rise to a species of constructive trust, this being "the concept employed by a court of equity to prevent a person from relying on his legal rights where it would be unconscionable for him to do so".[69] More strikingly, in *Sen v. Headley*,[70] Nourse L.J. opined that where the doctrine of proprietary estoppel gives the promisee a right to call for a conveyance of the land, "no doubt it could be said ... that that right is the consequence of an implied or constructive trust which arises once all the requirements of the doctrine have been satisfied".[71]

On the other hand, in *Stokes v. Anderson*,[72] Nourse L.J. considered that the two concepts had not yet been assimilated and that constructive trust principles still applied in the context of claims by marital and non-marital partners.[73] In many of the cases, a constructive trust and proprietary estoppel are pleaded in the alternative and treated as distinct doctrines.[74] It has even been held[75] that the

---

[63] [1991] 1 A.C. 107, H.L.
[64] *ibid.* 132–133.
[65] *ibid.* 132.
[66] [1987] A.L.J.R. 605, P.C. See also, *Walton Stores (Interstate) Ltd v. Maher* (1988) 62 A.L.J.R. 110, High Court of Australia and *Baumgartner v. Baumgartner* (1988) 62 A.L.J.R. 29, High Court of Australia, discussed in Chap. 8 at pp. 168–170.
[67] *ibid.* 609.
[68] [1986] 1 W.L.R. 1498.
[69] *ibid.* 1504.
[70] [1991] Ch. 425, C.A.
[71] *ibid.* 440.
[72] [1991] 1 FLR 391, C.A.
[73] See further, Chap. 8.
[74] See, *e.g. Walker v. Walker*, April 12, 1984, C.A., unreported, available on Lexis; *Warnes v. Hedley*, January 31, 1984, C.A., unreported, available on Lexis; *Bristol and West Building Society v. Henning* [1985] 1 W.L.R. 778, C.A.; *Philip Lowe (Chinese Restaurant) Ltd v. Sau Man Lee*, July 9, 1985, C.A., unreported, available on Lexis.
[75] *Preston and Henderson v. St Helens Metropolitan Borough Council* (1989) 58 P. & C.R. 500 at 505, (Lands Tribunal).

two types of claim may operate together so as to confer on the claimant a 50 per cent beneficial share in property on each basis, thereby establishing beneficial entitlement to the whole.

It is submitted that, under current English law, the two concepts remain separate and distinct.[76] Thus, to establish a constructive trust, a common intention (whether express or inferred) must be established whereas, in the case of proprietary estoppel, a mere assurance is sufficient. More particularly, in the unilateral mistake category,[77] proprietary estoppel requires proof that the claimant acted to his or her detriment in reliance on a mistaken belief encouraged by the legal owner. As Hayton[78] has observed, the common intention constructive trust involves a "bilateral understanding or agreement" whereas, for a successful claim based on proprietary estoppel, the claimant need only show "unilateral conduct" by the legal owner which leads the former to believe that he or she has or will acquire an interest in the the latter's property. As Gray[79] puts it, "the constructive trust is ultimately based upon some concept of frustrated 'bargain' . . . the equity of estoppel is more clearly founded upon a concept of frustrated 'expectation' in circumstances where some 'holding out to the claimant that she had a beneficial interest' has comprised 'part of the inducement to her to do the acts relied on' ".[80]

Another major difference between the two doctrines is that an interest arising under a constructive trust exists from the date of its creation, whereas proprietary estoppel is more in the nature of a remedy than a right and comes into existence only from when it is declared by the court.[81] In constructive trust cases, the court's order merely confirms an existing right so that the decree has retrospective effect capable of binding third parties.[82] The court is simply giving effect to the express common intention of the parties. In estoppel cases, on the other hand, the claimant's equity merely attracts the discretion of the court—in other words, it remains "inchoate" until such time as the court actually decrees a specific interest or award in favour of the estoppel claimant. Only at this point (*i.e.* the date of the court order) may the equity materialise into a full property right. The decree of the court is prospective only. As Hayton[83] puts it:

> "The 'minimum equity to do justice' to [the claimant] and prevent [the legal owner's] unconscionable assertion of his proprietary rights is not known till the date of the court decree: until then the remedy is wholly uncertain and it is not even known whether the remedy will be proprietary or personal. The court is therefore tailoring the remedy to fit the wrong and

---

[76] But see, S. Gardner, (1993) 109 L.Q.R. 263 at pp. 266–269, who points to a number of similarities between the two doctrines.

[77] See, Chap. 6, pp. 115–127.

[78] D. Hayton, [1990] Conv. 370 at p. 371.

[79] Gray, *Elements of Land Law*, (2nd ed.) at p. 357.

[80] Citing, *Grant v. Edwards* [1986] Ch. 638 at 657, C.A., *per* Nicholas Browne-Wilkinson V.-C.

[81] See further, Chap. 7, pp. 130–132.

[82] See, *e.g. Midland Bank plc v. Dobson* [1986] 1 FLR 171, C.A.; *Lloyds Bank plc v. Rosset* [1989] Ch. 350, (C.A); *Williams & Glyn's Bank Ltd v. Boland* [1981] A.C. 487, H.L. The interest probably arises once the claimant has acted to his or her detriment in reliance on the common intention: *Coombes v. Smith* [1986] 1 W.L.R. 808 at 819, *per* Mr Jonathan Parker Q.C. (sitting as a deputy High Court judge); *Pascoe v. Turner* [1979] 1 W.L.R. 431 at 435, C.A., *per* Cumming-Bruce L.J.

[83] D. Hayton, [1990] Conv. 370 at p. 372.

not really upholding already existing rights of a proprietary nature. [The claimant] may request a particular remedy but she cannot insist upon it: she is a supplicant for the court's discretionary mercy."

Confusion arises because in some cases the courts, in satisfaction of the estoppel-based equity, grant the estoppel claimant an equitable interest in the land behind a constructive trust. A good illustration of this is to be found in *Re Sharpe, (A Bankrupt)*,[84] where the claimant had provided some £12,000 towards the purchase price of the house on the understanding that she would be able to stay in the property for as long as she liked. She also expended her own money on decorations and fittings for the property. Browne-Wilkinson J. held that, although the £12,000 had been provided as a loan (and not as a gift), nevertheless, it was an essential feature of the loan that the claimant was to make her home in the property to be acquired with the money lent and, accordingly, she had a right to occupy the premises for as long as she liked while the loan remained unpaid. Moreover, it was held that this right of occupation conferred an interest in the property under a constructive trust. It is thus important to distinguish, in this context, between what may be termed a "substantive" (or "intention-based")[85] constructive trust on the one hand and a "remedial" constructive trust, on the other. As Ferguson[86] points out:

"The so-called 'remedial constructive trust' is merely the satisfaction of an established proprietary estoppel by means of a court-imposed (hence 'constructive'), prospective (hence 'remedial') trust. It is to be carefully distinguished from the common intention constructive trust so long as the constructive trust and proprietary estoppel continue to be differentiated, and it is invalid to suggest that its characteristics (*i.e.* prospective interests originating in the court's order) apply equally to the common intention constructive trust".

The underlying conceptual difference recognised by Ferguson is that "estoppel is purely a *remedial* concept centred on the intervention of the court" whilst "the constructive trust is a *means of creating a proprietary right* which operates entirely independently of the court".[87] On this basis, Ferguson argues that the constructive trust is closer conceptually to the resulting trust, both being mechanisms "whereby the conduct of the parties leads by operation of law[88] to the creation of a proprietary interest".[89] As such, they form part of the general scheme of creation of proprietary interests in land. It is the element of discretion which, according to Ferguson, distinguishes proprietary estoppel from the category of implied, resulting and constructive trusts. In proprietary estoppel cases, the court intervenes to determine what is the "minimum equity to do justice"[90] between the parties. This means that the court must look at all the

---

[84] [1980] 1 W.L.R. 219.
[85] See further, P.T. Evans, [1989] Conv. 418 at pp. 423–424.
[86] P. Ferguson, (1993) 109 L.Q.R. 114 at p. 121.
[87] P. Ferguson, (1993) 109 L.Q.R. 114 at p. 124, but see, D. Hayton in reply, (1993) 109 L.Q.R. 485.
[88] See, s.53(2) of the Law of Property Act 1925.
[89] *ibid.* 124.
[90] *Crabb v. Arun District Council* [1976] Ch. 179 at 198, C.A., *per* Scarman L.J. See also, *Pascoe v. Turner* [1979] 1 W.L.R. 431 at 438, C.A., *per* Cumming-Bruce L.J. See further, Chap. 5.

circumstances in each case to decide in what way the equity can best be satisfied. The nature and extent of the remedy will depend upon the parties' conduct right up to the date of the hearing.[91] Estoppel does not always generate a proprietary interest—it may be sufficient to satisfy the equity by simply denying the legal owner's claim to possession of the property.[92] In other cases, however, the circumstances may justify the ordering of a conveyance of the fee simple in favour of the claimant.[93] By contrast, an interest arising under a constructive trust is always proprietary in nature involving a beneficial share in the property.

Another difference between the two concepts is that the evidentiary requirements for a constructive trust are more stringent than for proprietary estoppel. Thus, for example, in the absence of an express agreement between the parties, only direct financial contributions to the purchase price by the non-owning partner (either initially or by payment of the mortgage instalments) will be sufficient to raise the necessary inference for the creation of a constructive trust. In the words of Lord Bridge in *Lloyds Bank plc v. Rosset*,[94] "it is at least extremely doubtful whether anything less will do".[95] By contrast, the detrimental reliance necessary to support a proprietary estoppel claim need not necessarily take the form of financial contributions. For example, in *Jones (A.E.) v. Jones (F.W.)*,[96] a step-mother was held estopped from evicting her step-son from the house by virtue of his father's conduct which had led him to leave his job and pay money to his father in the belief that the house would be his home for the rest of his life. In this case, the son's act of giving up his job and moving house was held to constitute detrimental reliance so as to found an estoppel. There are other estoppel cases to the same effect.[97] It is also apparent that, for inferred common intention constructive trusts,[98] the required financial contribution must be referable to the acquisition of the house[99] so that

---

[91] See Chap. 5, pp. 73—76.

[92] See further, Chap. 5, pp. 82–84.

[93] See *e.g.*, *Pascoe v. Turner* [1979] 1 W.L.R. 431, C.A.

[94] [1991] 1 A.C. 107, H.L.

[95] *ibid.* 133. But see also the recent Court of Appeal decision in *Midland Bank plc v. Cooke* [1995] 4 All E.R. 562, C.A., where it was held that, where a partner in a matrimonial home without legal title had established an equitable interest through direct contribution, the court would assess (in the absence of express evidence of intention) the proportions the parties were to be assumed to have intended for their beneficial ownership by undertaking a survey of the whole course of dealing between the parties relevant to their ownership and occupation of the property and their sharing of its burdens and advantages and would take into consideration all conduct which threw light on the question what shares were intended. In particular, the court was not bound to deal with the matter on the strict basis of the trust resulting from the cash contribution to the purchase price.

[96] [1977] 1 W.L.R. 438, C.A.

[97] See further, Chap. 4, pp. 65–71.

[98] If there is an express common intention between the parties, it appears from the decision in *Grant v. Edwards* [1986] Ch. 638, C.A., that detrimental conduct must be such upon which the non-owning partner could not reasonably have been expected to embark unless s/he was to have an interest in the house: *ibid.* 648, *per* Nourse L.J. Moreover, the decision in *Eves v. Eves* [1975] 1 W.L.R. 1338, C.A., indicates that there has to be some link between the common intention and the acts relied on as a detriment. However, once an express common intention is shown that the claimant should have an interest in the house, it seems that any detrimental act done by him or her relating to the joint lives of the parties will be sufficient to qualify for the purposes of a constructive trust: *Grant v. Edwards* [1986] Ch. 638 at 675, C.A., *per* Nicholas Browne-Wilkinson V.-C.

[99] *Burns v. Burns* [1984] Ch. 317 at 328, C.A., *per* Fox L.J. See also, *Gissing v. Gissing* [1971] A.C.

expenditure of money on domestic appliances and performing domestic services will not give rise to beneficial entitlement on constructive trust principles.[1] It is apparent, however, that a purely "spousal" form of contribution may be enough to provide the necessary detriment to support an estoppel-based equity in the claimant.[2]

Another potential distinction lies in the location of the onus of proof. In estoppel cases, the decision in *Greasley v. Cooke*[3] establishes that there is a presumption of reliance once an assurance on the part of the legal owner has been shown. In the absence of proof to the contrary, the court would infer that the claimant's conduct was induced by the assurances given to her. In constructive trust cases, no such presumption applies. There is no suggestion in the constructive trust cases that, once the requisite representation and detrimental conduct has been proved, the court will infer the requisite link between the two.

According to Ferguson,[4] the higher evidentiary requirements and different onus of proof in constructive trust cases complement the inherent conceptual distinction between the two doctrines:

"Since the result of establishing a constructive trust is the automatic recognition of a pre-existing proprietary right belonging to [the claimant], whereas the remedy for an estoppel is discretionary and may be merely personal, it is entirely logical that [the claimant] should be required to satisfy higher evidentiary standards and without the benefit of any presumption in her favour. The higher standards act as a filter, only allowing clearly deserving claimants to obtain an interest in the land in question without the intervention of the court. The lower standards applicable in proprietary estoppel cases, by contrast, allow all cases to be considered by the court: the discretionary nature of the estoppel jurisdiction provides the filter necessary to separate out those cases deserving a proprietary right. On this formulation the two concepts may be seen to complement each other very neatly".

It is apparent also that, in estoppel cases, the precise nature or quantum of the interest or right to be received need not be formulated at the time when the claimant is induced to act to his or her detriment.[5] It is enough that there is an expectation of *some* future entitlement of a recognisable kind, at this stage.[6] In the context of a purely domestic arrangement, for example, it is unlikely that the claimant will have formulated his or her expectation of entitlement in precise

---

886 at 909, H.L., *per* Lord Diplock.
[1] See, *e.g. Burns v. Burns* [1984] Chap. 317, C.A., discussed in Chap. 8.
[2] See Chap. 8, pp. 149–157.
[3] [1980] 1 W.L.R. 1306, C.A. See further, Chap. 3, pp. 44–47.
[4] (1993) 109 L.Q.R. 114 at pp. 124–125.
[5] See, *e.g.*, *Plimmer v. The Mayor, Councillors and Citizens of the City of Wellington* (1884) 9 App. Cas. 699, P.C., where Sir Arthur Hobhouse said: " ... the equity arising from the expenditure on land need not fail merely on the ground that the interest to be secured has not been expressly indicated": *ibid.* 713.
[6] See further, Chap. 6, pp. 111–112.

legal terms. The estoppel rules reflect the likelihood of this informal state of affairs by providing that it is not essential that the claimant proves an express indication of the interest created by the conduct of the parties. Where an equity arises because of that conduct, the court may define the interest which satisfies the equity. By contrast, the common intention constructive trust requires clear evidence of an express agreement, arrangement or understanding between the parties that the property was to be shared beneficially. In the absence of an express agreement, arrangement, etc., the court may *infer* a constructive trust but only from evidence of direct contributions to the purchase price by the non-legal owner. In other words, constructive trust theory requires evidence of a more precise legal or equitable entitlement in the property.

(E) Proprietary Estoppel as a Cause of Action

It is well established that the doctrine of proprietary estoppel may be used not only as a "shield" in defence of an action by the legal owner but also as a "sword" capable of grounding an independent cause of action.[7] In the leading case of *Crabb v. Arun District Council*,[8] Lord Denning M.R. put the matter succinctly[9]:

> " . . . it is commonly supposed that estoppel is not itself a cause of action. But that is because there are estoppels and estoppels. Some do give rise to a cause of action. Some do not. In the species of estoppel called proprietary estoppel, it does give rise to a cause of action".

Thus, in *J.T. Developments Ltd v. Quinn*,[10] it was common ground that the defendants were asserting a right in equity by estoppel to a new lease of their shop and were not merely denying the plaintiffs' right to possession. As such, the defendants were relying upon proprietary estoppel as a basis for their cause of action.[11]

Although proprietary estoppel is not, as a contract is, a source of legal obligation, nevertheless, it acts as a sword in the sense that it may have the effect that a party can enforce a cause of action which, without the estoppel, he would not be able to do.[12] Essentially, the proprietary estoppel claimant, who is led to believe that he will be granted a right or interest in land and who acts to his detriment in that belief, is enabled to obtain that interest through the

---

[7] *Pascoe v. Turner* [1979] 1 W.L.R. 431 at 436, C.A., *per* Cumming-Bruce L.J.; *Bennett v. Bennett*, May 18, 1990, C.A., unreported, available on Lexis, *per* Slade L.J.; *Durant v. Heritage* [1994] EGCS 134, *per* Mr Andrew Park Q.C., (sitting as a deputy judge of the High Court). See generally, M.P. Thompson, (1983) 42 C.L.J. 257 at pp. 266–272; L. Kirk, (1991) 13 Adel. L.R. 225. See also, Spencer Bower and Turner, *The Law Relating to Estoppel by Representation*, (3rd ed., 1977), Chap. 12 at pp. 303–306.

[8] [1976] Ch. 179, C.A. See further, M. Vitoria, (1976) 126 New L.J. 772, 773.

[9] *ibid.* 187.

[10] (1991) 62 P. & C.R. 33, C.A.

[11] *ibid.* 45, *per* Ralph Gibson L.J.

[12] See, *Amalgamated Investment & Property Co. Ltd v. Texas Commerce International Bank Ltd* [1982] Q.B. 84 at 105, *per* Robert Goff J.

intervention of equity. This is in contrast to promissory estoppel, which is concerned essentialy with a representation by a party that he will not enforce his strict legal rights and, therefore, of its very nature, does not enable a party to enforce a cause of action.[13] In the words of Pennell J. in *Classic Communications Ltd v. Lascar*[14]:

> "It was for long supposed that estoppel, at least the familiar species known as promissory estoppel, could only be used as a defence and not to found an action. In its enlarged and elevated nature as proprietary estoppel, equity stands ready to strike or defend as and when conscience commands".

(F) Does the Doctrine Apply to Chattels?

There is no direct English authority on the question whether the doctrine of proprietary estoppel is applicable to chattels as well as land. All the cases concern the application of the doctrine to rights and interests created in and over land.[15] In *Moorgate Mercantile Co. Ltd v. Twitchings*,[16] however, Lord Denning M.R. drew no distinction between goods or land when discussing the application of the doctrine. He said[17]:

> "There are many cases where the true owner of goods or of land has led another to believe that he is not the owner, or, at any rate, is not claiming an interest therein, or that there is no obejction to what the other is doing. In such cases it has been held repeatedly that the owner is not to be allowed to go back on what he has led the other to believe. So much so that his own title to the property, be it land or goods, has been held to be limited or extinguished, and new rights and interests have been created therein. And this operates by reason of his conduct—what he has led the other to believe—even though he never intended it".

Lord Denning cited one example of this principle as being surrender by operation of law. Thus, when the owner of a particular estate creates a new estate which is inconsistent with it, thus leading to the belief that the estate has ceased to exist, he is not allowed to go back on it.[18] Another illustration given by Lord Denning M.R. is "when a man, by his words or by his silence, or acquiescence, leads another to believe that he is not the owner and has no interest in the goods, whereupon the other buys them or sells them to an innocent purchaser".[19] In these circumstances, the true owner cannot subsequently assert that the goods belonged to him and title will pass to the buyer.[20] These examples have an obvious parallel with estoppel doctrine and it is interesting to note that Lord Denning M.R.'s observations were cited with

---

[13] See, *e.g. Coombe v. Coombe* [1951] 2 K.B. 215, C.A.
[14] (1986) 21 D.L.R. (4th) 579 at 587, Ontario High Court of Justice.
[15] But see, *Re Foster, Hudson v. Foster (No. 2)* [1938] 3 All E.R. 610, where the doctrine was applied to an insurance policy.
[16] [1976] Q.B. 225, C.A.
[17] *ibid.* 242.
[18] See, *e.g. Foster v. Robinson* [1951] 1 K.B. 149, C.A.
[19] *ibid.* 242.
[20] See, *e.g. Eastern Distributors Ltd v. Goldring* [1957] 2 Q.B. 600, C.A.

apparent approval in *Western Fish Products Ltd v. Penwith District Council*,[21] where Megaw L.J., delivering the judgment of the Court of Appeal, opined that the principle of proprietary estoppel "may extend to other forms of property".[22]

Although there is no English case where an owner has stood by and allowed another to improve a chattel knowing that the other was acting under a mistake, there is no reason why in principle an improver of a chattel should not be entitled to equitable relief on similar principles to those which apply to proprietary estoppel.[23] Indeed, reference may be made, in this connection, to section 6(1) of the Torts (Interference with Goods) Act 1977, which provides as follows:

> "If in proceedings for wrongful interference against a person (the 'improver') who has improved the goods, it is shown that the improver acted in the mistaken but honest belief that he had a good title to them, an allowance shall be made for the extent to which, at the time as at which the goods fall to be valued in assessing damages,[24] the value of the goods is attributable to the improvement".

The sub-section generally restates the common law[25] and permits a person who has acted honestly in making improvements to goods to which he believes he is entitled, to claim an allowance to the extent of the improved value. The value may consist in physical additions or repairs to goods, but it seems that any expenditure of work or materials which enhances saleability constitutes an improvement. Moreover, section 6(2) extends the availability of the allowance from the original wrongdoer effecting an improvement to a *bona fide* purchaser who has derived his supposed title from the improver. Thus, if a stolen car is fitted with a new engine and then sold to a *bona fide* purchaser, the purchaser can claim an allowance. Although he is not an improver, he will normally have paid a price reflecting the improved value and, accordingly, it is right that he should be able to retain that part of the value.

(G) Proprietary Estoppel and Public Law Matters

It is evident that the doctrine of proprietary estoppel does not apply to public law matters such as planning permission. In *Western Fish Products Ltd v. Penwith District Council*,[26] the Court of Appeal held that the doctrine only applied where the plaintiff, encouraged by the defendant, acted to his detriment in relation to his own land in the expectation of acquiring a right over the

---

[21] [1981] 2 All E.R. 204, C.A. See also *Re Basham, (dec'd)* [1986] Ch. 1498 at 1508, *per* Mr Edward Nugee Q.C., (sitting as a High Court judge).

[22] *ibid.* 218.

[23] Alternatively, the improver should, in principle, be entitled to restitution (*i.e.* to recover the reasonable value of the services rendered on the basis that the owner has freely accepted them): see *e.g. Constanzo v. Stewart* 453 P. 2d 526 (1969).

[24] This means the date of conversion or wrongful interference with the goods.

[25] See, *e.g. Greenwood v. Bennett* [1973] 1 Q.B. 195, C.A., (innocent purchaser of stolen motor car held entitled to an allowance (£226) for extensive repairs and improvements carried out to it, which he honestly believed was his own property). See further, P. Matthews, (1981) 40 C.L.J. 340.

[26] [1981] 2 All E.R. 204, C.A.

defendant's land. In the instant case, although the plaintiffs had, to their detriment, spent money on their own land at the encouragement of the Council that planning permission would be forthcoming, they had not done so in the expectation of acquiring any rights in relation to the Council's or any other person's land and, accordingly, their claim based on proprietary estoppel failed. Moreover, it was held that an estoppel could not be raised to prevent a statutory body exercising its statutory discretion or performing its statutory duty.[27]

---

[27] See further, Chap. 2, p. 35.

2. ASSURANCE

(A) Introduction

Although the modern approach is to explain the doctrine of proprietary estoppel in terms of the general concept of "unconscionability",[1] it is evident that a claim of this nature will fail unless the court is satisfied that the claimant has proven three essential elements, namely, (1) assurance, (2) reliance, and (3) detriment or change of position. In *Attorney-General of Hong Kong v. Humphreys Estate (Queen's Gardens) Ltd*,[2] for example, the Privy Council, whilst recognising the trend away from any strict application of rigid criteria in this context towards a more flexibe test of unconscionability, nevertheless, held that all three elements of estoppel had to be satisfied. Thus, while the Hong Kong government in that case had acted to its detriment, the other two essential elements were not present (*i.e.* the creation or encouragement of a belief or expectation by the company and a reliance on that by the government).

This and the next two chapters are devoted to examining each of these three vital ingredients in turn.

(B) Types of Assurance

In order to establish a proprietary estoppel equity, it is essential[3] for the claimant to show that the legal owner has made a representation or created an expectation[4] that the claimant is or will become entitled to some right or interest in the former's land. In the absence of any encouragement[5] or acquiescence on the part of the legal owner (or promise of reward), the claimant's expenditure on

---

[1] See, Chap. 10.

[2] [1987] A.C. 114, P.C.

[3] See, *e.g. Rodgers v. Moonta Town Corporation* (1981) 37 A.L.R. 49 at 53, High Court of Australia, where Gibbs C.J. said: "It is, of course, not enough to give rise to an equitable estoppel in the present case that the appellants should have spent money on the faith of an expectation that they would get a 10 year lease. It would be necessary that the expectation was created or encouraged by the council". See also, *Easterbrook v. The King* [1931] 1 D.L.R. 628 at 636, Supreme Court of Canada, where it was held that, since the defendant occupied the land under a lease from the Indians, they could not have believed that they owned the land, and that the Crown had not given them any reason by act or representation for such a belief.

[4] *Savva v. Costa and Harymode Investments Ltd* (1981) 131 New L.J. 1114, C.A., *per* Oliver L.J. In this case, the court concluded that the most that could be inferred from the facts of the case was that the female claimant, a cohabitee, expended monies on improvements to the house in the expectation that she would be permitted to live in the improved property with her children. This, however, did not empower the court to confer upon her any proprietary interest in the property so long as her expectation was fulfilled, which it had been.

[5] See, *e.g. Ward v. Gold* (1969) 211 EG 155 at 161, where Plowman J. held that there was no estoppel in a neighbour's expression of pleasure at the general impression of a developer's plans.

the land is treated as purely voluntary[6]. It is not a requirement that the legal owner should have acted unconscionably at the time of making the assurance— the element of unconscionability arises only when the legal owner seeks to resile from his representation and insist on his strict legal rights. In the words of Scarman L.J. in *Crabb v. Arun District Council*[7]:

" . . . the fraud or injustice alleged does not take place during the course of negotiation, but only when the defendant decides to refuse to allow the plaintiff to set up his claim against the defendant's undoubted right. The fraud, if it be such, arises after the event, when the defendant seeks by relying on his right to defeat the expectation which he by his conduct encouraged the plaintiff to have. There need not be anything fraudulent or unjust in the conduct of the actual negotiations—the conduct of the transaction by the defendants".

Similarly, in *Lim Teng Huan v. Ang Swee Chuan*,[8] Lord Browne-Wilkinson opined[9]:

" . . . in order to found a proprietary estoppel, it is not essential that the representor should have been guilty of unconscionable conduct in permitting the representee to assume that he could act as he did: it is enough if, in all the circumstances, it is unconscionable for the representor to go back on the assumption which he permitted the representee to make".

Moreover, although in cases of promissory estoppel, it is a prerequisite that there should be an existing legal relationship between the parties, there is no requirement that the underlying transaction between the parties should constitute a pre-existing binding relationship in cases of proprietary estoppel.[10] Nor, indeed, need the assurance be made so as to give rise to contractual liability on the claimant.

The encouragement or acquiescence may take a variety of forms. As was indicated by Oliver J. in *Taylor Fashions Ltd v. Liverpool Victoria Trustees Co. Ltd*,[11] it may involve simply standing by in silence (*i.e.* silent abstention) whilst one party unwittingly infringes the other's legal rights. Alternatively, it may take the form of passive or active encouragement of expenditure or alteration of legal position upon the footing of some unilateral or shared legal or factual supposition. The range of activity (or inactivity) which may qualify as a relevant assurance is both wide and far-reaching. Essentially, the question is whether there was "anything done or left to be done"[12] by the legal owner which encouraged a belief in the claimant that he had or would acquire an entitlement

---

[6] See, *e.g. Ezekiel v. Orakpo*, February 20, 1980, C.A., unreported, available on Lexis, (no evidence that legal owner had encouraged the claimant to expend money on improving the property).

[7] [1976] Ch. 179, 195, C.A.

[8] [1992] 1 W.L.R. 113, P.C.

[9] *ibid.* 117.

[10] See *Holiday Inns Inc. v. Broadhead* (1974) 232 EG 951 at 1087, where Goff J. said: " . . . this relief can be granted although the arrangement or understanding between the parties was not sufficiently certain to be enforceable as a contract": *ibid.* 1087.

[11] [1982] Q.B. 133 at 148.

[12] *E. & L. Berg Homes Ltd v. Grey* (1979) 253 EG 473 at 477, C.A., *per* Sir David Cairns.

in the owner's land. An assurance may even be spelt out of an agreement which is legally unenforceable for uncertainty. Thus, in *Lim Teng Huan v. Ang Swee Chuan*,[13] the agreement (which was void for uncertainty) was, nevertheless, held to constitute evidence of the parties' intentions and it was to be inferred that the claimant had completed the construction of the subject house in reliance on that agreement.

The right or interest assured must, however, be one relating to land[14] and within the legal owner's capacity to grant.[15] It may, therefore, give rise to an expectation of fee-simple ownership,[16] equitable entitlement,[17] a first option to purchase,[18] grant of a lease,[19] licence to occupy for life[20] and the grant of an incorporeal interest (*e.g.* an easement) over the land.[21] It is evident that a claim will not fail simply because the right or interest to be secured has not been precisely or expressly identified at the time of the assurance.[22] It is enough that the representation leads to an expectation that some right is being or will be acquired by the estoppel claimant. It is not, therefore, a requirement that there be an expectation of some precise legal term.[23] In *Inwards v. Baker*,[24] for example, the son had spent money on building a bungalow on his father's land in the expectation, induced by his father, that he would be allowed to stay there as his home. Lord Denning M.R. said[25]:

"... even though there is no binding contract to grant any particular interest to the licensee, nevertheless the court can look at the circum-

---

[13] [1992] 1 W.L.R. 113, P.C.

[14] As to whether proprietary estoppel doctrine can be invoked in respect of chattels, see Chap. 1, pp. 17–18.

[15] *Ezekiel v. Orakpo*, February 20, 1980, C.A., unreported, available on Lexis, where Brightman L.J. said: "I think one has to ask oneself, what was the spender relying on? Was he relying on an interest to which he was entitled or on an interest which he could not get without the concurrence of the landowner? If the latter is right, the question then arises whether the circumstances are such that it would be inequitable for the landowner to withhold his concurrence. But if the spender of the money is not relying on an interest which the landowner can give or withhold, then there is no place for the equity ... [The claimant] fails that test, because there is no evidence that he was relying on some interest which the landlord was at liberty to give or withhold during the period of the option, which was the time when the expenditure was made."

[16] See, *e.g. Dillwyn v. Llewelyn* (1862) 4 De G.F. & J. 517; 45 E.R. 1285; *Pascoe v. Turner* [1979] 1 W.L.R. 431, C.A.; *Voyce v. Voyce* (1991) 62 P. & C.R. 290, C.A.

[17] *Hussey v. Palmer* [1972] 1 W.L.R. 1286, C.A.; *Lim Teng Huan v. Ang Swee Chuan* [1992] 1 W.L.R. 113, P.C.

[18] *Stilwell v. Simpson* (1983) 133 New L.J. 894. See also, *Wellington City Council v. New Zealand Law Society* [1988] 2 N.Z.L.R. 614 at 631–632, High Court of Wellington, where the estoppel claim failed.

[19] *Watson v. Goldsbrough* [1986] 1 EGLR 265, C.A.; *Siew Soon Wah v. Yong Tong Hong* [1973] A.C. 836, P.C.; *J.T. Developments Ltd v. Quinn* (1991) 62 P. & C.R. 33, C.A.; *Andrews v. Colonial Mutual Life Assurance Society Ltd* [1982] 2 N.Z.L.R. 556, High Court of Auckland.

[20] *Griffiths v. Williams* (1978) 248 EG 947, C.A.; *Inwards v. Baker* [1965] 2 Q.B. 29, C.A.; *Greasley v. Cooke* [1980] 1 W.L.R. 1306, C.A.; *Maharaj v. Chand* [1986] A.C. 898, P.C.; *Matharu v. Matharu* (1994) 68 P. & C.R. 93, C.A.

[21] *Crabb v. Arun District Council* [1976] Ch. 179, C.A.; *Soames-Forsythe Properties Ltd v. Tesco Stores Ltd* [1991] EGCS 22; *E.R. Ives Investment Ltd v. High* [1967] 2 Q.B. 379, C.A.; *Ward v. Kirkland* [1967] Ch. 194; *Dewhirst v. Edwards* [1983] 1 N.S.W.L.R. 34; *Classic Communications Ltd v. Lascar* (1986) 21 D.L.R. (4th) 579, Ontario High Court.

[22] *Plimmer v. Mayor, Councillors and Citizens of the City of Wellington* (1884) 9 App. Cas. 699 at 713, *per* Sir Arthur Hobhouse.

[23] *Inwards v. Baker* [1965] 2 Q.B. 29 at 37, C.A., *per* Lord Denning M.R.

[24] [1965] 2 Q.B. 29, C.A.

[25] *ibid.* 37.

stances and see whether there is an equity arising out of the expenditure of money."

In *Coombes v. Smith*,[26] however, an assurance given by the defendant to his female cohabitee that he would always "provide her with a roof over her head" was held insufficient to constitute a representation that she was legally entitled to security of tenure against his wishes.

The assurance itself must be clear and unequivocal[27] and *intended* to be relied upon by the claimant to his (or her) detriment. A mere expression of opinion, therefore, is not a sufficient assurance for estoppel purposes.[28] Statements made in the course of commercial negotiations prior to entering into a contract may give rise to an estoppel provided that they fairly created an expectation in the mind of the claimant that he would be granted an interest in land. In *J.T. Developments Ltd v. Quinn*,[29] the defendants were the tenants of a coffee shop under a lease which was due to expire on June 24, 1989. Their landlords served notice under section 25 of the Landlord and Tenant Act 1954, terminating the tenancy. The defendants did not respond to this notice. In November 1988, the landlords' surveyor, Mr Clayton, visited the shop and was told by defendants that they were planning to make improvements to the kitchen. At that time, the defendants still had time to serve a counternotice under the 1954 Act (advising the landlords that they did not wish to give up possession) but they subsequently failed to do so within the two-month time limit prescribed by the 1954 Act. In January 1989, there was a telephone conversation between Mr Clayton and the defendants, the former stating that the landlords were prepared to grant a new tenancy on the same terms as those contained in a new tenancy of a nearby shop also owned by the landlords. In January and February 1989, the defendants carried out the kitchen improvements. The landlords then sold the shop to the plaintiffs who sought possession against the defendants. The Court of Appeal[30] held that the defendants were entitled to a new tenancy of the shop by virtue of proprietary estoppel. In order to found an estoppel in the instant case, it had to be shown that the plaintiffs had created or encouraged an expectation that the defendants would have a new lease and that the defendants had expended money on the shop in reliance on the expectation and with the knowledge of the plaintiffs. The decisive question was whether the plaintiffs were free to resile from the telephone statement without telling the defendants before the defendants had acted to their detriment in reliance on the statement. In the context of commercial negotiations which, if successful, would lead to a binding contract, a statement of intention to make an agreement was capable of forming the basis of an estoppel by which the defendant could claim the benefit of the agreement provided that the statement did fairly create such an expectation, bearing in mind that the parties to commercial negotiations did not normally intend such statements to give rise to any legal rights until an actual agreement was concluded. In the instant case, the trial judge had found as a fact

---

[26] [1986] 1 W.L.R. 808.

[27] See, *e.g. Sidney Bolsom Investment Trust Ltd v. E. Karmios & Co. (London) Ltd* [1956] 1 Q.B. 529 at 540, C.A., *per* Denning L.J.

[28] See, *e.g. E. & L. Berg Homes Ltd v. Grey* (1979) 253 EG 473 at 477, C.A., *per* Sir David Cairns.

[29] (1991) 62 P. & C.R. 33, C.A.

[30] Ralph Gibson L.J. and Lord Donaldson M.R., Glidewell L.J. dissenting.

that the statements of Mr Clayton did not merely contain an offer to negotiate but constituted an assurance that, irrespective of the making of an agreement for a new lease, the defendants would be granted an interest in land, namely a new tenancy. The Court of Appeal endorsed this finding of fact and held the defendants to be entitled to a new tenancy.

The case may be contrasted with *Attorney-General of Hong Kong v. Humphreys Estate (Queen's Gardens) Ltd,*[31] where a contract in writing between the government and the Hong Kong Land Company (HKL) was expressly made "subject to contract". Pursuant to that contract, the government took possession of a number of residential flats and spent money on them. HKL later refused to proceed with the contract. The government contended that HKL were bound in equity to proceed because the government had spent money under an expectation, created or encouraged by HKL, that HKL would carry out the contract and transfer the flats. The claim failed because the evidence showed that, although the government had acted in "the confident and not unreasonable hope"[32] that a voluntray agreement in principle, expressly made subject to contract, and therefore not binding, would eventually be followed by the achievement of legal relationships in the form of grants and transfers of property, nevertheless, at no time did HKL indicate expressly or by implication that they had surrendered their right to change their minds and to withdraw from the contract. It is important to note that in the *Humphreys* case, the contract was expressly made "subject to contract" and its effect was fully understood by both sides. In *Quinn*, there were no such words. Moreover, in *Humphreys*, the evidence did not show that HKL had actually created or encouraged a belief or expectation in the government that the agreement in principle would be carried into effect and that HKL would not withdraw. In this connection, it is important to bear in mind that an estoppel claim cannot be founded on a mere expectation of entitlement—there must be some *encouragement* of a belief by means of either an express or implied representation.[33] This has led Gray to comment that "detrimental reliance upon a self-induced expectation cannot give rise to a valid claim of estoppel".[34] He contrasts Australian caselaw[35] where there has been "a willingness to order that the owner compensate spontaneously incurred detriment where a failure to do so would be 'unconscionable' or would lead to unjust enrichment of the owner".[36]

The decision in *Humphreys* may also be contrasted with *Crabb v. Arun District Council,*[37] where the claimant, Mr Crabb, owned some land with a right of access to the public road over an adjoining piece of land held by the Council. He wanted to divide his land into two portions and to sell them separately. For

---

[31] [1987] A.C. 114, P.C.
[32] *ibid.* 124.
[33] See further, Chap. 8, pp. 158–161.
[34] Gray, *Elements of Land Law*, (2nd ed), p. 330.
[35] *Nepean District Tennis Association Inc. v. Council of the City of Penrith* (1989) N.S.W. Conv. R. 55–438, at 58, 180, where a "reasonable expectation" unsupported by any representation, was held to found an estoppel claim for compensation. Gray also cites *Beaton v. McDivitt* (1987) 13 N.S.W.L.R. 162, where Kirby P. states: "Even where the owner may not request or excite that behaviour, where the expenditure is induced by an expectation of obtaining protection, equity will intervene to ensure that an injustice may not be perpetrated": *ibid.* 171.
[36] *ibid.* 330.
[37] [1876] Ch. 179, C.A.

this purpose, he needed a second point of access. At a meeting between Mr Crabb's architect and the Council, who knew of Mr Crabb's intention to sell and why he needed the second access, there was an "agreement in principle" that Mr Crabb should have a second access point. He later sold a portion of his land without reserving any right of way over it to gain access to the public road. The Court of Appeal held that there was, at the meeting, a firm agreement or undertaking to grant Mr Crabb the second access point.

Lord Denning M.R. said[38]:

> "The judge found that there was 'no definite assurance' by the defendants' representative, and 'no firm commitment', but only an 'agreement in principle', meaning, I suppose that . . . there were 'some further processes' to be gone through before it would become binding. But if there were any such processes in the mind of the parties, the subsequent conduct of the [Council] was such as to dispense with them. The [Council] actually put up the gates at point B at considerable expense. That certainly led the plaintiff to believe that they agreed that he should have the right of access through point B without more ado".

It is evident, therefore, that there is no rule that an "agreement in principle" (or a clear statement of intention in the course of negotiations) can never provide the basis for an estoppel claim. The authorities show that a statement made in the course of negotiations must be carefully examined to see whether it can fairly be held to have been capable of creating or encouraging the expectation upon which the claimant relied.[39] However, an assurance cannot operate to give rise to an estoppel claim where the claimant is already owner of the land which is the subject-matter of the representation. Thus, in *Avondale Printers & Stationers Ltd v. Haggie*,[40] a proprietary estoppel claim was not established because the claimant had not spent the money in the expectation, encouraged by the defendants, that it would become the beneficial owner of the land. At the relevant time of the assurance, the claimant was already contractually entitled to become the beneficial owner of the land in question, and after it had relinquished that right, the defendants had notified the claimant that any further expenditure was at his own risk.

The decision in *Quinn*, mentioned above, also highlights the importance of showing that the assurance given was, in the circumstances, such that would operate on the mind of a reasonable person. In the words of Denning L.J., "a man must be taken to intend what a reasonable person would understand him to intend".[41] Thus, in *Quinn*, it was accepted that the claimant believed that he had received during the telephone conversation with Mr Clayton, the landlords' surveyor, a firm assurance that he would obtain a new tenancy and that he acted in the belief that the landlords would not go back on it. It was pointed out, however, by Ralph Gibson L.J. that the claimant's *subjective* belief could not be

---

[38] *ibid*. 189.
[39] *J.T. Developments Ltd v. Quinn* (1991) 62 P. & C.R. 33 at 49, C.A., *per* Ralph Gibson L.J.
[40] [1979] 2 N.Z.L.R. 124, Supreme Court of Auckland.
[41] *Sidney Bolsom Investment Trust Ltd v. E. Karmios & Co (London) Ltd* [1956] 1 Q.B. 529 at 540–541, C.A.

decisive.[42] It was necessary to consider what effect the assurance had on the claimant as a reasonable person. Conversely, it is immaterial that the reperesentor did not realise the consequence of his words or acts as giving rise to a legitimate expectation of entitlement on the part of the claimant.[43] It is always the effect of the assurance on the mind of the representee as a reasonable man (or woman) that is crucial—the representation must be sufficiently clear, that is, it must be one which is either reasonably understood in the material sense by the claimant or which is intended by the legal owner to be so understood and is, in fact, so understood.[44]

If, however, the representor, shortly before the representee acts to his detriment, asserts his claim to the land, no equity will arise against him, even if he claims a greater interest than he in fact had, and gave no details of his title. Nor, it appears, is he obliged to reassert his title to the land before any expenditure on the land actually begins. In *The Master, Fellows and Scholars of Clare Hall v. Harding*,[45] the plaintiffs, who believed themselves to be the owners of a house and shop, entered into a lease agreement of the premises with a tenant, who proceeded to expend money in pulling the property down and rebuilding it. The defendant, who was the true owner of the property, asserted his title to it, which assertion he repeated a few days before the improvements were begun. Thereafter, knowing the tenant was acting under a mistake, he permitted the works to be carried out without raising any objection. It was held that the defendant, having once given notice of his claim to the property, was not bound, in order to exclude any equity arising against him on the ground of acquiescence, to assert his claim again when the expenditure began or while it was going on.

The assurance may constitute either "active" encouragement (*i.e.* by words or deeds) or, alternatively, mere "passive" (silent) acquiescence. In some cases, the representation may consist of an actual denial of any rights in the land in favour of the estoppel claimant. In these circumstances, of course, no estoppel will operate.[46] A good example is to be found in the New Zealand case of *Gillies v. Keogh*,[47] where the female partner (who had purchased a house in her sole name) had made it quite clear to her male partner throughout their relationship that she asserted the house was hers alone and, accordingly, he was held to have acquired no beneficial interest in it on estoppel principles. Richardson J. stated[48]:

"If one party has insisted throughout that a particular item of property in that party's name is his (or hers) to the exclusion of the other, he (or she)

---

[42] (1991) 62 P. & C.R. 33 at 50, C.A.
[43] See *Preston and Henderson v. St Helens Metropolitan Borough Council* (1989) 58 P. & C.R. 500 at 503, (Lands Tribunal). See also, *Taylors Fashions Ltd v. Liverpool Victoria Trustees Co. Ltd* [1982] Q.B. 133 at 151–152, where Oliver J. concluded that the legal owner may act "knowingly or unknowingly" in encouraging the claimant to act to his detriment.
[44] *Wellington City Council v. New Zealand Law Society* [1988] 2 N.Z.L.R. 614 at 627, High Court of Wellington, *per* Davison C.J.
[45] (1848) 6 Hare 273; 67 E.R. 1169.
[46] See, *e.g. Haughan v. Rutledge* [1988] I.R. 295 at 301, where an express refusal to agree to grant a lease rebutted any expectation of a grant.
[47] [1989] 2 N.Z.L.R. 327, Court of Appeal of Wellington.
[48] *ibid.* 347.

cannot be said to have encouraged the other to a belief or expectation that it would be shared ... "

It will be convenient to examine the two types of assurance (*i.e.* active and passive) separately. It should be noted, however, that both types of assurance, whether express or implied, will attract equity's intervention. In the words of Ungoed-Thomas J. in *Ward v. Kirkland*[49]:

> "The fundamental principle of the equity is unconscionable behaviour, and unconscionable behaviour can arise where there is knowledge by the legal owner of the circumstances in which the claimant is incurring the expenditure as much as if he was himself requesting or inciting that expenditure. It seems to me that abstension as well as a request or incitement can fall within the principle from which the claimant's equity arises".

(i) Words or Deeds

In the typical case, the legal owner will have verbally represented to the claimant that he or she already has or will acquire some right or interest in the owner's land. A good example is *Inwards v. Baker*,[50] where a father told his son, who wished to build a bungalow as his home, "Why don't you build the bungalow on my land and make it a bit bigger?" So encouraged, the son gave up his plan to buy other land and built the bungalow on his father's land, largely by his own labour. The cost was about £300, of which the son provided £150 and the father the balance. The Court of Appeal held that the father's representation had induced an expectation in the son that he would be allowed to remain there for his lifetime or for as long as he wished. This gave rise to a successful claim based on proprietary estoppel. The equity arising from the expenditure on the land did not fail simply because the interest to be secured had not been expressly indicated by the father. It was unnecessary for the claimant to show that he had an expectation of some precise legal term.

In *Michaud v. City of Montreal*,[51] the plaintiff, who was the owner of a strip of land, verbally offered to give it to a city council for the purpose of widening a city street. He presided as mayor at a meeting of the council at which a resolution was passed accepting the gift. The council, while the plaintiff was still mayor, took possession of the land and expended money in fitting it for public use. The plaintiff subsequently claimed the land back, alleging that the gift was subject to a condition which had not been fulfilled. The Privy Council held that the plaintiff was estopped by his conduct from alleging that the gift was subject to a condition.

In *Pascoe v. Turner*,[52] the plaintiff assured his mistress that she had nothing to worry about as his house and everything in it was hers. In reliance upon this

---

[49] [1967] Ch. 194 at 239.
[50] [1965] 2 Q.B. 29, C.A. See also, *Ward v. Kirkland* [1967] Ch. 194, where the claimant laid drains over a farmyard acting on the express permission of the legal owner thereof.
[51] (1923) 129 L.T. 417, P.C.
[52] [1979] 1 W.L.R., C.A.

declaration (which was made on several occasions), the defendant spent money on redecorations, improvements and repairs to the house. The Court of Appeal held that the plaintiff's encouragement of the defendant improving the house, in the belief that it belonged to her, gave rise to a successful plea of proprietary estoppel. In *Griffiths v. Williams*,[53] a mother had repeatedly assured her daughter that she would be allowed to live in her house for the rest of her life. On the faith of these assurances, the daughter had expended £2,000 of her own monies on improvements to the property which consisted of putting in a bathroom and indoor toilet, electrical rewiring, concreting the yard and repairs to the yard. It was held that the daughter had a clear equitable right to occupy the house during her lifetime.

Again, in *Stevens v. Stevens*,[54] the plaintiff told the defendant (his daughter-in-law) that she and her children could have his house for the rest of their lives. This assurance was repeated by the plaintiff on subsequent occasions using words such as "the house is yours" and "the house is for you and the children" and "I have given it to you". In reliance upon these statements, the defendant moved into the plaintiff's house with her children, paid the outgoings and carried out certain repairs and decorations thereat over several years. The Court of Appeal held, on these facts, that the defendant's claim based on proprietary estoppel was made out.

In *Bennett v. Bennett*,[55] however, the estoppel claim failed for lack of the requisite element of assurance. In this case, it was held that the bare verbal statement by the legal owner that he "didn't want [the claimant] out" could not possibly have been reasonably understood by her, or anyone else, as an assurance that she could remain there for the rest of her life. The only way in which the claimant could reasonably have understood this statement was that he (the legal owner) was prepared to allow her to remain in the property *for the time being*—in other words, it was implicit in this arrangement that the legal owner would have the right to ask the claimant to leave on reasonable notice. A similar conclusion was reached in *Bostock v. Bryant*,[56] where the claimant was told by her uncle: "Don't worry about the future, you'll be all right". This was held by the Court of Appeal to be too vague to amount to an assurance that she could live in the house as long as she wished.[57]

(ii) Silent Acquiescence

It seems that a successful proprietary estoppel claim may be founded on the legal owner's passive acquiescence in the claimant's conduct.[58] In other words, it is sufficient if the legal owner has simply stood by whilst the claimant acts to his detriment or changes his position in the mistaken belief that he is entitled to a

---

[53] (1977) 248 EG 947, C.A.
[54] Unreported, March 3, 1989, C.A., available on Lexis.
[55] Unreported, May 18, 1990, C.A., available on Lexis.
[56] (1990) 61 P. & C.R. 23, C.A.
[57] *ibid.* 31–32, *per* Stuart-Smith L.J.
[58] An early case is *Dann v. Spurrier* (1802) 7 Ves. Jun. 232 at 235–236; 32 E.R. 94 at 95, where Lord Eldon said: "this Court will not permit a man knowingly, though but passively, to encourage another to lay out money under an erroneous opinion of title; and the circumstance of looking on is in many cases as strong as using terms of encouragement". See also, *Steed v. Whitaker* (1740) Barn. Ch. 220; 27 E.R. 621, where a mortgagee stood silently by while a purchaser, in ignorance of the mortgage, built on the land.

right or interest in the owner's land. However, "strong and cogent"[59] evidence is necessary to prove an estoppel based on passive encouragement. The classic statement of this principle is to be found in the judgment of Lord Wensleydale in *Ramsden v. Dyson*[60]:

"If a stranger build on my land, supposing it to be his own, and I, knowing it to be mine, do not interfere, but leave him to go on, equity considers it to be dishonest in me to remain passive and afterwards to interfere and take the profit. But if a stranger build knowingly upon my land, there is no principle of equity which prevents me from insisting on having back my land, with all the additional value which the occupier has imprudently added to it."

Similarly, in the more recent case of *Warnes v. Hedley*,[61] Slade L.J. said:

"... in some circumstances passive conduct, even if unaccompanied by any words, may suffice to constitute the relevant encouragement, if the facts are such that it is reasonable for the other party so to construe it."

In this case, however, there was nothing on the evidence to suggest that, when making the expenditure on the house, the claimant had any belief or expectation that she was being offered an interest in the house other than simply a licence to occupy terminable by the owner on reasonable notice.

In *Salvation Army Trustee Co. Ltd v. West Yorkshire Metropolitan County Council*,[62] "conscious silence" was held sufficient to give rise to a proprietary estoppel. In this case, the plaintiff's owned a site (the old site) on which was a meeting hall used by the Salvation Army. The Council informed the plaintiffs that the old site was affected by a proposed road-widening scheme. It also informed the plaintiffs that they intended to acquire the old site and that an alternative site (the new site) would be made available to the plaintiffs for a replacement meeting hall. The plaintiffs then proceeded to engage contractors for the building of the new hall on the new site. They later took possession of the new site and a new hall was built. Subsequently, the Council informed the plaintiffs that the highway improvement scheme would not be carried out for some years and that they no longer wished to purchase the old site. Woolf J. held that the inactivity of the Council, whilst the new hall was being constructed, amounted to "conscious silence" raising an equity in the plaintiffs' favour. He said[63]:

"The defendant authority either actually knew, or certainly, on the material

---

[59] *Dann v. Spurrier* (1802) 7 Ves. Jun. 232 at 236; 32 E.R. 94 at 96, *per* Lord Eldon. The evidence must "leave no reasonable doubt" that the claimant "acted upon that sort of encouragement": *ibid.* 236; 96.

[60] (1866) L.R. 1 H.L. 129, 168, H.L.

[61] Unreported, January 31, 1984, C.A., available on Lexis. See also, *Holiday Inns Inc. v. Broadhead* (1974) 232 EG 951 at 1087, where Goff J. said: "... there is a head of equity under which relief will be given where the owner of property seeks to take an unconscionable advantage of another by *allowing* or encouraging him to spend money ...": *ibid.* 1087, (emphasis added).

[62] (1981) 41 P. & C.R. 179.

[63] *ibid.* 196.

before me, ought to have known, that the plaintiffs were continuing to incur expenditure under the mistaken belief to which I have referred, and, although they were not entitled to stop building work on the new site, they could have indicated that they did not regard themselves as committed to the purchase of the old site. Instead, they stood by without enlightening the plaintiffs".

In *Midland Bank Ltd v. Farmpride Hatcheries Ltd*,[64] the appellant was the director of a company which owned a mansion house and chicken hatchery in Norfolk. The respondent bank had granted a mortgage upon the security of the house, unaware of an express licence for occupation of the house rent-free for 20 years in favour of the appellant. In due course, the bank was obliged to seek possession of the house, pursuant to the mortgage, and was met with a claim to a right of occupation by the appellant. The trial judge held that the appellant should be refused an injunction restraining the order for possession because of his unconscionable failure to inform the bank of his interest at the time of the loan. The Court of Appeal, agreeing with the decision, held that the appellant was clearly estopped from relying on his claim since he himself had procured the mortgage on behalf of the company. It was unconscionable for a negotiating agent to remain silent about an adverse interest to which he laid claim in the mortgaged property and subsequently to assert that interest when the other party had irrevocably altered its position. The principle of proprietary estoppel was, accordingly, held to apply to the facts of the case.

It is possible, however, for the legal owner's silence to be explained on grounds other than the endorsement of the claimant's alleged entitlement. A good example is to be found in the case of *Williams v. Coleman*,[65] where the person claimed to be estopped was a middle-aged lady who was physically disabled and confined to a wheelchair. The Court of Appeal explained her silence in the face of adverse occupation as being motivated by a desire not to make a fuss and to avoid trouble. In *Rogers v. Eller*,[66] the claimant argued that the requisite encouragement on the part of the legal owner could be inferred from his conduct.

Firstly permitting his sister to reside in the subject property for about 40 years; secondly allowing her (and her former husband) to maintain it; thirdly allowing them to improve it and to incur substantial expenditure in so doing; fourthly permitting her to care for him and to look after him (particularly, at a period during which he was ill for some six months); and fifthly failing to take any action to recover possession of the house.

In particular, stress was placed on the long period of time during which the claimant had been allowed to occupy the property without any express indication, on the part of the plaintiff, that she would ever be turned out. The Court of Apeal, however, rejected these five factors, taken individually or

---

[64] (1981) 260 EG 493, C.A.
[65] Unreported, June 27, 1984, C.A., available on Lexis. See also, *Pennell v. Nunn*, unreported, April 2, 1982, available on Lexis, where mere inactivity by a liquidator whilst a bankrupt improved his property was held insufficient to give rise to a proprietary estoppel.
[66] Unreported, May 20, 1986, C.A., available on Lexis.

cumulatively, as being sufficient to raise the inference that the claimant could remain in the premises for as long as she wished. Slade L.J., giving the leading judgment of the court, concluded that these factors were perfectly consistent with an arrangement between the parties that the claimant should be allowed to live rent-free in the property without a definite time limit, but only so long as the plaintiff so desired.

There is considerable debate as to whether the legal owner's knowledge of the claimant's action and mistaken belief (and of his own legal rights to intervene) is strictly necessary in a case involving passive acquiescence. In *Shaw v. Appelgate*,[67] a case involving acquiescence in a continuing breach of covenant, the Court of Appeal held that to deprive the possessor of a legal right of that right on the ground of his acquiescence, the situation must have become such that it would be dishonest or unconscionable for him to continue to seek to enforce it. Buckley L.J. suggested that it may be "open to doubt"[68] whether, in order to establish dishonesty or unconscionability, it was strictly necessary to comply with all the five *probanda* listed by Fry J. in *Willmott v. Barber*[69] although "no doubt if all those five tests were satisfied there would be shown to be a state of affairs in which it would be dishonest or unconscionable for the owner of the right to insist upon it".[70] Goff L.J., agreeing with Buckley L.J., also had doubts as to whether, in an acquiescence case, it was strictly necessary to establish all five *Willmott* criteria and agreed that the test was essentially whether, in all the circumstances, it had become unconscionable for the plaintiff to rely upon his strict legal rights. In the earlier case of *Electrolux Ltd v. Electrix Ltd*,[71] cited with approval by Buckley L.J., similar reservations were expressed by Sir Raymond Evereshed M.R., who also indicated that not all the five requisites stated by Fry J. in *Willmott* had to be present in every case in which it was sought to deprive the legal owner of his right to succeed in an action on the ground of acquiescence.[72]

The point was also addressed by Oliver J. in *Taylor Fashions Ltd v. Liverpool Victoria Trustee Co Ltd*,[73] who suggested that strict adherence to the five *probanda* "must now be considered open to doubt"[74] where all that has happened is that the party estopped has stood by without protest while his rights have been infringed.

By contrast, the Court of Appeal in *Armstrong v. Sheppard & Short Ltd*,[75]

---

[67] [1977] 1 W.L.R. 970, C.A.
[68] *ibid.* 978.
[69] (1880) 15 Ch.D. 96. See, Chap. 6, pp. 117–118.
[70] *ibid.* 978.
[71] (1954) 71 R.P.C. 23.
[72] *ibid.* 33.
[73] [1982] Q.B. 133. See further, Chap. 6, pp. 124–127.
[74] *ibid.* 147.
[75] [1959] 2 Q.B. 384, C.A. See also, *Denny v. Jensen* [1977] 1 N.Z.L.R. 635, Supreme Court of Dunedin, where White J. said: "Conscious silence implies knowledge on the part of the defendant that the plaintiff was incurring the expenditure and in the mistaken belief that there was a contract to purchase and that the defendant "stood by" without enlightening the plaintiff. In short, the plaintiff must establish fraud or unconscionable behaviour": *ibid.* 638. There is also authority for the proposition that the legal owner should know that his property was being improved: see, *Brand v. Chris Building Co. Ltd* [1957] V.R. 625, Supreme Court of Victoria, where the plaintiff had no knowledge that building work had been undertaken on his land. It is also suggested that the legal owner should have, at least, knowledge that he was entitled to interfere: *Svenson v. Payne* (1945) 71 C.L.R. 531.

relying on the judgment of Fry J. in *Willmott*, held that an owner of land was not debarred from asserting his legal right on the ground of acquiescence unless it was clear that, at the time he acquiesced, he was aware of his proprietary right. In this case, the plaintiff owned a small strip of land at the rear of his premises on which the defendants had entered and constructed a sewer for the discharge of sewage and effluent. The plaintiff's claim was for damages for trespass and an injunction to restrain the discharge of effluent through the sewer. The trial judge found as a fact that (1) the plaintiff had orally informed the defendants that he did not object to the construction of the sewer and (2) that the plaintiff, when he made the statement, was not aware that he was the owner of the strip of land or that he had a right to object to the construction of the sewer. On appeal, the Court of Appeal held that there was no equity which barred the plaintiff from asserting his legal title. Lord Evershed M.R. said[76]:

> "... it is true to say that a proprietor will not be debarred from asserting his legal right, against one who is shown to have infirnged it, on the ground of acquiescence, unless it is also clear that, at the time he did so acquiesce, the proprietor was aware of his proprietary rights".

The above-cited passage was applied by Ungoed-Thomas J. in *Ward v. Kirkland*,[77] who reiterated the principle that "knowledge by the legal owner of his own proprietary right is essential to found an equity which will prevent him exercising that legal right".[78] According to Snell, *Principles of Equity*[79]:

> "Before the equity can arise in [a case of passive acquiescence], O [the representor] must have known of A's [the representee's] expenditure. Further, normally he must also have known that the property was his, or that his property was being improved, or that he was entitled to interfere, for such knowledge makes it dishonest for him to remain wilfully passive and thereby afterwards profit by a mistake which he might have prevented.[80] But this knowledge is not essential, for even without it, O's encouraging conduct considered in conjunction with A's actions and belief, may be such that it would be dishonest and unconscionable for O to seek to stand on his legal rights".

In the Canadian case of *The Queen v. Smith*,[81] the Crown was held, by virtue of its long inaction with knowledge that the subject land was being occupied by non-Indians, to have stood by and acquiesced in various improvements made by the respondent and his predecessor in occupation. The Crown, through both the provincial and federal government, knew of the occupation of the land by non-Indians from 1838 onwards but never took steps to regularise the position. In view of the Crown's passive conduct, it was held unconscionable for it to

---

[76] *ibid.* 396.
[77] [1967] Ch. 194.
[78] *ibid.* 240.
[79] (29th ed.), pp. 575–576.
[80] Citing *Ramsden v. Dyson* (1866) L.R. 1 H.L. 129 at 141, (H.L.), *per* Lord Cranworth L.C. See also, *Proctor v. Bennis* (1887) 36 Ch. D. 740 at 760, *per* Cotton L.J.
[81] (1981) 113 D.L.R. (3d) 522, Federal Court of Appeal.

recover the land from the respondent without compensation for the improvements made.[82]

(C) Who Must Give the Assurance?

Generally speaking, the relevant assurance must emanate from the freehold owner of the land against which the estoppel equity is being claimed.[83] There may, however, be special circumstances where the assurance need not strictly be given by the legal owner. In *Matharu v. Matharu*,[84] for example, the claimant's husband had assured her that the subject property was as much hers at it was his. The husband's father, however, was the freehold owner of the property. Despite this apparent obstacle to relief, Roch L.J. accepted the claimant's argument that, in the context of an Indian family, anything said by a son to his wife was to be taken as said with the authority of his father. Accordingly, the father was saddled with his son's assurance.

It is not enough that the assurance was given by a tenant of the freeholder.[85] It may, however, be given by his employee or agent.[86] Thus, in *Attorney-General to H.R.H. Prince of Wales v. Collom*,[87] the defendant was in possession of a house and garden, the site of which she had purchased in 1902. The house was subsequently enlarged to the knowledge of the mineral agent of the Duchy of Cornwall, which subsequently claimed ownership of the house by virtue of the Assessionable Manors Act 1844. The defendant was held to have a good equitable defence based on proprietary estoppel against the Duchy, her expenditure on the house having been made to the knowledge of the agent to the Duchy and on property which she reasonably believed to be her own. The defence was, accordingly, held to be good against the Crown.[88] Atkin J. said[89]:

> "... in a case where it can only be contemplated that the Duke of Cornwall can act through agents, the knowledge or conduct of the agent whose special duty it is to look after mine buildings, such as this is, must bind the Duchy".

---

[82] *ibid.* 583.

[83] *Ward v. Kirkland* [1967] Ch. 194 at 241, *per* Ungoed-Thomas J.

[84] (1994) 68 P. & C.R. 93, C.A.

[85] *Ward v. Kirkland* [1967] Ch. 194 at 241, *per* Ungoed-Thomas J.

[86] *Ivory v. Palmer* (1976) 237 EG 411, C.A.; *Swallow Securities Ltd v. Isenberg* [1985] 1 EGLR 132, C.A.; *Moorgate Mercantile Co Ltd v. Twitchings* [1976] Q.B. 225 at 243, C.A. In this latter case, Lord Denning M.R. opined that "the owner is estopped by the conduct of anyone to whom he entrusts the task of looking after his property and interests ... Whenever the true owner puts someone in his place to answer questions as to his property, he must be bound by his answers just as if he gave them himself": *ibid.* 243. See also, *Moorgate Mercantile Co. Ltd v. Twitchings* [1977] A.C. 890, H.L., (limited agency only) and *Eastern Distributors Ltd v. Goldring* [1957] 2 Q.B. 600 at 606–607, C.A., *per* Devlin J.

[87] [1916] 2 K.B. 193.

[88] See also, *Easterbrook v. The King* [1931] 1 D.L.R. 628, where the Supreme Court of Canada assumed that the doctrine of proprietary estoppel applied to the Crown. See, in particular, the judgment of Newcombe J. at 636. See also, *The Queen v. Smith* (1981) 113 D.L.R. (3d) 522 at 582–583, Federal Court of Appeal, where the Crown, by its standing by and acquiescing in improvements made by the respondent and his predecessor over a long period of time, was held estopped from recovering possession of the land without compensation for the improvements.

[89] *ibid.* 203.

It should be borne in mind, however, that an estoppel cannot be raised to prevent a statutory body exercising its statutory discretion or performing its statutory duty. The point arose in *Western Fish Products Ltd v. Penwith District Council*,[90] where it was held that the council's planning officers, even though acting in the apparent scope of their authority, could not bind the council in the determination of the plaintiffs' planning applications because the council alone had the statutory power, under the Town and Country Planning Act 1971, to determine planning applications. Although a planning authority might be bound by the decisions of a planning officer if the power to decide the particular matter had been (or appeared to be) delegated to the officer, for an estoppel to arise in such circumstances it was necessary to show something over and above the mere fact of the officer's position, on which the applicant was justified in thinking that the officer's statements would bind the council. In the instant case, there was nothing, apart from the position held by the planning officer, on which the plaintiffs could have assumed that the officer could bind the council and, accordingly, the council was held not to be estopped by anything the planning officer had said from refusing the plaintiffs' applications for planning consent.

The relevant assurance may be given by a company through one of its agents or employees.[91] This was implicitly recognised in *Swallow Securities Ltd v. Isenberg*,[92] where the claimant had caused major works (costing some £40,000) to be carried out to a flat (in which she was living without the knowledge of the landlords), works which were known to the landlords' resident porter but not known at the time to the managing agents or the landlords. The Court of Appeal, agreeing with the trial judge, rejected the claimant's submission that the landlords were estopped from asserting a right to possession of the flat against her. Although the resident porter was aware of the refurbishment works, there was nothing to put him on inquiry that they were being carried out on behalf of the claimant rather than on the order of the persons who were still assumed to be the lawful tenants of the flat. Accordingly, there was no evidence of any action on the part of the landlords, or their servants or agents, inducing an expectation on the part of the claimant that she had rights more extensive than she actually had.

The relevant assurance may have been made by the plaintiff's predecessor in title.[93] In *Jones (A.E.) v. Jones (F.W.)*,[94] for example, the defendant's father bought a house near his own home for the defendant, who left a job and council house and moved with his family into the house. The defendant gave his father sums amounting to one-quarter of the purchase price of the house. The defendant understood from his father that the house was his. When the father died, the house vested in the plaintiff, the defendant's step-mother. The Court of Appeal held that the plaintiff was estopped from turning the defendant out of the

---

[90] [1981] 2 All E.R. 204, C.A.
[91] But not if the assurance is given to an associated company with identical shareholders and management: *Te Rama Engineering Ltd v. Shortlands Properties Ltd* [1982] B.C.L. 692, High Court of New Zealand.
[92] [1985] 1 EGLR 132, C.A. See also, *Crabb v. Arun District Council* [1976] Ch. 179 at 189, C.A., *per* Lord Denning M.R., (Council representative).
[93] *Hopgood v. Brown* [1955] 1 W.L.R. 213 at 224–225, 229, 231, C.A., *per* Lord Evershed M.R., Jenkins and Morrris L.JJ., respectively, relying on *Taylor v. Needham* (1810) 2 Taunt. 278; 127 E.R. 1084.
[94] [1977] 1 W.L.R. 438, C.A.

house by the father's conduct which had led the defendant to leave his job and pay money to his father in the belief that the house would be his home for the rest of his life. The representation made by the father to the defendant was held to be just as binding upon the plaintiff, who was the administratrix of his will, as upon the deceased father.

It is not essential that the representor should already own the land at the time when the assurance is made.[95] It will be sufficient if the estoppel is subsequently "fed" when the representor acquires the legal estate at a later date. The point arose in *Watson v. Goldsbrough*,[96] where a dispute arose between members of an angling club and owners as to rights to fish in certain ponds. No lease, licence (or other legal document) had been executed conferring fishing rights on the anglers but, at one time, a form of lease had been executed by the plaintiff, a member of the club. This lease was never executed by the owners but the plaintiff claimed that there was an informal agreement that the club could have a lease or option to purchase the ponds in question. In these circumstances, the club proceeded to spend substantial sums of money in dredging and improving the ponds and stocking them with fish. Matters came to a head when the first and second defendants, who had originally been licensees, became the freehold owners of the land (which included the ponds) and entered into negotiations to sell the ponds to a third party (the third defendant). The plaintiff's claim based *inter alia* on proprietary estoppel succeeded. The Court of Appeal emphatically rejected an argument that the estoppel could not be established against persons who were mere licensees at the material time. The estoppel had been "fed" when the licensees, who had stood by watching the work being done, acquired the legal estate.

(D) Non-specific Assets and Future Entitlement

There is also some controversy as to whether an equity can be raised where the assurance relates to non-specific assets. In *Layton v. Martin*,[97] the deceased, a maried man, asked the plaintiff to come and live with him offering "what emotional security I can give, plus financial security during my life and financial security after my death". In reliance on this assurance, the plaintiff provided wifely services and was paid a salary plus an amount for housekeeping. Later, the parties separated but kept in touch until the deceased's death in 1982. The plaintiff's claim for financial provision based on proprietary estoppel was dismissed on the gound that the deceased's representations did not relate to any specific assets. Scott J. said[98]:

> "A representation that 'financial security' would be provided by the deceased to the plaintiff, and on which I will assume she acted, is not a

---

[95] See, *e.g. Riches v. Hogben* [1986] 1 Qd. R. 315, where a mother promised that she would buy a house and place it in her son's name if he emigrated to Australia to live near her.

[96] [1986] 1 EGLR 265, C.A. See also, *Abbey National Building Society v. Cann* [1991] A.C. 56, H.L.

[97] [1986] 2 FLR 227. Compare *Baumgartner v. Baumgartner* (1988) 62 A.L.J.R. 29, High Court of Australia, where oral assurances that quasi-matrimonial home would be "a security" for female partner held to give rise to an expectation of an indefinite right of residence. See further, Chap. 8, pp. 168–170. See generally C.J. Davis [1996] Conv. 193.

[98] *ibid.* 238–239.

representation that she is to have some equitable or legal interest in any particular asset or assets. It is unthinkable that either the plaintiff or the deceased would have supposed that, on her return to live at 12 Clifton Villas, induced, let it be supposed, by that representation, she thereby acquired some sort of equitable interest in his assets. What assets? His assets for the time being, answered counsel for the plaintiff. The proposition has only, in my view, to be put to be seen to be untenable".

In *Philip Lowe (Chinese Restaurant) Ltd v. Sau Man Lee*,[99] the plaintiff assured the defendant, his mistress (a "second wife" or "little wife" under Chinese custom), that she would inherit half his business and any cash and the proceeds of an insurance policy, when he died. In reliance on this assurance, the defendant did various works of repair and redecoration at the plaintiff's house. When the plaintiff later claimed possession of the house, the defendant raised the defence of proprietary estoppel. The claim was based on the plaintiff's representation as to what was to happen to the property when he died. It was submitted that this comprised a clear intimation by him to the defendant that she would have a future interest in the property. Since she had acted upon that representation to her prejudice or detriment by doing work to the property, it was argued that she had thereby acquired an equity sufficient to defeat the plaintiff's claim to possession. Her claim, however, was rejected by the Court of Appeal largely on the ground that the defendant had not relied upon the plaintiff's representation. She had caried out the various works, not on the basis of any right to live there, but simply because she considered herself part of the plaintiff's family. It was also doubted whether any representation as to what would happen upon the plaintiff's death (or what would be in his will) could be construed as involving an intention that there should be a present acquisition of that future right by the defendant. In the words of May L.J., giving the leading judgment of the Court, "in some respects, if one considers the alleged representation to take effect only upon death, the two are indeed inconsistent". However, May L.J. considered it unnecessary to decide the point.

The decisions in *Layton* and *Lowe* were not cited in the subsequent case of *Re Basham (dec'd)*,[1] where Mr Edward Nugee Q.C. (sitting as a High Court judge) held that the principle of proprietary estoppel was not limited to acts done in reliance on a belief relating to an existing right, but extended to acts done in reliance on a belief that future rights would be granted. Accordingly, an estoppel could be raised in relation to the grant of rights over a residuary estate. In this case, the deceased had assured the plaintiff that she would inherit the deceased's property. It was argued that the deceased's representation had to relate to an existing right (*i.e.* a present right or interest) in order to found an estoppel claim. Since, it was argued, it had to relate to a particular property it could not extend to property as indefinite and fluctuating as the whole of a deceased's estate. In rejecting this argument, the learned judge said[2]:

"It is clear that the doctrine which bears the label 'proprietary estoppel' is

---

[99] Unreported, July 9, 1985, C.A., available on Lexis.
[1] [1986] 1 W.L.R. 1498. See, D. Hayton, [1987] 46 C.L.J. 215; J. Martin, [1987] Conv. 211; M. Davey, (1988) 8 L.S. 92 at pp. 101–108. See also *Burrows & Burrows v. Sharp* (1991) 23 H.L.R. 82, C.A.
[2] *ibid.* 1510.

not limited to cases ... where A believes that he already has the interest which he asks the court to confirm, but extends to cases in which A believes that he will obtain an interest in the future; and this being so, I see no justification for importing a requirement that he should in addition already be in enjoyment of some lesser interest".

Similar reasoning led Mr Edward Nugee Q.C. to reject the submission that the claimant's belief must relate to some clearly identified piece of property, movable or immovable. By analogy with constructive trust cases, in particular those arising from mutual wills, it was evident that the trust could bind the whole of the deceased's estate. On this basis, there was no reason in principle why "the doctrine of proprietary estoppel should not apply so as to raise an equity against B in favour of A extending to the whole of B's estate".[3] It seems apparent, therefore, that an assurance may relate to a future grant of rights. Indeed, in *Durant v. Heritage*,[4] the decision in *Re Basham, (Deceased)* was expressly followed by Mr Andrew Park Q.C. (sitting as a deputy judge of the High Court). In this case, a Mr Robinson, who died on March 30, 1989, left Holme Farm, a house and garden in the village of Normanton, by his will to one of his nieces, the first defendant. Another niece, the plaintiff, claimed that, by virtue of proprietary estoppel, she was entitled to have the property transferred to her. The plaintiff and her husband moved into the property in 1970 as tenants at a very low rent and carried out substantial works to the property over the years, in their own time and at their own expense, in the belief that Mr Robinson would leave the property to her on his death. The plaintiff brought an action against the first defendant as well as against the second defendant, as executors of Mr Robinson's will,[5] seeking the transfer of the property to her. In the course of his judgment, Mr Andrew Park Q.C., applying *Re Basham (dec'd)*, concluded that the doctrine of proprietary estoppel was not confined to a case where the claimant is encouraged to believe he or she has a presently subsisting right or interest. The doctrine can extend to a case where the claimant has a belief, knowingly encouraged by the legal owner, that, although he or she does not presently have an interest in the property, he or she will acquire one in the future (*e.g.* by will). Similarly, in *Needham v. Bowner*,[6] the plaintiff, a daughter of the deceased, successfully claimed that she was entitled to the freehold of her father's house, 19 Capbell Street, Belpher, Derbyshire, on the basis of proprietary estoppel. She argued that she had lived in the house since 1940 with her husband looking after her father until his death in 1976. She was led to believe that, on her father's death, the house would pass to her. Originally, the father held only a tenancy but, in 1975, he purchased the house, the plaintiff (and her sister, now also deceased) contributing to the legal expenses and to some extensive repairs over the years. Mervyn Davies J. held that (1) the father had allowed and encouraged the plaintiff (and her sister) to assume that the

---

[3] *ibid.* 1510.
[4] [1994] EGCS 134.
[5] Mr Andrew Park Q.C. made it clear, in the course of his judgment, that the equity was being claimed against the personal representatives of Mr Robinson, not against the beneficiaries of his will. In other words, the first defendant was being sued in her representative capacity as an executrix of the testator, not in her persoanl capacity as the devisee of Holme Farm.
[6] [1989] EGCS 73.

house would be theirs after his death; (2) in that expectation, the sisters spent money on the property incurring a detriment; and (3) it was unconscionable to disappoint or deny their expectations.

In *Shaida v. Kindlane Ltd*,[7] the defendants represented to the plaintiff that they would transfer the freehold interest of a house to him and, on the faith of that representation, the plaintiff carried out various works to the property and also contributed to the purchase price. H.H. Judge Baker Q.C. (sitting as a judge of the High Court) held that, on these facts, the plaintiff was entitled to have the house transferred to him under the doctrine of proprietary estoppel. It is interesting to observe that in this case the assurance raised an expectation that the claimant would become entitled to the freehold interest in the property at some future time. In the more typical case, the assurance takes the form of an expectation of present entitlement.

(E) Knowledge of the Legal Owner

Knowledge by the legal owner that his assurance is being relied upon by the estoppel claimant is essential[8] to found a successful estoppel claim. It must be shown that the legal owner either knew[9] or ought to have known[10] that the claimant was acting in reliance upon the assurance given. Thus, in *Costagliola v. English*,[11] the defendant had expended money in the improvement of her house in reliance upon there being no vehicular right of way across her land in favour of the plaintiff. She contended that she would not have spent the money if she had known that the plaintiff would claim that such a right of way still existed. The defendant gave evidence that she would have bought the house in any event, as it was her parent's home, but she would not have modernised it if there had been a right for vehicles past it. Her claim based on proprietray estoppel failed since there was no evidence to suggest that the owner of the dominant tenement knew anything about the defendant's intentions. On this point, Megarry J. said[12]:

"Even on the footing that that there was some knowledge of the execution of some or other of the improvements, there was not a shred of evidence that Mrs Runciman or anyone on her behalf knew that the defendant was doing the work in reliance on there being no right of way for vehicles".

It is not a necessary prerequisite, however, that the party estopped should

---

[7] Unreported, June 22, 1982, H.H. Judge Baker Q.C., available on Lexis.
[8] It should be noted, however, that in *Shaida v. Kindlane Ltd*, unreported, June 22, 1982, H.H. Judge Baker Q.C. indicated that "it is important, though not crucial ... that the true owner of the land, normally the person who has made the representation, knew that the person to whom he had made it was so acting to his detriment". See also, above, pp. 32–34, in relation to cases on passive acquiescence.
[9] See, *e.g. Griffiths v. Williams* (1978) 248 EG 947 at 949, C.A., *per* Goff L.J.; *Ward v. Gold* (1969) 211 EG 155 at 161, *per* Plowman J.; *Gross v. Grench* (1976) 238 EG 39 at 41, C.A., *per* Scarman L.J.; *Savva v. Costa and Harymode Investments Ltd* (1981) 131 New L.J. 1114, C.A.
[10] *Salvation Army Trustee Co. Ltd v. West Yorkshire Metropolitan County Council* (1981) 41 P. & C.R. 179 at 196, *per* Woolf J.; *Swallow Securities Ltd v. Isenberg* [1985] 1 EGLR 132 at 134, *per* Cumming-Bruce L.J.
[11] (1969) 210 EG 1425.
[12] *ibid.* 1431.

know the precise nature of the detriment (or change of position) suffered by the claimant. Thus, in *Crabb v. Arun District Council*,[13] it was not crucial for the plaintiff, in order to establish his equity, to show that the defendants knew that he was actually selling the front portion of his land without reserving a right of access for the back portion. It was enough that the defendants knew that the plaintiff *intended* to sell the two portions separately and that he would need an additional access point. In the words of Lord Denning M.R., "seeing that they knew of his intention—and they did nothing to disabuse him but rather confirmed it by erecting gates at point B -it was their conduct which led him to act as he did: and this raises an equity in his favour against them".[14] Scarman L.J. was of the same view, holding that it was immaterial that the defendants's only knew of the plaintiff's "intention"[15] to sell a portion of the land but was unaware of "the realisation of that intention".[16] Moreover, there was no obligation on the part of the plaintiff claimant to give notice of the sale to the defendants so as to afford them the opportunity to disabuse him of his mistaken belief before he acted to his detriment. On this point, Scarman L.J. said[17]:

> "I can conceive of cases in which it would be absolutely appropriate for a defendant to say: 'But you should not have acted to your detriment until you had a word with me and I could have put you right.' But there are cases in which it is far too late for a defendant to get himself out of his pickle by putting upon the plaintiff that sort of duty; and this, in my judgment, is one of those cases".

A good example of a claim failing for want of knowledge on the part of the legal owner that his assurance is being relied upon by the estoppel claimant is to be found in *Savva v. Costa and Harymode Investments Ltd*,[18] where the plaintiff was the first defendant's mistress and had two children by him. The second defendant, a company, was under the control of the first defendant and owned the freehold property upon which the plaintiff had spent an appreciable sum in improvements. Whilst the first defendant offered the plaintiff the property for occupation by herself and the children, the Court of Appeal found that he gave her no expectation that she would obtain an interest in the property and, moreover, there was no knowledge on his part that the plaintiff believed that she was going to obtain such an interest. Her claim based on proprietary estoppel accordingly failed. Reference may also be made to *Brinnard v. Ewens*,[19] where the first appellant had been the tenant of the ground floor and back bedroom on the first floor of a house. The respondent was her landlord. Until 1978 or 1979,

---

[13] [1976] Ch. 179, C.A.

[14] *ibid*. 189.

[15] If the evidence does not support any knowledge of even an intention to rely upon the representation, the estoppel is bound to fail: See, *Costagliola v. English* (1969) 210 EG 1425 at 1431, *per* Megarry J.

[16] *ibid*. 197–198.

[17] *ibid*. 198. See further, Chap. 6, pp. 113–114.

[18] (1981) 131 New L.J. 1114, C.A.

[19] (1987) 19 H.L.R. 415, C.A.

the remainder of the house was occupied but, at that time, the last occupant left and the first appellant (and her husband, the second appellant) moved into the whole house. From that time onwards, the appellants expended considerable sums of money in carrying out repairs and improvements to the property which they claimed amounted to £30,000. They brought proceedings claiming an interest in the remainder of the house under the doctrine of proprietary estoppel.

The trial judge found as a fact that the main reason for occupying the whole house was to enable the local authority to exercise their statutory powers to compel the landlord to repair the house. Much of the work had been done simply to make the house more comfortable to live in. It was also found that the landlord did not know or have any reason to know that the work was being done by the appellants with the view that a tenancy of the whole house was being granted by her. The Court of Appeal, agreeing with the trial judge, held that the appellants could not establish that their expenditure had taken place in the belief that they would obtain an interest in the property. Moreover, it could not be said that the landlord had encouraged any such belief since she had no knowledge of it. Accordingly, the appellants' claim failed. Nourse L.J. said[20]:

"You cannot encourage a belief of which you do not have any knowledge".

There is now considerable doubt as to whether the legal owner's knowledge of his own legal rights at the time of making the assurance is essential to found every type of proprietary estoppel claim. In *Willmott v. Barber*,[21] Fry J. listed five criteria for the establishment of a claim based on acquiescence. His third prerequisite was that the legal owner "must have known of the existence of his own right which is inconsistent with the right claimed by the plaintiff".[22] If he is unaware of his own legal right, "he is in the same position as the plaintiff, and the doctrine of acquiescence is founded upon conduct with a knowledge of your legal rights".[23] It appears from recent judicial pronouncements[24] that this requirement of knowledge is confined to cases of pure acquiescence where the assurance takes the form of mere silence or passive abstention. Thus, the fact that the legal owner is ignorant of his own legal rights will, it seems, provide no bar to a claim of proprietary estoppel founded upon active encouragement by words or conduct. In the Canadian case of *Canadian Superior Oil Ltd v. Paddon-Hughes Development Co. Ltd*,[25] there is clear recognition that, in a case involving estoppel by words or conduct (as opposed to mere acquiesc-

---

[20] *ibid.* 418.
[21] (1880) 15 Ch.D. 96.
[22] *ibid.* 105–106.
[23] *ibid.* 105–106.
[24] See, in particular, Oliver J. in *Taylors Fashions Ltd v. Liverpool Victoria Trustees Co. Ltd* [1982] Q.B. 133 at 147, where he considered it "open to doubt" that the strict *Willmott v. Barber* criteria "are applicable as necessary requirements in those cases where all that has happened is that the party alleged to be estopped has stood by without protest while his rights have been infringed". In *Hopgood v. Brown* [1955] 1 W.L.R. 213, C.A., Lord Evershed M.R. observed that "the formulation [by Fry J. in *Willmott v. Barber*] was addressed to and limited to cases where the party is alleged to be estopped by acquiescence": *ibid.* 223. See further, Chap. 6, pp. 124–127. By contrast, see the judgment of Ungoed-Thomas J. in *Ward v. Kirkland* [1967] Ch. 194, where he said: "knowledge by the legal owner of his own proprietary right is essential to found an equity": *ibid.* 240.
[25] (1969) 3 D.L.R. (3d) 10, Alberta Supreme Court.

ence), knowledge of his rights is not essential in a person against whom such a defence is raised.[26]

Similarly, it appears that Fry J.'s fourth *probandum* in *Willmott v. Barber*, namely, that the legal owner has knowledge of the claimant's mistaken belief of his rights, is no longer an essential element in cases involving an estoppel by encouragement.[27] Here again, Oliver J. in *Taylors Fashions Ltd v. Liverpool Victoria Trustees Co. Ltd*[28] indicated that "knowledge of the true position by the party alleged to be estopped, becomes merely one of the relevant factors – it may even be a determining factor in certain cases—in the overall inquiry".[29] It will still, however, continue to be of strict relevance in cases involving unilateral mistake.[30]

---

[26] *ibid.* 16, *per* Johnson J.A. See also, on appeal, (1970) 12 D.L.R. (3d) 247 at 253, Supreme Court of Canada, *per* Martland J.
[27] See further, Chap. 6, pp. 124–127.
[28] [1982] Q.B. 133.
[29] *ibid.* 152.
[30] See further, Chap. 6, pp. 115–127. See, in particular, *Coombes v. Smith* [1986] 1 W.L.R. 808, discussed in detail, below, at pp. 120–122.

3. RELIANCE

(A) Introduction

The second ingredient necessary to found a proprietary estoppel claim is the claimant's *reliance* on the legal owner's assurance that he or she has or will acquire some right or interest in the land. It is the element of reliance which demonstrates that it was the legal owner's assurance which caused the estoppel claimant to act to his detriment or change his position.

In *Attorney-General of Hong Kong v. Humphreys Estate (Queen's Gardens) Ltd*,[1] the Privy Council held that it was necessary for the estoppel claimants to "show"[2] that they had relied on the belief or expectation which had been encouraged. In this case, an agreement in principle expressed to be "subject to contract" was reached between the defendants (H.K.), as the representatives of the government of Hong Kong, and a group of companies (H.E.), which included the plaintiff company, to the effect that, in exchange for acquiring 83 flats from H.E., H.K. would grant a Crown lease of certain land and a permission to develop. H.K. moved some civil servants into the flats, spending some money on them, and H.E. did some work on the land, the subject of the intended lease. H.E. subsequently withdrew from the agreement. The Privy Council held that H.E. were entitled to withdraw. On the evidence, it had not been shown by H.K. that H.E. had encouraged an expectation that it would not withdraw from the agreement since H.E. had always retained a right to resile from it. Moreover, nothwithstanding that H.K. had acted to its detriment, it had not been shown that it had relied on an expectation that H.E. would carry out the agreement and transfer the flats to H.K.. Accordingly, no estoppel operated to prevent H.E. from exercising its legal right to refuse to execute the transfer documents and to withdraw from the transaction. Lord Templeman, giving judgment, said[3]:

> "First the government must show that H.K.L created or encouraged a belief or expectation on the part of the government that H.K.L would not withdraw from the agreement in principle. Secondly the government must show that the government relied on that belief or expectation. Their Lordships agree with the courts of Hong Kong that the government fail on both counts".

It appears, however, that the requirement of reliance is not strict. Reliance

---

[1] [1987] A.C. 114, P.C.
[2] *ibid.* 124.
[3] *ibid.* 124.

may be presumed or inferred once it has been shown that an assurance was calculated to influence the judgment of a reasonable man (or woman).[4]

(B) Presumption of Reliance

It is apparent that there is a presumption of reliance once an assurance on the part of the legal owner has been established. In *Greasley v. Cooke*,[5] the defendant came as a maid in 1938 to live in the house of a widower. He died in 1948 and, after his death, the defendant stayed on in the house looking after his son and daughter until their deaths in 1975, receiving no payment for doing so. She and the son lived together as husband and wife throughout this period, and she was treated as one of the family. The county court judge held that she believed, because of what was said to her by the son, that she would be allowed to live in and remain in the house as long as she wished, though the judge said that she might have expected the son to make provision for her to this effect by his will. However, he held that she failed to prove that the reason why she looked after the son and daughter without payment was because of her belief that she would be entitled to live in the house as long as she wished, and he dismissed her claim based on proprietary estoppel. The Court of Appeal, reversing this decision, concluded that, once it was shown that the defendant had relied on the representations made to her, the burden of proving that she acted to her detriment in staying on to look after the house and family did not rest on her. In the absence of proof to the contrary, the court would infer that her conduct was induced by the assurances given to her. Lord Denning M.R. said on this point[6]:

> "So, instead of looking for another job, she stayed on in the house looking after Kenneth and Clarice. There is a presumption that she did so, relying on the assurances given to her by Kenneth and Hedley. The burden is not on her, but on them, to prove that she did not rely on their assurances. They did not prove it, nor did their representatives. So she is presumed to have relied on them".

According to Lord Denning M.R., reliance could be presumed simply from the fact that a promise or representation was made provided that it was "calculated to influence"[7] the claimant. According to Waller L.J. in the same case, it was enough if the assurances were of such a nature as to "tend to

---

[4] *Brikom Investments Ltd v. Carr* [1979] Q.B. 467 at 483, C.A., *per* Lord Denning M.R.

[5] [1980] 1 W.L.R. 1306, C.A.

[6] *ibid.* 1311. Lord Denning M.R. relied on his earlier statements in *Brikom Investments Ltd v. Carr* [1979] Q.B. 467 at 482–483, C.A., that, where a person makes a representation intending that another should act on it: "It is no answer for the maker to say: 'You would have gone on with the transaction anyway'. That must be mere speculation. No one can be sure what he would, or would not, have done in a hypothetical state of affairs which never took place . . . Once it is shown that a representation was calculated to influence the judgment of a reasonable man, the presumption is that he was so influenced". In *Stevens & Cutting Ltd v. Anderson* [1990] 1 EGLR 95, 97, C.A., Stuart-Smith L.J. states that the headnote in *Greasley* is misleading in suggesting that it was concerned with the onus of proving detriment—it was concerned with the burden of proving reliance on a representation. See also, *Smith v. Chadwick* (1882) 20 Ch.D. 27 at 44–45, *per* Sir George Jessel M.R.

[7] *ibid.* 1311. See also, *Layton v. Martin* [1986] 2 FLR 227 at 253, *per* Scott J.

induce"[8] a course of conduct on the claimant's part. This reasoning was applied by Mr Edward Nugee Q.C. (sitting as a High Court judge) in *Re Basham (dec'd)*,[9] who, although satisfied on the evidence that one reason why the plaintiff did so much for the deceased in that case was her belief that, although she was not a blood relative of his, he would leave his estate to her on his death, nevertheless, went on to conclude that "if the evidence was not sufficient to establish this positively, the plaintiff would still be entitled to succeed [on the authority of *Greasley v. Cooke*] . . . in the absence of proof that she did not rely on the deceased's statements".[10]

The observations of Lord Denning M.R. in *Greasley* on the burden of proof have since been judicially interpreted as meaning that "where, following assurances made by the other party, the claimant has adopted a course of conduct which is prejudicial or otherwise detrimental to her, there is a rebuttable presumption that she adopted that course of conduct in reliance on the assurances".[11] The argument that, once the plaintiff proves that she changed her position in reliance on the alleged assurances, the onus shifts to the defendant to prove the absence of detriment, was firmly rejected. In *Watts & Ready v. Story*,[12] Dunn L.J., with reference to the *Greasley* case, said:

"There was some discussion at the Bar as to what Lord Denning M.R. meant in [*Greasley v. Cooke*]. In that case there was no doubt on the evidence that Miss Cooke had been given assurances by the Greasley family that she could regard the property as her home for the rest of her life. Equally, there was no doubt on the facts that she had suffered a detriment, because she had devoted her life to looking after the Greasley family without payment instead of getting a paid job. The only question in the case was whether that admitted detriment was caused by the assurances, or whether she would have continued to look after the family anyway because she was fond of Kenneth Greasley . . . It is in that context that the words of Lord Denning . . . should be read . . . All that Lord Denning was saying was that, the assurances having been established, there was no need for Doris Cooke to prove that the obvious detriment had resulted from them".

The issue regarding the burden of proof was also considered in *Wayling v. Jones*,[13] where the trial judge rejected a claim based on proprietary estoppel on the ground that the plaintiff was unable to prove that the promises that he would

---

[8] *ibid.* 1313.
[9] [1986] 1 W.L.R. 1498.
[10] *ibid.* 1507. See also, *Hamp v. Bygrave* (1983) 266 EG 720, where Boreham J., citing *Greasley v. Cooke*, said: " . . . it is for the defendants to show that the plaintiffs did not rely upon the defendants' assertions": *ibid.* 726; *Habib Bank Ltd v. Habib Bank AG Zurich* [1981] 1 W.L.R. 1265 at 1287, C.A., *per* Oliver L.J.; *Durant v. Heritage* [1994] EGCS 134, *per* Mr Andrew Park Q.C., (sitting as a deputy judge of the High Court). The *Greasley* principle is not, however, without its academic critics: see, *e.g.* M.P. Thompson, (1981) 125 S.J. 539, where it is suggested that the decision was incorrect.
[11] *Coombes v. Smith* [1986] 1 W.L.R. 808 at 821, *per* Mr Jonathan Parker Q.C. (sitting as a deputy High Court judge).
[12] [1984] 134 New L.J. 631, available on Lexis.
[13] (1995) 69 P. & C.R. 170, C.A. The case was actually decided in July 1993. See, C.J. Davis [1995] Conv. 409.

inherit property after the death of the deceased influenced him to remain in the deceased's service. This decision was reversed on appeal. Balcombe L.J, giving the leading judgment, concluded that (1) there must be a sufficient causal link between the promises relied upon and the conduct which constitutes the detriment,[14] (2) the promises relied upon do not have to be the sole inducement for the conduct—it is sufficient if they are an inducement[15] and (3) once it has been established that promises were made, and that there has been conduct by the plaintiff of such a nature that inducement may be inferred, then the burden of proof shifts to the defendant to establish that he did not rely on the promises.[16] On the facts in *Wayling*, the Court of Appeal was satisfied that the plaintiff's conduct in helping the deceased to run his cafe and hotel businesses in return for pocket money was conduct from which his reliance on the deceased's promises of inheritance could be inferred. The real issue was whether the defendants had established that the plaintiff did not rely on these promises. On the evidence, they were held not to have done so. In the words of Leggatt L.J. in the same case[17]:

> "In my judgment the effect of the evidence ... is that: (a) if the deceased had made no promise, the plaintiff would have stayed with him; (b) the deceased did make a promise; and (c) if the deceased had reneged on his promise, the plaintiff would have left. From this it must be inferred that it was because the plaintiff relied on the promise that he would have left if he had learned that it was not going to be kept."

It was recognised by Browne-Wilkinson V.-C. in *Grant v. Edwards*[18] that, in many cases involving cohabitees, it may be virtually impossible to say whether or not the claimant would have done the acts relied on as detriment even if he or she had thought she had no interest in the legal owner's property. His conclusion, therefore, was that "the holding out to the claimant that she had a beneficial interest in the house is an act of such a nature as to be part of the inducement to her to do the acts relied on".[19] Accordingly, in his view (relying on the *Greasley* case), in the absence of evidence to the contrary, the correct inference was that the claimant acted in reliance on such holding out and the burden was on the legal owner to show that she did not do so.

In *Lim Teng Huan v. Ang Swee Chuan*,[20] the Privy Council held that the requirement of reliance could be established by an "inevitable"[21] inference that could be drawn from the facts. Here, the plaintiff and the defendant jointly purchased land which was transferred into their fathers' names. In 1982, the defendant decided to build a house on the land for himself. In 1985, when the

---

[14] See below, pp. 47–53.

[15] See below, p. 53.

[16] This formulation, which requires a promise *and* "conduct by the plaintiff of such a nature that inducement may be inferred", has been criticised as being unduly restrictive: C.J. Davis, [1995] Conv. 409 at pp. 411–412: "It suggests an objective approach where the courts would not infer reliance where the claimant's acts were of such a nature that they would probably have been done anyway. In such a case, the burden of proof of reliance would remain with the claimant".

[17] *ibid*. 176.

[18] [1986] Ch. 638 at 657, C.A.

[19] *ibid*. 657.

[20] [1992] 1 W.L.R. 113, P.C.

[21] *ibid*. 118, *per* Lord Browne-Wilkinson, giving the judgment of the Privy Council.

house was partially built, the parties entered into a written agreement wherein the plaintiff acknowledged that the construction was with his consent and agreed to exchange his undivided share in the land for unspecified land expected to be allotted to the defendant by the government. Subsequently, when the house was complete and fenced in, the plaintiff sought a declaration that he was the owner of a one-half undivided share. The defendant counterclaimed that he was the sole beneficial owner of the plaintiff's share. The Privy Council, affirming that a proprietary estoppel had been established, held that it was to be inferred that the defendant had completed the construction of the house relying on the unenforceable agreement made between the parties. In these circumstances, it would be unconscionable for the plaintiff to renege on the agreement and he was, therefore, estopped from denying the defendant's title to the whole of the land, conditional upon payment of suitable compensation.[22] In the course of his judgment, Lord Browne-Wilkinson said[23]:

> "Although the defendant did not give direct evidence of such reliance, the sole purpose of the agreement was to regularise the position so that the defendant's house would be built on land to which he was solely entitled: the inference that thereafter the defendant proceeded in reliance on that agreed arrangement is inevitable . . . "

Finally, reference may be made to *Durant v. Heritage*,[24] where Mr Andrew Park Q.C. (sitting as a deputy judge of the High Court) usefully expressed the *Greasley* presumption of reliance in a double negative form, namely, that the legal owner must be *unable* to prove that the claimant, in relying on the belief, did *not* rely on it to his or her prejudice or detriment.

(C) Sufficient Causal Link Between Assurance and Detriment

It was stated in *Wayling v. Jones*[25] that there must be a sufficient causal link between the promises relied upon by the estoppel claimant and the conduct which constitutes the detriment. In other words, the promises or representations made must be an *effective cause* of the detrimental conduct. If the claimant was motivated to act as he did for reasons other than the promise or representation made, his claim will not succeed. What must be shown is that the legal owner's assurances *induced* the claimant's expectations that he (or she) has or will acquire a right or interest in the former's property. It is this "inducing an expectation"[26] which renders it unconscionable for the legal owner to go back on his assurances and insist upon his strict legal rights.

In *Wayling*, Balcombe L.J., giving the leading judgment of the Court of

---

[22] As to compensation, see Chap. 5, pp. 91–95.
[23] *ibid.* 118.
[24] [1994] EGCS 134.
[25] (1995) 69 P. & C.R. 170 at 173, C.A., *per* Balcombe L.J. See further, C.J. Davis, [1995] Conv. 409 at pp. 410–411.
[26] *Swallow Securities Ltd v. Isenberg* [1985] 1 EGLR 132 at 134, C.A., *per* Cumming-Bruce L.J. See also, *Dodsworth v. Dodsworth* (1973) 228 EG 115 at 1117, C.A., where Russell L.J. spoke in terms of an "induced expectation".

Appeal, relied upon several constructive trust cases (concerning the acquisition of a beneficial interest in the family home) in support of the proposition requiring a causal link between the assurance and detriment. For example, in *Eves v. Eves*,[27] a decision based on the common intention constructive trust, Brightman J. found it difficult to imagine that the claimant (Janet Eves) would have wielded a 14lb sledge hammer, broken up a large area of concrete, filled the skip and done other things which were carried out when the couple moved into the property, except in pursuance of some expressed or implied arrangement and on the understanding that she was helping to improve her male partner's house in which she was promised that she had an interest.

Similarly, in *Grant v. Edwards*,[28] the Court of Appeal referred to the necessity of establishing a "sufficient link"[29] between the common intention necessary to support a constructive trust and the claimant's conduct in contributing towards the mortgage instalments and housekeeping expenses. In *Layton v. Martin*,[30] a case also involving constructive trust principles, the plaintiff, who was 29, met the deceased and became his mistress. He was a married man, aged 50, whose wife was in poor health. By a letter, the deceased asked the plaintiff to come and live with him offering "what emotional security I can give, plus financial security during my life and financial security after my death". The plaintiff provided wifely services and was paid a modest salary plus an amount for housekeeping. He made some provision for her in his will but later cut her out of his inheritance and gave her written notice of dismissal. The couple parted amicably and kept in touch until the deceased's death. The plaintiff's claim for financial provision, based on the contents of the deceased's letter, failed. There was nothing to suggest, on the evidence, that she had been influenced in any way by the deceased's offer of financial security or that she was induced by his promise to embark on a course of conduct that she would not otherwise have embarked upon. She had gone to live with the deceased on the footing that she would be his *de facto* wife and, accordingly, relied on him to provide for her as a partner in a quasi-marriage and not on account of the content of his letter.

It should be noted, however, that the requirements of proprietary estoppel and constructive trusts in relation to detrimental reliance are not necessarily the same, and it has been suggested[31] that Balcombe L.J.'s judgment in *Wayling*, relying as it does on cases involving the acquisition of an interest in the quasi-matrimonial home by means of a constructive trust, may be misleading in so far it may suggest limitations on what types of detrimental conduct will be accepted as having been done in reliance on assurances given in the proprietary estoppel context.

To found a claim on constructive trust principles, it is evident that the courts require the claimant to have done acts which, in its opinion, would not have been done were it not for the common intention. Any acts that it is considered the claimant would have done anyway (*e.g.* out of natural love and affection)

---

[27] [1975] 1 W.L.R. 1338, C.A.
[28] [1986] Ch. 638, C.A.
[29] *ibid*. 656, *per* Sir Nicholas Browne-Wilkinson V.-C.
[30] [1986] 2 FLR 227.
[31] C.J. Davis, [1995] Conv. 409 at pp. 410–411.

will be treated as insufficient.[32] There appears to be no such explicit limitation on the acts that will be regarded as sufficient detrimental reliance in a case of proprietary estoppel. Any acts will suffice so long as the estoppel claimant can show that he or she would suffer prejudice if the legal owner were allowed to enforce his strict legal rights. Thus, in *Pascoe v. Turner*,[33] the female claimant had spent her own monies on decorations, improvements and repairs to her male partner's house. This was held to be sufficient to accord her an estoppel-based equity. More notably, in *Greasley v. Cooke*,[34] the female claimant had looked after the legal owner's house and family and, in particular, cared for his daughter who was mentally ill. None of her acts were directly referable to the property. Again, in *Maharaj v. Chand*,[35] involving an unmarried couple, the defendant gave up her flat to live with the plaintiff and used her earnings for household requirements and looked after the family. In *Re Basham (dec'd)*,[36] the plaintiff had provided unpaid services in looking after her step-father's house. This was held sufficient detrimental reliance to support an equity on the basis of proprietary estoppel. It is interesting to observe, in passing, that in this case acts by the claimant's husband were also accepted as detrimental reliance on the part of the claimant herself. The decision in *Wayling v. Jones*[37] has already been mentioned earlier. More recently, in *Matharu v. Matharu*,[38] the claimant was able to show detrimental reliance in a number of ways. First, she had abandoned divorce proceedings in order to resume her matrimonial relationship with her husband in reliance on her mistaken belief that the property was as much hers as his. She argued that had she not abandoned those proceedings, she might have claimed accommodation from the local authority as a homeless person with a priority need.[39] Secondly, Roch L.J. accepted that the son's expenditure in improving the property could rank as detrimental reliance on the part of his wife. Such expenditure meant that the amount of income available to benefit the claimant and her children would be less than it

---

[32] See, *e.g. Midland Bank plc v. Dobson* [1986] 1 FLR 171 at pp. 176–177, C.A., *per* Fox L.J.; *Burns v. Burns* [1984] Ch. 317 at 331, C.A., *per* Fox L.J.; *Lloyds Bank plc v. Rosset* [1991] 1 A.C. 107 at 131, H.L., *per* Lord Bridge. In *Grant v. Edwards* [1986] Ch. 638, C.A., Sir Nicholas Browne-Wilkinson V.-C. stated: "In many cases of this sort, it is impossible to say whether or not the claimant would have done the acts relied on as a detriment even if she thought she had no interest in the house. Setting up house together, having a baby, making payments to general housekeeping expenses (not strictly necessary to enable the mortgage to be paid) may all be referable to the mutual love and affection of the parties and not specifically referable to the claimant's belief that she has an interest in the house": *ibid.* 657. By analogy with the proprietary estoppel cases, however, he was prepared to accept such acts as sufficient reliance where it was shown that there was a common intention that the claimant should have an interest in the house: "... any act done by her to her detriment relating to the joint lives of the parties is, in my judgment, sufficient detriment to qualify. The acts do not have to be inherently referable to the house": *ibid.* 657.

[33] [1979] 1 W.L.R. 431, C.A.

[34] [1980] 1 W.L.R. 1306, C.A.

[35] [1986] A.C. 898, P.C.

[36] [1986] 1 W.L.R. 1498.

[37] (1995) 69 P. & C.R. 170, C.A.

[38] (1994) 68 P. & C.R. 93, C.A.

[39] It has been questioned whether this sort of conduct can legitimately be viewed as detrimental: see, M. Welstead, [1995] Conv. 61 at p. 64, who suggests that the claimant's "original change of position had not resulted in any financially quantifiable loss as a result of the [legal owner's] subsequent change of mind. After all, it remained open to her, at all times, to reinstitute proceedings for divorce and attempt to claim local authority accommodation".

would otherwise have been. As Welstead has commented,[40] this seems to "introduce, somewhat prematurely, the concept of a joint regime of matrimonial property into English law". Lastly, money spent by the claimant on renovating a kitchen, even after she had become aware that the property belonged to her husband's father, was held to be a relevant detrimental reliance. According to Roch L.J., the father had induced a belief in the claimant both during and after this expenditure because he had continually, albeit passively, led her to believe that he would abstain from enforcing his legal rights in the property.

By contrast, in *Coombes v. Smith*,[41] Mr Jonathan Parker Q.C. (sitting as a deputy judge of the High Court) held that, even if an assurance had been made by the legal owner, the female claimant had not acted in reliance on it. As to her becoming pregnant, the deputy judge concluded that "it would be wholly unreal, to put it mildly, to find on the evidence adduced before me that the plaintiff allowed herself to become pregnant by the defendant in reliance on some mistaken belief as to her legal rights".[42] She had become pregnant because she wished to live with the defendant and to bear his child. The act of giving birth to her child was rejected on similar grounds. The act of leaving her husband and moving to the defendant's house was also dismissed: "There is no evidence that she left her husband in reliance on the defendant's assurance that he would provide for her if and when their relationship came to an end".[43] The plaintiff's course of conduct in looking after the defendant's house (ready for his visits) and looking after her child was also rejected as being things which "were done by the plaintiff as occupier of the property, as the defendant's mistress, and as Clare's mother, in the context of a continuing relationship with the defendant".[44] The same observations were made in relation to decorating the property and installing decorative beams. Finally, it was argued that, in reliance on the defendant's assurances, the plaintiff took no other steps to provide for herself and her child (*i.e.* she did not look for a job). This also was treated by the deputy judge as insufficient on the basis that there was no evidence that she had actually foreborne to look for employment on the faith of a belief that she was legally entitled to security of tenure.

A proprietary estoppel claim also failed in *Philip Lowe (Chinese Restaurant) Ltd v. Sau Man Lee*,[45] where the Court of Appeal held that the female claimant had carried out works of repair, not in the belief that she was acquiring an interest in the property, but merely because she was part of the legal owner's family. In this case, the parties were Chinese. Under Chinese custom, it was permissible for a married man to take a woman as his second or "little wife" even though he was already married. The plaintiff, Mr Lowe, was married to his first wife and he continued throughout to live with her. The defendant, Miss Lowe, had also been married. In the course of their relationship, she was divorced and became Mr Lowe's "little wife" with the expectation that she would be looked after by the plaintiff as if she were his lawful wife. A

---

[40] M. Welstead, [1995] Conv. 61 at p. 64.
[41] [1986] 1 W.L.R. 808. See further, Chap. 6, pp. 120–122.
[42] *ibid.* 820.
[43] *ibid.* 820.
[44] *ibid.* 820.
[45] Unreported, July 9, 1985, C.A., available on Lexis.

discussion took place between the parties in which the plaintiff stated that he had given instructions that his business should be divided equally between his two wives, together with any cash and the proceeds of an insurance policy, when he died. Thereafter, the defendant did various works of repair and redecoration to the defendant's property, where she lived. She claimed an equity in the property on the ground of proprietary estoppel. The Court of Appeal rejected her claim on the ground that, even if there was an assurance as to her future entitlement, it had not been relied upon by the defendant. She had undertaken the improvement work not on the basis of any right to live there, but simply because she was part of the plaintiff's family.

The court may also be inclined to refuse relief where the improvements have been effected for reasons of purely domestic convenience or comfort. In *E. & L. Berg Homes Ltd v. Grey*,[46] for example, possession was sought against persons who had occupied a caravan by licence of the owners of the site used as a brickworks until it became derelict. The occupation lasted for 26 years. The brick company had arranged for water and electricity to be supplied to the caravan but, after the brickworks closed down, the occupiers installed their own electric generator, later purchased a replacement caravan, had main electricity laid on and a telephone installed. The site was subsequently conveyed to the plaintiffs, an associated company. The plaintiffs' claim for possession was upheld. Sir David Cairns, in the course of his judgment, referred to the transient nature of the development works[47]:

"I cannot accept that the developments were of such a character that a reasonable person would suppose the defendants believed themselves to have any right greater than that of licensees. The home is a mobile home; the services were such as licensees would wish to have, even if there was a risk of their not being able to stay there very long. The carport is the only item of which it can possibly be said that it was of a permanent character, but I do not consider that it was of such magnitude as to raise an equity".

A similar conclusion was reached in *Rogers v. Eller*,[48] where the Court of Appeal, agreeing with the trial judge, held that the arrangement between the parties was that the defendants should simply be allowed to reside in the plaintiff's house indefinitely but with the clear implication that they should only do so so long as they wished and it suited the plaintiff. The defendants had spent considerable sums of money on redecorating and maintaining the property, as well as carrying out alterations which comprised extending the central heating system and renewing the boiler. In relation to these works, Slade L.J. said:

---

[46] (1980) 253 EG 473, C.A.

[47] *ibid.* 479.

[48] Unreported, May 20, 1986, C.A., available on Lexis. See also, *Warnes v. Hedley*, unreported, January 31, 1984, C.A., available on Lexis, where a house was purchased for a young married couple as a family home by the husband's mother. The couple did work on the house to provide nursery accommodation for their first child and also redecorated the property and modernised the kitchen. It was held that this work was "just as consistent with a belief that they had a licence from [the legal owner], a belief that the house was bought for them to occupy as licensees, as it was with any suggestion that they had been given or acquired a beneficial equitable interest": *per* May L.J.

" ... it is to be expected that in such circumstances closer relatives in the position of the defendants, no doubt hoping and expecting that they would continue to live in the property, by keeping the plaintiff well satisfied with their continued presence and wishing to improve their own comfort at the same time, would contribute by carrying out work to the property, even at substantial expense, and also by giving other assistance to the plaintiff in one way or another".

Another illustrative case is *Stilwell v. Simpson.*[49] Here, the defendant granted a tenancy of part of a house to the plaintiff, a jobbing builder, and his wife. The plaintiff carried out various repairs and improvements to the property which was in a bad condition. The plaintiff's claim for a beneficial interest in the property based on proprietary estoppel failed since it was held that the plaintiff had not acted to his detriment by carrying out the work in reliance on the defendant's assurance that he would be entitled to a first option to purchase the property, but for his own benefit (by way of improvement to his home) because he knew that the defendant could not afford to pay for it to be done.

The claimants also failed in *Brinnard v. Ewens.*[50] Here, the appellants had originally been tenants of the ground floor and back bedroom on the first floor of a house owned by the respondents. When the rest of the house became vacant, they moved into all of it. From that time onwards, they expended some £30,000 in works of repair and improvement. The Court of Appeal, agreeing with the trial judge, held that, on the evidence, the appellants could not establish that their expenditure had taken place in reliance on the landlord granting them a tenancy of the whole house. The primary reason for doing the work was because it was their home and they hoped it might be possible to acquire it as owners or tenants at some time in the future. Moreover, the landlord did not know (or had any reason to know) that the work was being done by the appellants with the view that it would grant them a tenancy of the whole house.

By contrast to the foregoing cases, in *Durant v. Heritage,*[51] Mr Andrew Park Q.C. (sitting as a deputy judge of the High Court) held that the various improvement works carried out by the claimant went far beyond what one would expect a Rent Act protected tenant to do. It was argued that the works were carried out simply for the claimant's own comfort and convenience and not in reliance on the expectation of inheriting the property. This argument was rejected by the deputy judge on the basis that the works done went "significantly beyond" what might have been expected of a monthly tenant, even a tenant with security of tenure under the Rent Act 1977. In the words of the deputy judge:

"The extent of the works makes sense if Mrs Durant had expectations of inheriting the property -over £12,000 worth of materials (at 1992 values)

[49] (1983) 133 New L.J. 894.
[50] (1987) 19 H.L.R. 415, C.A. See also, *Avondale Printers & Stationers Ltd v. Haggie* [1979] 2 N.Z.L.R. 124, Supreme Court of Auckland, where a claim based on proprietary estoppel failed because the plaintiff had not spent the money in the expectation, encouraged by the defendants, that it would become the beneficial owner of the land. In fact, the expenditure was carried out when the plaintiff was either contractually entitled to become the beneficial owner or, alternatively, after he had relinquished that right and the defendants had notified the plaintiff that any further expenditure was at its own risk.
[51] [1994] EGCS 134.

and fifty-eight skilled man-hours of work worth £9,400 (at 1992 values) but provided free. It makes very little sense if Mrs Durant merely had a protected tenancy and no expectations of inheritance".

(D) Assurance Need Not Be Sole Inducement

In *Wayling v. Jones*,[52] Balcombe L.J. also stated that the promises relied on by the estoppel claimant do not have to be the sole inducement for the detrimental conduct. It is sufficient if they are an inducement. In *Amalgamated Investment & Property Co. Ltd v. Texas Commerce International Bank Ltd*,[53] Robert Goff J. observed that, where an estoppel is alleged to be founded upon encouragment, it could only be unconscionable for the encouragor to enforce his strict legal rights if the claimant's conduct had been influenced by the encouragement. It was no bar, however, to a conclusion that the claimant was so influenced, that his conduct did not derive its origin exclusively from the encouragement of the first party. Thus:

> "There may be cases where the representee has proceeded initially on the basis of a belief derived from another source independent of the representor, but his belief has subsequently been confirmed by the encouragement or representation of the representor. In such a case, the question is not whether the representee acted, or desisted from acting, solely in reliance on the encouragement or representation of the other party; the question is rather whether his conduct was so *influenced* by the encouragement or representation ... that it would be unconscionable for the representor thereafter to enforce his strict legal rights".[54]

Robert Goff J. cited the following example by way of illustration. Suppose that A and B are neighbours, and that A proposes to build a wall, on what is in fact B's land, though both parties mistakenly believe it to be A's land. A invites B's co-operation in the building of the wall, for example, by providing a means of access over his land for the purposes of building work or by supporting an application for planning permission. B co-operates as requested and the wall is built at A's expense. In such circumstances, it may well be unconscionable for B thereafter to assert his strict legal rights.

---

[52] (1995) 69 P. & C.R. 170, C.A.
[53] [1982] Q.B. 84, C.A.
[54] *ibid*. 105.

4. DETRIMENT/CHANGE OF POSITION

(A) Introduction

In addition to establishing an assurance and a reliance on that assurance, the estoppel claimant must show that he acted to his or her detriment. Although there is a suggestion in the judgment of Lord Denning M.R. in *Greasley v. Cooke*[1] that there is no need for detriment to be proved in order to establish proprietary estoppel, the statement must be read in the context in which it was made, namely, in relation to the burden of proof. Lord Denning M.R. accepted that expenditure of money was not a necessary element since it was sufficient "if the party, to whom the assurance is given, acts on the faith of it—in such circumstances that it would be unjust and inequitable for the party making the assurance to go back on it".[2] In *Watts & Ready v. Storey*,[3] Dunn L.J. expressly renounced the suggestion that no detriment was required to raise an estoppel equity. This was not what Lord Denning M.R, was saying. According to Dunn L.J., it was immaterial whether one spoke in terms of detriment or in terms of it being unjust or inequitable for the party giving the assurance to go back on it -it would be difficult to envisage circumstances in which it would be inequitable for the party giving the assurance to go back on it unless the person to whom the assurance was given had suffered some prejudice or detriment. Both formulations meant the same thing.

According to Mr Jonathan Parker Q.C. (sitting as a deputy High Court judge) in *Coombes v. Smith*,[4] Lord Denning M.R.'s statement should be taken to mean merely that where, following an assurance made by the legal owner, the claimant adopts a course of conduct which is prejudicial or otherwise detrimental to him, there is a rebuttable presumption that he adopted that course of conduct in reliance on the assurance. Such an interpretation is certainly consistent with earlier authority and in line with the judgments of Waller and Dunn L.JJ. in the *Greasley* case. The argument that, once the plaintiff proves that she changed her position in reliance on the alleged assurances, the onus shifts to the defendant to prove the absence of detriment, was firmly rejected.

As we shall see, detriment can take a variety of forms and is not limited to an expenditure of money on the land in question. It is the element of detriment

---

[1] [1980] 1 W.L.R. 1306 at 1311–1312, C.A. See, J.E.M., [1988] Conv. 59.
[2] *ibid.* 1311.
[3] [1984] 134 New L.J. 631, C.A.
[4] [1986] 1 W.L.R. 808 at 821.

which renders it unconscionable for the legal owner to insist on his strict legal rights.[5] In *Stevens v. Stevens*,[6] Slade L.J. observed:

> "Where the court invokes and applies the doctrine of proprietary estoppel, it is, in the exercise of its equitable jurisdiction, acting upon the conscience of the owner who has the paper title to the land because, broadly it considers that, in all the circumstances of the case, it would be against conscience for the owner with the paper title, who has made the relevant representations, to be permitted to go back on them and to decline to give effect to the interest which he has led the other party to believe he or she will have. If the other party has suffered no detriment, in other words if he or she has not been prejudiced in any significant way by the representations, it will not ordinarily be against conscience to allow the plaintiff to resile from his promise, which *ex hypothesi* is not of a contractual nature."

Thus, mere encouragment by the legal owner without any detrimental response by the claimant does not give rise to any equity. The legal owner, in these circumstances, is free to exercise his legal rights without equity's intervention. The point was addressed by Dixon J. in *Grundt v. Great Boulder Property Gold Mines Ltd*,[7] who referred to the element of detriment as "indispensable"[8]:

> "[The other party] must have so acted or abstained from acting upon the footing of the state of affairs assumed that he would suffer a detriment if the opposite party were afterwards allowed to set up rights against him inconsistent with the assumption."

It is not enough, however, for the estoppel claimant to have been induced to act to his detriment. The essential purpose of the estoppel doctrine, according to Dixon J., is to "avoid or prevent a detriment to the party asserting the estoppel by compelling the opposite party to adhere to the assumption upon which the former acted or abstained from acting".[9] The real detriment or harm, therefore, is that which would flow from the change of position if the relevant assumption were discarded or removed. Thus[10]:

> "So long as the assumption is adhered to, the party who altered his situation upon the faith of it cannot complain. His complaint is that when afterwards the other party makes a different state of affairs, the basis of an assertion of right against him then, if it is allowed, his own original change of position will operate as a detriment."

---

[5] See, *e.g. Bennett v. Bennett*, May 18, 1990, C.A., unreported, available on Lexis, where it was held that the defendant had suffered no detriment sufficient to render it unconscionable for the plaintiff to determine her licence to occupy the property on reasonable notice. Contributing towards a joint drive and access road to the rear of the premises was held not to qualify since this was merely a "necessary adjunct to the occupation" of the property: *per* Slade L.J. As such, it was equated with the payment of rates by an occupier.

[6] Unreported, March 3, 1989, C.A., available on Lexis.

[7] (1937) 59 C.L.R. 641, High Court of Australia.

[8] *ibid*. 674.

[9] *ibid*. 674.

[10] *ibid*. 674.

In essence, the claimant's action or inaction must be such that, if the assumption upon which he proceeded were shown to be wrong and an inconsistent state of affairs were accepted, the consequence would be to make his original act or failure to act "a source of prejudice".[11] To take a simple example, suppose the defendant spent the money he was being sued for, believing it to be his own to spend, and this was treated as a sufficient alteration of his position to estop the plaintiff from departing from the assumption which he had induced the defendant to believe. The harm or detriment giving rise to the estoppel would, according to Dixon J., be that which would be done by requiring the defendant to repay the money which he no longer had. The point was also addressed by Mason C.J. in *Commonwealth v. Verwayen*,[12] where he drew a distinction between essentially two quite different types of detriment. In a "broad sense", there is the legal detriment which would result from the denial of the correctness of the assumption upon which the estoppel claimant has relied. In a "narrower sense", there is factual detriment (or disadvantage) which the claimant has suffered as a result of his reliance upon the correctness of the assumption. While legal detriment in the broad sense is certainly required in order to found an estoppel, the actual relief or remedy which is granted in order to satisfy the equity will often be closer in scope to the factual detriment suffered in the narrower sense.

In some cases, the English courts refer to the element of detriment in terms of a wider notion of "change of position". In *E.R. Ives Investment Ltd v. High*,[13] for example, Winn L.J.[14] stated that the person entitled to an estoppel must show he has "suffered a past detriment or other change of position". In *Bhimji v. Salih*,[15] Brightman L.J. expressed the view that proprietary estoppel could only apply where "the promisee has in fact acted to his detriment in the sense that ... the promisee has altered his position in a way which would be to his disadvantage if the strict legal position remain unqualified". In *Re Basham (dec'd)*,[16] Mr Edward Nugee Q.C. (sitting as a High Court judge) referred to the factor which gave rise to the equitable obligation as "A's alteration of his position"[17] on the faith of an understanding. Similarly, Lord Bridge in *Lloyds Bank plc v. Rosset*[18] opined that a cohabitee asserting a claim to a beneficial interest in her partner's house was obliged to show that "he or she has acted to his or her detriment or significantly altered his or her position in reliance on the agreement"[19] in order to give rise to a constructive trust or proprietary estoppel. In *Stevens v. Stevens*,[20] Sir Roger Ormrod stated that there was a danger in using the word "detriment" too narrowly so as to unduly limit the scope of the doctrine—in his view, the claimant had to show that, in reliance on the legal owner's assurances, he has acted "in such a way that he has been prejudiced or disadvantaged, otherwise no equity would arise".

---

[11] *ibid.* 674–675.
[12] (1990) 170 C.L.R. 394 at 415, High Court of Australia.
[13] [1967] 2 Q.B. 379, C.A.
[14] *ibid.* 405.
[15] Unreported, Court of Appeal, February 4, 1981, available on Lexis.
[16] [1986] 1 W.L.R. 1498.
[17] *ibid.* 1504.
[18] [1991] 1 A.C. 107, H.L.
[19] *ibid.* 132.
[20] Unreported, March 3, 1989, C.A., available on Lexis.

(B) Counter-balancing Benefits

In assessing whether the requirement of detriment has been proved, the courts may have regard to any counter-balancing advantages enjoyed by the estoppel claimant during the relevant period of expenditure or occupation. The principle of offsetting counter-balancing benefits against detriment suffered by the claimant has been discussed in several cases. The net result of such a balancing process may be that the claimant is held not to have suffered any detriment at all in financial or material terms. In *Watts & Ready v. Storey*,[21] the defendant had been persuaded by his grandmother to give up the tenancy of his home in Leeds (and the prospects of finding employment there) to live in her home in Nottinghamshire. The defendant was misled, by a letter shown to him by his grandmother, into believing that her house would be left to him under her will. Within weeks of the defendant moving into the house, his grandmother died. In dismissing his claim based on proprietary estoppel, the Court of Appeal held that, in considering what detriment had been suffered by the defendant, regard had to be made to countervailing benefits that he had received, namely, the occupation of a rent-free house of which he was very fond. On the facts, therefore, the requirement of detriment had not been satisfied. In *E. & L. Berg Homes Ltd v. Grey*,[22] a landowner was a successor in title to a brick company who had allowed a then employee, Grey and his wife, to occupy part of the company's site in about 1953. The Greys put a caravan on the site and, over a period of 26 years, occupied the site residentially and carried out substantial works thereon (*e.g.* fencing, the installation of a carport, etc.). In 1969, the brick company ceased trading and the remainder of the site became derelict. A claim based on proprietary estoppel failed because, on the evidence, the Greys had never made a mistake as to their legal rights as required by the first test propounded by Fry J. in *Willmott v. Barber*.[23] Neither had they been encouraged in the carrying-out of the works within Fry J.'s fifth test. The Greys were simply bare licencees of the site. In the course of his judgment, Brandon L.J. alluded[24] to the fact that, although great hardship would be suffered by the Greys as a result of the court's order for possession, nevertheless, there were "certain factors which fall to be weighed on the other side". In particular, it was stressed that the couple had been extremely fortunate to be allowed to occupy the site, without any payment of rent or other consideration of any kind, for over 26 years.

Another example of the court taking into account rent-free occupation in assessing the claimant's overall entitlement is to be found in the Canadian case of *Hink v. Lhenen*.[25] Here, the claimant had resided with the deceased from 1940 until 1954 and again from 1958 until his death in 1972. When the claimant (and her sister) first resided with the deceased, they were under the impression that he

---

[21] [1984] 134 New L.J. 631, C.A., available on Lexis.

[22] (1979) 253 EG 473, C.A.

[23] (1880) 15 Ch. D. 96. See also, *Bennett v. Bennett*, May 18, 1990, C.A., unreported, available on Lexis, where the Court of Appeal observed that the defendant, who failed in her estoppel claim for lack of detriment, had been very fortunate in enjoying rent-free accommodation in the property for over 25 years. See further, Chap. 6, pp. 117–118.

[24] *ibid*. 477. See also, Sir David Cairns and Ormrod L.JJ., 479.

[25] (1975) 52 D.L.R. (3d) 301, Alberta Supreme Court.

was their father. Although he was not, a father and daughter relationship subsisted between them until the deceased's death. She left the deceased in 1954 to work and was subsequently married. She returned to live with the deceased at his house in 1958 at his request after her marriage had broken up. At that time, she had one child and was pregnant with another. Since that time until his death, she looked after the deceased and the house, contributing from her salary for this purpose. In awarding the claimant a *quantum meruit* for her services rendered to the deceased, the Alberta Supreme Court took into account the benefit which the claimant had received by being able to live rent-free in the house with her children and by being able to leave her children with the deceased while she went out to work. The fact that she had retained some of the rental income from the house (part of which was tenanted) in excess of expenses during the last two years' of the deceased's lifetime and thereafter was also brought into account in calculating her entitlement.

In the Irish case of *Cullen v. Cullen*,[26] Kenny J. refused to order a transfer of the legal owner's land since the only act relied on by the claimant to create the estoppel equity was the putting of £403 into the former's business. As against this, the claimant had been in receipt of the profits of the business and these sums were considerably more than the amount which she paid in. The learned judge said on this point[27]:

"The equity ... is a discretionary one and when I consider the circumstances in which the plaintiff made the statement that he was about to transfer the property at Adamstown to his wife ... I have no doubt whatever that it would be grossly inequitable to regard [the claimant] as being entitled to a transfer of the property at Adamstown or as having acquired any proprietary interest, legal or equitable, in the property as a result of what was said. The use [by the claimant] of her own monies for the running of the business, particularly when she could have repaid this advance at any time [from the profits of the business], does not, in my opinion, create any claim in conscience or in equity which the Court should enforce or give any ground for disregarding the general principle that equity will not aid an imperfect gift".

Again, in the Australian case of *Beaton v. McDivitt*,[28] Young J. considered that "the case may be that the claimant has already had a sufficient satisfaction for his expenditure, so may be entitled to no relief" and that "there would be a lot to be said for the proposition that rent and rate free occupation of this land for seven years has already satisfied any equity that the plaintiff may have had".[29]

Apart fron rent-free occupation, the court may consider as relevant the fact that the party estopped has shown past forebearance in some way towards the

[26] [1962] I.R. 268.
[27] *ibid.* 282–283.
[28] (1985) 13 N.S.W.L.R. 134, Supreme Court of New South Wales. See also, *Bostock v. Bryant* (1990) 61 P. & C.R. 23, C.A., where Stuart-Smith L.J. said: "It was to their advantage that they should remain in the house on these very favourable terms and conditions, living rent-free simply on the payment of the outgoings in respect of the gas and electricity bills, and that there really was no detriment to her at all": *ibid.* 32.
[29] *ibid.* 158.

estoppel claimant. In *Appleby v. Cowley*,[30] for example, Sir Robert Megarry V.-C. held that the proprietary estoppel claim could not succeed because the expenditure on various works had been counter-balanced by a prolonged forebearance to charge a full rent. In these circumstances, the claimants had received "sufficient satisfaction" for their expenditure on improvements.

On similar principles, a claim will fail if the estoppel claimant has received ample reward for his services or expenditure. Thus, in *Re Basham (dec'd)*,[31] it is suggested by Mr Edward Nugee Q.C. (sitting as a High Court judge) that no estoppel claim would have succeeded in that case had the claimant "received any commensurate reward for [her services] during [the deceased's] lifetime".[32]

(C) Categories of Detriment

It will now be convenient to examine the various categories of detriment recognised by the courts. The list is by no means exhaustive and it has been judicially recognised that the categories of detriment are not closed. In *Watts & Ready v. Storey*,[33] the Court of Appeal reiterated that, whilst in many of the cases on proprietary estoppel there has been an expenditure of money, this was not a necessary element. Dunn L.J. accepted that it was sufficient if the claimant acted on the faith of the assurance in such circumstances that it would be unjust and inequitable for the party making the assurance to go back on it. It did not matter whether one spoke in terms of "detriment" or in terms of it being "unjust or inequitable for the party giving the assurance to go back on it" since it would be difficult to envisage circumstances in which it would be inequitable for a party to go back on an assurance given by him other than where the person to whom the assurance was given had suffered some prejudice or detriment.

(i) Expenditure of Money on Improvements

In *Shaida v. Kindlane Ltd*,[34] H.H. Judge Paul Baker Q.C. remarked that the claimant's expenditure of money on improvement of the land in reliance on an assurance was the "classic way" in which a detriment could be established. A number of cases may be mentioned by way of illustration.

In *Pascoe v. Turner*,[35] a case involving an unmarried couple, the female claimant, in reliance upon her partner's declaration that he had given her his house and its contents, spent approximately £230 on redecorations, improvements and repairs. The claimant knew that she was improving what she thought to be her property. The work done was characterised by the court as substantial. Although the sum laid out on the improvements was comparatively small, the court viewed the matter subjectively from the point of view of the claimant's limited financial resources. It was noted, for example, that the claimant had devoted a quarter of her remaining capital and her personal effort upon the house and its fixtures.

---

[30] *The Times*, April 14, 1982; [1982] C.L.Y. 1150, available on Lexis.
[31] [1986] 1 W.L.R. 1498.
[32] *ibid*. 1505.
[33] [1984] 134 New L.J. 631, C.A.
[34] Unreported, June 22, 1982, available on Lexis.
[35] [1979] 1 W.L.R. 431, C.A.

In *Dillwyn v. Llewelyn*,[36] a father had encouraged his son to build a house on his (the father's) land for some £14,000. Lord Westbury L.C. said[37]:

" . . . if A puts B in possession of a piece of land, and tells him, 'I give it to you that you may build a house on it', and B on the strength of that promise, with the knowledge of A, expends a large sum of money in building a house accordingly, I cannot doubt that the donee acquires a right from the subsequent transaction to call on the donor to perform that contract and complete the imperfect donation which was made".

Similarly, in *Inwards v. Baker*,[38] the son had built a bungalow on his father's land at a cost of some £300, of which the son provided £150 and the father the balance. The son had been encouraged to build the bungalow in reliance on his father's assurance that he would be allowed to remain there for as long as he wished. The Court of Appeal held that the son was held entitled to an equity in the form of an irrevocable licence to occupy the bungalow rent-free for life. In *Griffiths v. Williams*,[39] a house was left by the testatrix to a granddaughter, who had been assured by the testatrix that it was her home for life. She spent considerable sums of money (*i.e.* £2,000) on improvements to the house on the faith of this assurance. The improvements[40] consisted of putting in a bathroom and an indoor toilet, electrical rewiring, concreting the yard and repairs to one of the walls. This was held to constitute detriment giving the granddaughter an equitable right in her favour. She had also spent money in paying the outgoings but these were discounted as raising an equity because they could be regarded simply as current payments for the benefits which she was enjoying by being allowed to live in the house.

In *Appleby v. Cowley*,[41] the remedial works to the building comprised some rewiring, decoration and remedying of dampness costing £7,000. These were treated by the court as representing not much more than keeping the building in a usable state while it was being occupied and, accordingly, insufficient to give the claimants a proprietary right in the building. Although such expenditure was not to be ignored, it carried little weight. It seems evident, therefore, that the improvement must be of a permanent and substantial character. It has been suggested, however, by Slade L.J. in *Stevens v. Stevens*[42] that the court could, in principle, regard expenditure on current repairs (*e.g.* maintenance and decoration, fitting new carpets, etc.) as capable of constituting a detriment if it was satisfied that it was expenditure which, but for the assurances given, the claimant would not have incurred.

In *Voyce v. Voyce*,[43] the defendant's mother gave him a cottage and land as a

---

[36] (1862) 4 De G.F. & J. 517; 45 E.R. 1285.
[37] *ibid.* 521; 1286.
[38] [1965] 2 Q.B. 29, C.A.
[39] (1977) 248 EG 947, C.A.
[40] Goff L.J. appears to have considered that a distinction could be drawn between expenditure on "improvements" and expenditure on "current repairs", because he expressly observed that the evidence before him failed to show how the money should be broken down between those two categories: *ibid.* 947.
[41] *The Times*, April 14, 1982; [1982] C.L.Y. 1150.
[42] Unreported, March 3, 1989, C.A., available on Lexis.
[43] (1991) 62 P. & C.R. 290, C.A.

gift provided that he "did it up", which he did do at considerable expense. The gift was never executed by deed. The improvement work consisted of substantial modernisation of the property. The Court of Appeal had no difficulty in ordering that the freehold of the cottage and land be transferred to the defendant in order to perfect the imperfect gift. In the New Zealand case of *Stratulatos v. Stratulatos*,[44] the detriment comprised substantial expenditure ($22,000) on renovating and upgrading the property owned by the defendant. The works were carried out over a period of three years and enhanced its capital value and rental value significantly. The defendant was aware of the work being carried out, to some degree encouraged it and also acquiesced in it. The High Court of Wellington held that to allow the defendant to go back on her assurance that the house belonged to the plaintiff and her husband, would be to permit her to take a windfall advantage of the expenditure and effort of the claimants. Accordingly, a proprietary estoppel was made out since it would have been unconscionable, in the circumstances, for the defendant to go back on her word.

In the recent case of *Matharu v. Matharu*,[45] the claimant's husband made substantial improvements to his father's house at his own expense. The work involved the construction of a through lounge and kitchen/diner, installation of central heating, replacement of an old staircase, refurbishment of the cellar, the removal of two chimney breasts and subsequent repair, and the replacement of all doors throughout the premises and the bathroom. Roch L.J., giving the leading judgment of the majority of the Court of Appeal, held that these various alterations and improvements to the house were acts done which the claimant herself was entitled to take advantage.[46] In the result, she was held entitled to an equity despite the fact that there was no evidence to suggest that the claimant's husband had ever agreed or intended to share his money with his wife.

In *Durant v. Heritage*,[47] the deceased's niece successfully claimed that, by virtue of proprietary estoppel, she was entitled to have the deceased's cottage transferred to her. The niece and her husband moved into the property in 1970 as tenants at a very low rent and carried out substantial works to the property over the years, at their own expense, in the belief that the deceased would leave the property to her on his death. The improvement works were regarded by the court as "important and substantial, going far beyond what one would expect a Rent Act protected tenant to do".[48] The works included the construction of an extension to the house at ground floor level, the reconstruction of the roof and the raising of the height of the walls in the upper rooms, the general rearrangement of the downstairs accommodation of the house, and the building of a substantial triple-garage where previously there had been a dilapidated shed. The work was done by the claimant and her husband, who was a builder by trade, personally in their spare time. They also paid for the materials themselves. The amount of time put in was agreed in evidence as being the equivalent of 58 weeks of work by one craftsman, valued at about £9,400. The cost of the materials was estimated at just over £12,000 and the property was

---

[44] [1988] 2 N.Z.L.R. 424, High Court of Wellington.
[45] (1994) 68 P. & C.R. 93, C.A.
[46] For further analysis of this point, see Chap. 6, pp. 122–124.
[47] [1994] EGCS 134.
[48] *ibid. per* Mr Andrew Park Q.C., (sitting as a deputy judge of the High Court).

estimated to be worth in the region of £30,000 more than it would have been if the improvement works had not been done.

The detriment may also consist of contributing to a joint business venture to be carried out on the representor's land,[49] or even the payment of premiums required to maintain the latter's policy of insurance.[50]

It seems that there is no strict requirement that the works done in reliance on the assurance should necessarily involve any qualitative enhancement of the land. In *Pennine Raceway Ltd v. Kirklees Metropolitan Borough Council*,[51] for example, the relevant works comprised the erection of about 400 yards of safety barriers on an airfield used for motor racing. Part of the land was cleared for pits and for a competitor's car park and laid with tarmacadam. In addition, about 3,000 cubic metres of soil was moved in order to create a bank for spectators and nylon cable was attached to existing posts in order to provide fencing. It is difficult to imagine that this work enhanced the utility of the land other than for the specific purpose of motor racing.

In some cases, the relevant expenditure involves the financing of an addition or extension to the legal owner's property. This is what happened in the well-known case of *Hussey v. Palmer*,[52] where the plaintiff, an elderly widow, was invited to live with her daughter and son-in-law, the defendant, in the house where they lived with their family. A bedroom was built on as an extension for the plaintiff at a cost of £607 which was paid for by the plaintiff herself. After living there for some time, differences arose and the plaintiff left. The majority of the Court of Appeal held that, since the payment for the extension was not intended as a gift or loan, it was against conscience for the defendant to retain the benefit of it without repayment. In the result, he held the house on a resulting/constructive trust for the plaintiff proportionate to her payment.

In the normal case, the claimant is held entitled to an equity on the basis of improvements carried out on the land of the legal owner. The claimant, however, will also have acted to his detriment if he improves *his own land* in reliance on the legal owner's assurance that he will be granted some right over the latter's land. In *Willmott v. Barber*,[53] Fry J. postulated his second test in terms that "the plaintiff must have expended some money or must have done some act (*not necessarily upon the defendant's land*) on the faith of his mistaken belief",[54] (emphasis added). This situation arose in *Rochdale Canal Co. v. King*,[55] where a mill owner built a mill on his land having applied to a canal company for permission to take canal water for generating his steam engines. The canal company did not refuse the application and the pipes were laid down in the presence of its engineers. It was held that the canal company was not entitled to an injunction to prevent the mill owner from using the water for the purpose of generating steam on the ground of their acquiescence. Similarly, in *Cotching v. Bassett*,[56] the owner of a house, in the course of

---

[49] *Holiday Inns Inc. v. Broadhead* (1974) 232 EG 951, C.A.
[50] *Re Foster, Hudson v. Foster (No. 2)* [1938] 3 All E.R. 610.
[51] [1983] Q.B. 382, C.A.
[52] [1972] 1 W.L.R. 1286, C.A.
[53] (1880) 15 Ch.D. 96. See also, *Holiday Inns Inc. v. Broadhead* (1974) 232 EG 951, 1087, *per* Goff J.
[54] *ibid.* 105.
[55] (1853) 16 Beav. 630; 51 E.R. 924.
[56] (1862) 32 Beav. 101; 55 E.R. 40.

rebuilding it, altered his ancient lights. This was done after communication with the adjacent owner and with the knowledge and under the inspection of his surveyor, but without any express agreement. It was held that, in equity, the lights (as altered) could not be interfered with. A recent example is to be found in *Cook v. Minion*,[57] where a claim for proprietary estoppel was upheld in favour of an owner who had installed water closets on his own land in reliance on permission received from his neighbour for ancillary rights of drainage.[58] In *E.R. Ives Investment Ltd v. High*,[59] the defendant, in reliance on an agreement with the adjacent owner that he would be entitled to a right of way across the latter's yard, built himself a garage which could only be entered over the adjacent owner's land. The Court of Appeal held that the defendant had in equity a good right of way across the yard which did not need to be registered under the Land Charges Act 1925. It is evident,[60] however, that the doctrine does not apply where the claimant does acts on his own land which are not done in the expectation of acquiring rights over the land of another.

The detriment may also consist of the acquisition of new land by the claimant in reliance on an assurance that its existing land is required by the Council for public purposes. In *Salvation Army Trustee Co Ltd v. West Yorkshire Metropolitan County Council*,[61] the plaintiffs owned a meeting hall used by the Salvation Army. The Council informed the plaintiffs that the hall was affected by a proposed road-widening scheme. In due course, the plaintiffs acquired a new site and engaged contractors for the building of a new hall on it. Subsequently, the Council informed the plaintiffs that the road-widening proposal was no longer to be carried out and that it did not wish to purchase the existing hall. Woolf J. held that the principle of proprietary estoppel was capable of extending to the disposal of an interest in land where the disposal was closely linked by an arrangement that also involved the acquisition of an interest in land. The only inference to be drawn from the facts was that what had motivated the plaintiffs into taking possession of the new site and entering into a contract with the builders to build the new hall was the belief that the old hall was to be purchased and that the new site was to be sold to them on terms that reflected their receiving compensation in respect of the old site under the Land Compensation Act 1961. Accordingly, the disposal of the old site and the acquisition of the new site were sufficiently closely linked for the principle of estoppel to apply. In effect, it would have been unconscionable for the Council to resile from its previously stated intention of acquiring the old site. Thus, the plaintiffs were held entitled to the agreed compensation under the 1961 Act upon tendering to the Council a duly executed transfer of the old site. Woolf J. was careful to point out, however, that he would not have been prepared to extend the principle of proprietary estoppel to a case involving the mere sale of an interest in property. There is no case where proprietary estoppel has been

---

[57] (1979) 37 P. & C.R. 58. In other cases, the claimant engages in some activity on his own land which require facilities from an adjacent owner: see, *e.g. Armstrong v. Sheppard & Short Ltd* [1959] 2 Q.B. 384, C.A., (defendant constructed a sewer over a strip of the plaintiff's land); *Ward v Kirkland* [1967] Ch. 194, (defendant laid drains across plaintiff's farmyard); *Hopgood v. Brown* [1955] 1 W.L.R. 213, C.A., (defendant encroached upon plaintiff's land in building a garage).
[58] *ibid.* 65.
[59] [1967] 2 Q.B. 379, C.A.
[60] See, *Western Fish Products Ltd v. Penwith District Council* [1981] 2 All E.R. 204, C.A.
[61] (1981) 41 P. & C.R. 179.

applied to enforce the *disposal* of an interest in property as opposed to the *acquisition* of an interest in property. In the instant case, the purchase of the new site was "inextricably woven"[62] into the disposal of the old site. However, in the case of a normal arrangement to sell property where there is no contract of sale, it is highly unlikely that reliance could be placed on the principle of proprietary estoppel.[63]

That the principle has no application in this context is borne out by the Court of Appeal decision in *Western Fish Products Ltd v. Penwith District Council*,[64] where Megaw L.J. held that the principle only applied where the plaintiff, encouraged by the defendant, acted to his detriment in relation to his own land in the expectation of acquiring a right over the defendant's land. It did not apply where, as in the *Western* case, the claimant had spent money on his own land in the expectation encouraged by an officer of the local authority that he would acquire planning permission in respect of his own land. In this case, even if the claimant had to its detriment spent money on its own land at the encouragement of the local authority, it had not done so in the expectation of acquiring any rights in relation to the council's or any other person's land. It had spent money in order to take advantage of existing rights over its own land which the authority by their officers had confirmed it possessed. There was no question of it acquiring any rights in relation to any other person's land.

It has been suggested[65] that there is no difference, in principle, between the case where the person claiming the equity has expended money on the land of the legal owner and the case where such person has transferred the land to the then legal owner for an inadequate consideration. In each case, the legal owner can be said to have been enriched at the expense of the person claiming the equity, unless provision is made for the latter's protection. In *Bannister v. Bannister*,[66] for example, the defendant had conveyed two adjoining cottages to the plaintiff for what was found to be a "bargain" price, on the plaintif's verbal undertaking to allow the defendant to occupy one of the cottages rent-free for as long as she desired. The undertaking was not included in the formal conveyance. Subsequently, the plaintiff gave the defendant notice to quit the premises she was then occupying and on her refusing to do so, took action for possession. It was held by the Court of Appeal that the defendant was entitled to a declaration that the plaintiff held the cottage on trust during the defendant's life to permit her to occupy the same for as long as she desired and that the plaintiff was not entitled to an order for possession.

(ii) Personal Disadvantage

It is well established that the requisite element of detriment need not be related to land nor must it have a financial quality. Thus, detriment can take other forms not necessarily involving the expenditure of money on land.

A classic illustration is to be found in the case of *Re Basham (dec'd)*.[67] Here,

---

[62] *ibid.* 191.
[63] *ibid.* 198–199.
[64] [1981] 2 All E.R. 204, C.A.
[65] *Timber Top Realty Property Ltd v. Mullens* [1974] V.L.R. 312, Supreme Court of Victoria.
[66] [1948] 2 All E.R. 133, C.A.
[67] [1986] 1 W.L.R. 1498.

the detriment comprised the provision by the claimant and her husband of unpaid domestic services to the deceased, her step-father. The "cumulative effect" of this work showed that "the plaintiff and her husband subordinated their own interests to the wishes of the deceased".[68] It was suggested that the claimant's conduct could be attributed to her natural love and affection for her step-father but this was rejected by the courts, since there was clear evidence of the fact that there was no great affection between the parties. The unpaid work was carried out solely on the basis of an expectation that the deceased's estate would, in due course, pass to the claimant. In the course of his judgment, Mr Edward Nugee Q.C. concluded that "the expenditure of A's money on B's property is not the only kind of detriment that gives rise to a proprietary estoppel".[69] The learned judge cited *Greasley v. Cooke*[70] as an example of a case in which the claimant was not shown to have incurred any expenditure. In this case, the female claimant had worked initially as a living-in maid but later cared for the deceased's family (in particular, the deceased's daughter who was mentally ill) without payment for a considerable number of years. She had not asked for payment for her services because she had been encouraged by members of the family to believe that she could regard the family house as her home for the rest of her life. Lord Denning M.R. concluded that, whilst in many of the cases, there had been an expenditure of money, "that is not a necessary element".[71] In his view, it was sufficient "if the party, to whom the assurance is given, acts on the faith of it—in such circumstances that it would be unjust and inequitable for the party making the assurance to go back on it".[72] According to Lord Denning M.R., therefore, there was no need for the claimant to prove that she acted to her detriment since it was enough that "she stayed on [at] the house—looking after [the family]—when otherwise she might have left and got a job elsewhere".[73] By contrast, Dunn L.J. had no doubt that for proprietary estoppel to arise the claimant must have incurred expenditure or otherwise have prejudiced himself or acted to his detriment. This, of course, represents the orthodox view.[74] In *Basham*, Mr Edward Nugee Q.C. also considered it unnecessary that the claimant should have been in occupation of the legal owner's land, or even in enjoyment of some right over it. Thus, for example, in *Crabb v. Arun District Council*,[75] the claimant acted to his detriment in parting with part of his land without having secured for himself a right of way to his

---

[68] *ibid.* 1505.

[69] *ibid.* 1509.

[70] [1980] 1 W.L.R. 1306, C.A. See further, G. Woodman, (1981) 44 M.L.R. 461. See also, *Hink v. Lhenen* (1975) 52 D.L.R. (3d) 301, Alberta Supreme Court, where the claimant, who had looked after the deceased, was awarded compensation on a *quantum meruit* basis. In calculating the amount of compensation for her services to the deceased, account was taken of all the benefits received by her, namely, the fact that she had occupied the property rent-free and that she had retained income in excess of expenses, not only during the deceased's lifetime but also since his death: *ibid.* 315–316.

[71] *ibid.* 1311.

[72] *ibid.* 1311. A concept of detriment based on an "acting" on the faith of an assurance is consistent with a general movement towards a broader-based philosophy underlying proprietary estoppel based on the notion of "unconscionability". See further, Chap. 10.

[73] *ibid.* 1312. This suggests that foregoing an opportunity of a job or career may constitute sufficient detriment. But see, *Coombes v. Smith* [1986] 1 W.L.R. 808 at 820–821, where Mr Jonathan Parker Q.C. rejected the claimant's omission to look for a job as constituting detriment.

[74] See further, Chap. 8, pp. 150–151.

[75] [1976] Ch. 179, C.A.

remaining land, which was thereby rendered landlocked. But because he did so in the belief, encouraged by an adjacent owner, that he would be granted a right of way over the latter's adjoining land, the Court of Appeal held that an equity arose in his favour and that he was entitled to be granted such a right of way. It is apparent that the claimant had not spent any money on the access road over the adjacent owner's land, and that he had not even been using the access road himself prior to parting with the portion of his own land.

Another good example where purely personal disadvantage was held sufficient to constitute detriment for the purpose of raising an estoppel-based equity is to be found in *Jones (A.E.) v. Jones (F.W.)*.[76] Here, the claimant's father bought a house near his own home for the claimant who left a job and council house and moved with his family into the house. The claimant gave his father sums amounting to one-quarter of the purchase price of the house. He understood from his father that the house was his. When the father died, the house vested in the plaintiff, the claimant's step-mother, who brought proceedings for possession. The Court of Appeal held that the plaintiff was estopped from turning the defendant out of the house by virtue of the father's conduct which had led the defendant to leave his job and pay money to his father in the belief that the house would be his home for the rest of his life. It is apparent, however, that mere abandonment of an existing job and home in order to live with the legal owner will not always afford sufficient detriment. Much will depend on the circumstances in any given case. Thus, for example, in *Watts & Ready v. Storey*,[77] referred to earlier, the defendant's conduct in giving up the tenancy of his home in Leeds and the prospects of finding employment there to live with his grandmother in her home in Nottinghamshire was held not enough to raise an estoppel in his favour. A similar conclusion was reached in *Hannaford v. Selby*,[78] where the claimants gave up their secure council house in London to go and live with their daughter and husband in Ipswich. Again, in *Stevens v. Stevens*,[79] the mere fact that the claimant had moved into the house following the plaintiff's promise to her that she could live there for the rest of her life was held by Slade L.J. not of itself sufficient to found a claim based on proprietary estoppel.[80] His Lordship said:

"[This proposition] appears to have been accepted by Mr Jonathan Parker Q.C. in *Coombes v. Smith* [1986] 1 W.L.R. 808, at pp. 816–817. Whenever A moves into B's house, he must have come from somewhere else and, to quote the words of Mr Parker, summarising the argument in that case, 'if the mere fact of that inevitable change was sufficient as a detriment, there would be a detriment in every case'."

---

[76] [1977] 1 W.L.R. 438, C.A.
[77] [1984] 134 New L.J. 631, C.A.
[78] (1976) 239 EG 811.
[79] Unreported, March 3, 1989, C.A., available on Lexis.
[80] However, the other member of the Court of Appeal, Sir Roger Ormrod, appears to have accepted that a moving into the property may be a detriment. He said: "But what I do think clearly raises an equity is the fact that, acting on an assurance that she would have the right to live in this house for the rest of her life, she moved in and has lived there since 1976 making her home there. If it turns out that her right to remain in the house is not a secure one, then, plainly, by moving in and acting on the assurance, she acted to her detriment. That, in my judgment, is quite sufficient."

In the context of cohabitees, the cases support both a wide and narrow interpretation of the meaning of detriment.[81] In *Maharaj v. Chand*,[82] involving an unmaried couple, the defendant gave up her flat to live with the plaintiff and used her earnings for household requirements and looked after her *de facto* husband and the children as wife and mother. The Privy Council held that, in these circumstances, "it would plainly be inequitable for the plaintiff to evict her".[83] Similarly, in *Wayling v. Jones*,[84] the claimant lived with the deceased in a homosexual relationship from 1971 until the latter's death in 1987. The claimant acted throughout this time as the deceased's companion and chauffeur and gave substantial help in running the deceased's cafe and hotel business. In return for his services, the claimant received pocket-money, living and clothing expenses and the express promise that he would inherit the business. In this case, sufficient detriment was found supporting the claimant's equity from the claimant's conduct in not asking for, or receiving, higher wages and continuing to serve the deceased until his death. It is apparent in all these cases that the detriment need not necessarily involve the expenditure of a sum of money. In the words of Browne-Wilkinson J. in *Re Sharpe (A Bankrupt)*[85]:

> "In a strict case of proprietary estoppel the plaintiff has expended his own money on the defendant's property in an expectation encouraged by or known to the defendant that the plaintiff either owns the property or is to have some interest conferred on him. Recent authorities have extended this doctrine and, in my judgment, it is now established that, if the parties have proceeded on a common assumption that the plaintiff is to enjoy a right to reside in a particular property and in reliance on that assumption the plaintiff has expended money or otherwise acted to his detriment, the defendant will not be allowed to go back on that common assumption and the court will imply an irrevocable licence or trust which will give effect to that common assumption."

More significantly, in the later case of *Grant v. Edwards*,[86] Sir Nicholas Browne-Wilkinson (now Vice-Chancellor) had occasion to give further guidance on the meaning of detriment, albeit in the context of common intention constructive trust doctrine[87]:

> "... once it has been shown that there was a common intention that the claimant should have an interest in the house, any act done by her to her detriment relating to the joint lives of the parties is, in my judgment,

---

[81] See further, Chap. 8, pp. 149–157.

[82] [1986] A.C. 898, P.C. See also, *Matharu v. Matharu* (1994) 68 P. & C.R. 93, C.A., where the claimant's abandonment of divorce proceedings in order to resume her matrimonial relationship with her husband was held to constitute detrimental reliance. She successfully argued that, had she not abandoned these proceedings, she might have claimed accommodation from the local authority as a homeless person with a priority need.

[83] *ibid.* 908.

[84] (1995) 69 P. & C.R. 170, C.A.

[85] [1980] 1 W.L.R. 219.

[86] [1986] Ch. 638, C.A. See further, J. Warburton, [1986] Conv. 291 and D. Hayton, [1986] C.L.J. 394.

[87] *ibid.* 657. See further, J. Warburton, (1992) Trust L.I. 9.

sufficient detriment to qualify. The acts do not have to be inherently referable to the house."

In support of this broad proposition, he cited in support the decisions in *Jones (A.E.) v. Jones (F.W.)* and *Pascoe v. Turner*, referred to above. This has led Grey[88] to comment that "it is likely that this broader approach to ordinary acts of domestic endeavour marks the path of future developments in the law of estoppel".

By contrast, reference may be made to *Coombes v. Smith*,[89] where the female claimant was held not to have acted to her detriment in becoming pregnant, leaving her husband, looking after the house and child or not looking for another job.[90] Such conduct was classified as being done by the claimant in her capacity as "occupier of the property, as the defendant's mistress, and as [the child's] mother, in the context of a continuing relationship with the defendant".[91] In this case, the only relevant expenditure (on the installation of central heating) was incurred after proceedings had been commenced and without the knowledge of the legal owner. The judgment of Mr Jonathan Parker Q.C. strongly suggests that purely "spousal acts" which form an integral part of the relationship between the parties are not to be treated as sufficient detriment to establish an estoppel equity. As Grey[92] puts it, the case confirms that "an alteration of personal lifestyle is not necessarily a relevant change of position in the law of proprietary estoppel".

It is apparent that mere contributions to general household expenses or bills will not qualify as detriment to raise an equity.[93] In *Hannaford v. Selby*,[94] a couple agreed to buy a house in Ipswich on a mortgage and that the wife's parents should give up their secure council house in London and move in with them, paying £5 per week, representing one-third of the total weekly outgoings for rates and mortgage repayments, but no capital expenses. The arrangement did not work and the couple put up the house for sale. The wife's parents claimed to be entitled to a beneficial interest due to their financial contribution and detriment in giving up their council accommodation. Goulding J. held that the parents could not expect a beneficial interest as they put up no capital

---

[88] Gray, *Elements of Land Law*, (2d ed.) at p. 337. See also, R. Pearce and J. Stevens, *The Law of Trusts and Equitable Obligations* at p. 672, where the learned authors state that by "applying the test of 'any act done by her relating to the joint lives of the parties' to proprietary estoppel claims a whole range of non-monetary detriment would be sufficient to raise an equity".

[89] [1986] 1 W.L.R. 1306, C.A. See further, Chap. 6, pp. 151–153. No detriment was found to exist in *Christian v. Christian* (1981) 131 New L.J. 43, where the claimant argued that she had suffered social embarrassment caused by living with her male partner in a house situated in close proximity to the defendant's wife's home. Brightman L.J. rejected this alleged detriment pointing out that equity is "concerned with the protection of property and proprietary interests, not with the protection of people's feelings". Mere emotional commitment to a joint venture does not represent a sufficient detriment.

[90] As to giving up her job, it is, perhaps, significant that the defendant had maintained the plaintiff and "the kind of employment she had formerly been engaged in and was now resuming required no qualifications and would not be affected by her years at home": see, J.E.M. [1988] Conv. 60.

[91] *ibid.* 820.

[92] Gray, *Elements of Land Law*, (2nd ed.) at p. 337.

[93] *Griffiths v. Williams* (1978) 248 EG 947, C.A., where Goff L.J. said: "In so far as the expenditure was of the latter category [*i.e.* outgoings], I doubt whether it would raise an equity in [the claimant's] favour, because it could be regarded simply as current payment for the benefits which she was enjoying by being allowed to live in the house": *ibid.* 947.

[94] (1976) 239 EG 811.

towards the purchase price—their £5 per week was only attributable to expenses in consideration of being allowed to live with the couple in the house. It could not be regarded as payment for the acquisition of a capital interest in the house. The point was also addressed in *Stevens v. Stevens*,[95] where the claimant, in reliance on her father-in-law's verbal assurances that his house was to be a permanent home for herself and her children, moved into the house and paid the outgoings (*i.e.* rates, electricity and water) and carried out minor repairs to the roof. It was argued that expenditure on outgoings could not possibly be regarded as detriment sufficient to found a claim based on proprietary estoppel since these items of expenditure were of a nature which the claimant necessarily had to incur in any event if she was to continue living in the property. On this point, Slade L.J. said:

> "I for my part feel no doubt that expenditure by the defendant on outgoings would not raise an equity in her favour, since it is money she would have expended whether or not the relevant assurances had been given to her by the plaintiff."

As to the claimant's expenditure on the roof (which only amounted to £80), this was also rejected as constituting detriment since this had been made by her husband rather than herself. Her expenditure on decorating the house throughout and putting new carpets in the kitchen and bathroom was also considered insufficient. Interestingly, however, Slade L.J. considered that the court could, in principle, regard such expenditure as capable of constituting detriment if it was satisfied that it was expenditure which, but for the assurances, the claimant would not have incurred. In the instant case, unfortunately, the claimant had accepted in cross-examination that she would have spent the money she did spend even if the owner (her father-in-law) had not said he was giving her the house. The Court of Appeal were not prepared to go behind that evidence. The claimant, however, was held to succeed on her claim by relying on the fact that she had taken no steps to secure alternative accommodation for herself and her children in reliance on her father-in-law's representations. In this connection, evidence was given by a senior letting officer of the local housing authority who told the court that, if the claimant had come in 1976 (when the assurances were made) and said she was homeless with two young children, the authority would have treated her as in priority need and would have given her accommodation, if she had a residential qualification in its area or a strong family or employment link. At the date of the trial, however, the claimant's prospects of obtaining alternative council accommodation were shown to be "substantially worse"[96] than they would have been in 1975/76 when the assurances were first made to her. By the date of trial, there was a much reduced stock of housing and there would be a 12-month average waiting list for council accommodation. Slade L.J. said:

---

[95] Unreported, March 3, 1989, C.A., available on Lexis. See also, *Bostock v. Bryant* (1990) 61 P. & C.R. 23 at 31–32, C.A. and *Bennett v. Bennett* May 18, 1990, unreported, C.A., available on Lexis, where there was no detriment sufficient to make it unconscionable for the occupational licence to be determined.

[96] *ibid. per* Slade L.J.

"I think it is a fair and proper inference that, on the balance of probabilties, the defendant refrained from seeking council accommodation in and after December 1975 because of the plaintiff's assurances which had led [her] to take up occupation at No. 115... but for the plaintiff's offer of accommodation and his assurances, the obvious course would have been for her to apply for council accommodation... If he had not made these representations she would, I infer, in all likelihood have sought council accommodation as the obvious alternative, and her prospects of obtaining it at that time would have been substantially more favourable than they are now. This, in my judgment, is clearly capable of constituting sufficient detriment to found the application of the doctrine of proprietary estoppel, and no authorities cited... have persuaded me to a contrary view."

It seems also that a failure to acquire other property for use as a home may be taken into account in determining detriment.[97] Thus, in *Re Basham, (dec'd)*,[98] Mr Edward Nugee Q.C. considered[99] that evidence of occasions when the claimant or her husband acted or refrained from acting in a way in which they might not have done but for their expectation of inheriting the deceased's estate, was significant, taken cumulatively, in assessing detriment. In particular, the husband had refrained from selling his building land and refrained from taking a job elsewhere which would have made it impossible for the claimant to continue caring for the deceased.

---

[97] *Cameron v. Murdoch* [1983] W.A.R. 321 at 360, Supreme Court of Western Australia; affirmed, (1986) 63 A.L.R. 575 at 595, P.C. In this case, the acts of detriment comprised *inter alia* the claimant's abstention from establishing himself and his family on other lands.
[98] [1986] 1 W.L.R. 1498. See also, *Watkins v. Emslie* (1982) 261 EG 1192, 1194, C.A., where the alleged detriment comprised the refraining from serving a notice of termination of a business lease, pursuant to s.25 of the Landlord and Tenant Act 1954. However, a claim based on proprietary estoppel failed for lack of any assurances being given: *ibid.* 1194.
[99] *ibid.* 1505.

5. SATISFYING THE EQUITY

In *Crabb v. Arun District Council*,[1] Scarman L.J. posed three questions at the beginning of his judgment which the court had to ask in relation to the law of estoppel, namely:

> (1) is there an equity established? (2) what is the extent of the equity,[2] if one is established? and (3) what is the relief appropriate to satisfy the equity?[3]

This chapter is concerned with the second and third of these questions. What is the extent of the equity and in what ways may the estoppel claimant's equity be satisfied?

(A) The Underlying Principles

It is apparent from the cases that the courts adopt a very broad discretion in determining the form of relief to be granted to an estoppel claimant. The underlying principle was stated by the Privy Council in *Plimmer v. The Mayor, Councillors and Citizens of the City of Wellington*[4]: "the Court must look at the circumstances in each case to decide in what way the equity can be satisfied". Essentially, the courts, in formulating the appropriate remedy, seek to do justice to the claimant's estoppel equity. It has been said[5] that the court "moulds the relief to give effect to the equity". In a normal case, whether there is an equity and its extent will depend upon the initial conduct alleged to give rise to the equity. However, the court is not confined to such conduct and may take into account supervening circumstances in determining how the equity can best be satisfied.[6] In the words of Nicholls L.J. in *Voyce v. Voyce*[7]:

---

[1] [1976] Ch. 179 at 192–193, C.A.

[2] *i.e.* the nature of the interest expected by the claimant (*e.g.* freehold ownership, a lease, a licence, or some other form of occupational interest).

[3] This formulation of the problem has been applied in a number of cases: See, *e.g. Durant v. Heritage* [1994] EGCS 134; *Jones (A.E.) v. Jones (F.W.)* [1977] 1 W.L.R. 438, C.A.; *Griffiths v. Williams* (1977) 251 EG 159, C.A.

[4] (1884) 9 App. Cas. 699 at 714, *per* Sir Arthur Hobhouse. See also, *Chalmers v. Pardoe* [1963] 1 W.L.R. 677 at 682, P.C., *per* Sir Terence Donovan; *Inwards v. Baker* [1965] 2 Q.B. 29 at 37, C.A., *per* Lord Denning M.R.; *E.R. Ives Investment Ltd v. High* [1967] 2 Q.B. 379 at 395, C.A., *per* Lord Denning M.R.; *Pascoe v. Turner* [1979] 1 W.L.R. 431 at 437–438, C.A., *per* Cumming-Bruce L.J.; *Amalgamated Investement & Property Co. Ltd. v. Texas Commerce International Bank Ltd* [1982] Q.B. 84 at 122, C.A., *per* Eveleigh L.J.; *Voyce v. Voyce* (1991) 62 P. & C.R. 290 at 293, C.A., *per* Dillon L.J.

[5] *Beaton v. McDivitt* (1985) 13 N.S.W.L.R. 134 at 158, *per* Young J.

[6] *Williams v. Staite* [1979] Ch. 291 at 298, C.A., *per* Lord Denning M.R.

[7] (1991) 62 P. & C.R. 290 at 296, C.A.

"The extent to which [the legal owner] is precluded or estopped depends on all the circumstances. Regard must be had to the subject-matter of the dispute, what was said and done by the parties at the time and what has happened since".

A good example of this principle is to be found in the case of *Crabb v. Arun District Council*,[8] where the court directed that the plaintiff setting up the equity should have an easement. Had the matter come before the court soon after the conduct which gave rise to the equity, the court would have ordered that the plaintiff should make compensation for the grant of the easement but, in view of the time lapse during which the plaintiff's land had been sterile for a number of years due to the high-handedness of the defendants in locking-up his land, the court considered that compensation was no longer appropriate. Similarly, in *Dodsworth v. Dodsworth*[9] the Court of Appeal took into account in determining how the equity should be satisfied the fact that, in the meantime, the plaintiff who had offered to share her house with the defendant claimants had died.

The estoppel claimant's misconduct towards the legal owner may also affect his/her equitable entitlement.[10] The court has the power to look at all the circumstances of the case as they exist at the time of the hearing in order to decide whether it is right to allow the claimant to seek equitable relief. In the words of Cumming-Bruce L.J. in *Williams v. Staite*[11]:

"I do not think that in a proper case the rights in equity of the defendants necessarily crystallise forever at the time when the equitable rights come into existence. On the contrary, I take the view . . . that the true analysis is that, when the plaintiff comes to court to enforce his legal rights, the defendant is then entitled to submit that in equity the plaintiff should not be allowed to enforce those rights and that the defendant, raising that equity, must then bring into play all the relevant maxims of equity so that the court is entitled then on the facts to look at all the circumstances and decide what order should be made, if any, to satisfy the equity."

It is apparent, therefore, that where impropriety is alleged against the party setting up the equity, the court must consider whether he comes with clean hands so as to be entitled to relief.[12] In some cases, this may leave the estoppel claimant with no right at all. Thus, in *Brynowen Estates Ltd v. Bourne*,[13] Mrs Bourne claimed that she had been granted a licence to occupy (together with her husband) a house owned by the company for their joint lives. The company sought to terminate the licence on the grounds of her behaviour which was adversely affecting the company's caravan park nearby. Evidence was given that Mrs Bourne had sworn at and made obscene gestures at visitors to the park and had on many occasions deliberately driven her car at high speed along the roads of the park, sometimes sounding her horn continually so as to disturb the

[8] [1976] Ch. 179, C.A.
[9] (1973) 228 EG 1115, C.A.
[10] See generally, M.P. Thompson, [1986] Conv. 406 at pp. 412–414.
[11] [1979] Ch. 291 at 300–301, C.A.
[12] *ibid.* 299, *per* Goff L.J.
[13] (1981) 131 New L.J. 1212, C.A.

sleep of the occupiers of the caravans. The trial judge held that, on the basis that there was an implied term in the licence, Mrs Bourne had conducted herself in such a way that the company's business premises were gravely prejudiced, and they had a right to determine the licence. The Court of Appeal, agreeing with the trial judge, held that, insofar as Mrs Bourne was claiming equitable relief on the strict enforcement of the company's legal rights, she so behaved herself as to make it right for the court to deny the equitable right (*i.e.*, an equitable licence) which she was seeking. Similarly, in *J. Willis & Son v. Willis*[14] the occupiers of a flat claimed that they had a right to remain in occupation by virtue of equitable estoppel. They claimed that, on the faith of repeated statements (made on behalf of the owners) that they could live rent-free in the flat as long as they wanted to, they had spent money on the improvement and repair of the premises. The assistant recorder, at first instance, rejected this plea on the ground of misconduct by the occupiers which violated the principle of equity that "he who comes to equity must come with clean hands". There was evidence that the occupiers had put forward, in support of particulars of alleged expenditure for the benefit of the premises, a letter from a third party about supposed work done which was wholly fictitious and fraudulent. The Court of Appeal held that the assistant recorder was fully justified in deciding that, in the circumstances, no court could grant equitable relief. In the course of his judgment, Parker L.J. observed[15]:

> "When the question is whether the equitable licence is established at all, it will normally be the case that the degree of misconduct required is less than would be required if it were sought to cancel a pre-existing equitable licence, if indeed ... such an equitable licence, once established, can be destroyed by such misconduct".

It seems that, once the court has granted the estoppel claimant a remedy, it will only be in a very rare case that the award is likely to be revoked. In *Williams v. Staite*,[16] the defendants' established equitable licence to occupy a cottage for life was held not to be determined by their subsequent misconduct towards the legal owner. According to Lord Denning M.R., only in an extreme case might an equitable licence be revoked. Similarly, Goff L.J. concluded that excessive user or bad behaviour towards the legal owner could not bring the equity, once established by a decision binding on the legal owner, to an end or forfeit it. The appropriate remedy in such cases is an action for nuisance, trespass or an injunction restraining the improper conduct. However, where the court's remedial order is, by its nature, for a limited period only or determinable upon a condition, the court would need to consider whether, in the events which had happened, the equity had determined or it had expired or been determined by the happening of the condition.[17]

It is possible for the claimant's misconduct to take the form of non-compliance with an agreement which forms the basis of the estoppel. This may

---

[14] (1986) 277 EG 1133, C.A.
[15] *ibid.* 1133.
[16] [1979] Ch. 291, C.A.
[17] See, *e.g. Williams v. Staite* [1979] Ch. 291 at 300, C.A., *per* Goff L.J. and *Hardwick v. Johnson* [1978] 1 W.L.R. 683, C.A. See further, Chap. 7, pp. 145–146.

be illustrated by the Australian case of *Vinden v. Vinden*[18] where Needham J. held that a licence, revocable at its inception, could become irrevocable as a result of the conduct of the parties. In that case, the plaintiff was unable to retire and continue to live in his home because he could not meet the financial obligations involved. The defendant, his son, offered to meet all those obligations, thus allowing his father to retire and keep the house. The plaintiff accepted the offer by retiring and allowing the defendant to make the payments. The defendant was allowed to live in the house. Needham J. concluded that, whilst the defendant continued to meet the financial obligations, his licence to occupy the house was irrevocable. The decision illustrates the principle that a party cannot enforce an equity of estoppel while being himself in default of an agreement which underlays the estoppel. Thus, in *Beaton v. McDivitt*,[19] another Australian case, the principle in *Vinden* was applied so as to deny the claimant equitable relief who had failed to maintain a road despite his agreement to do so with the legal owner.

It is also apparent that a breakdown in the relationship between the parties at the time of the trial may influence the court in the form of relief to be granted. Thus, whilst it will often be appropriate to satisfy the equity by granting the claimant the interest he or she was intended to have, if that is not practicable or unworkable, the court has to do the best it can even though this may mean granting a form of relief wholly different from what was envisaged when the parties were on good terms.[20] In circumstances where the parties relationship has broken down, a "clean break" may be the only solution.[21]

It should also be borne in mind that the court may well consider that there are sufficient counter-balancing advantages enjoyed by the claimant which may partially (or completely) offset the detriment which has been suffered. This may have a substantial effect on the nature and scope of the relief (if any) to be granted. In *Watts & Ready v. Storey*,[22] for example, the defendant had been persuaded by his grandmother, much against his initial inclinations, to give up the tenancy of his home in Leeds (and the prospects of finding employment there) to live in her home, Apple House, in Woodborough, Nottinghamshire, following her move to the Isle of Wight. The defendant was misled, by a letter shown to him by his grandmother, into believing that Apple House would be left to him under her will. Within weeks of the defendant moving into Apple House, his grandmother died. When it transpired that his grandmother had not left Apple House to him, he resisted, on grounds of proprietary estoppel, the plaintiff executors' claim for possession. In denying the defendant an equity, the Court of Appeal was influenced by the fact that the detriment which he had suffered was largely offset by the countervailing benefits that he had received from occupation of a rent-free house (of which he was very fond) and the

---

[18] [1982] 1 N.S.W.L.R. 618, Supreme Court of New South Wales.

[19] (1988) 13 N.S.W.L.R. 162.

[20] *Burrows & Burrows v. Sharp* (1991) 23 H.L.R. 82, C.A. J. Martin, [1992] Conv. 54. See also, *Dodsworth v. Dodsworth* (1973) 228 EG 1115, C.A., where Russell L.J. observed that the consequence of granting the claimants a right of occupancy would be that the plaintiff "would . . . have to continue sharing her home for the rest of her life with the defendants, with whom she was, or thought she was, at loggerheads": *ibid.* 1115. See further, pp. 92–93, below.

[21] See, *Baker v. Baker and Baker* (1993) 25 H.L.R. 408, C.A.

[22] [1984] 134 New L.J. 631, C.A., available on Lexis.

benefits that he did receive under his grandmother's will. The principle of offsetting counter-balancing benefits is discussed further elsewhere.[23]

Finally, it may be noted that, where the proprietary estoppel doctrine is being used as a sword rather than as a shield, there is an apparent judicial reluctance to grant the claimant equitable relief unless the circumstances of the case clearly warrant the court's equitable intervention. Gray[24] cites two examples of this phenomenon. In *Stilwell v. Simpson*,[25] the defendant granted (in 1971) a tenancy of part of a house to the plaintiff and his wife. From 1972 onwards, the plaintiff, who was a jobbing builder, carried out repairs and improvements to the property which was in bad condition. He subsequently issued a writ claiming a beneficial interest in the property on the basis of equitable estoppel. The action failed. What is significant is that "the court noted that the plaintiff was a protected tenant of the defendant and therefore had in any event 'a life interest by statute'. However, the court added significantly that if there had not been a protected tenancy and the defendant (or a purchaser) had 'sought to eject the plaintiff', that would have been a different matter".[26] Similarly, in *Savva v. Costa and Harymode Investments Ltd*,[27] the plaintiff had spent an appreciable sum in improvements to the premises owned by the defendant company. In this case, however, there was no immediate threat by the legal owner to dispossess the plaintiff and her family. Although her claim failed, Shaw L.J. pointed out that:

"If at some time it should be sought to turn [the plaintiff] out, there would arise the serious question as to the protection of an interest in the property on her behalf commensurate with the money she has spent on improving its condition so as to provide a proper degree of amenity for the accommodation of the children, who are intended to be the ultimate proprietors of the property."

This has led Gray to observe that "proprietary estoppel may still be more readily accepted by the courts as a shield rather than as a sword".[28]

(B) The Theoretical Basis of Relief

In his book, *Elements of Land Law*,[29] Gray highlights two alternative theoretical bases of relief in the context of estoppel doctrine. These may conveniently be referred to as "the expectation-oriented" principle of relief and the "detriment-oriented" approach. A simple illustration,[30] taken from the facts of *Pascoe v. Turner*,[31] will serve to explain the nature of the problem. Suppose that the plaintiff and defendant, an unmarried couple, decide to live together in a house

---

[23] See Chap. 4, pp. 58–60.
[24] *Elements of Land Law*, (2nd ed.) at pp. 350–351.
[25] (1983) 133 New L.J. 894.
[26] Gray, *Elements of Land Law*, (2nd ed.) at p. 350.
[27] (1981) 131 New L.J. 1114, C.A.
[28] Gray, *Elements of Land Law*, (2nd ed.) at p. 351.
[29] (2nd ed.), (Butterworths) at pp. 345–347.
[30] Gray cites the example postulated by Deane J. in *Commonwealth of Australia v. Verwayen* (1990) 170 C.L.R. 394 at 441, High Court of Australia.
[31] [1979] 1 W.L.R. 431, C.A.

owned by the plaintiff. After several years, the plaintiff decides to move out and informs his female partner, the defendant, that she has nothing to worry about as the house and its contents are entirely hers. The defendant continues to live in the house and carries out various (relatively minor) improvements to its fabric costing around £200. Subsequently, the plaintiff seeks possession of the house claiming that the defendant has only a revocable licence to occupy. Assuming that the defendant establishes an equity of estoppel, how should the court determine the nature and extent of the remedy to be granted? One solution is to give effect to the plaintiff's assurance on which the defendant has placed reliance. On this basis, "as soon as any convincing element of detrimental reliance [is] shown, the estoppel doctrine operate[s] effectively as a procedural mechanism for sanctioning or legitimising the informal creation of property rights in land".[32] In the *Pascoe* case itself, the Court of Appeal ordered a conveyance of the house into the sole name of the estoppel claimant. In so doing, the court was essentially using the estoppel doctrine as a means of perfecting the plaintiff's imperfect gift of land. This approach has been criticised on a number of fronts, in particular because it offends against established property and contractual principles which render unenforceable informal grant of rights in land and gratuitous promises.

By contrast, the "detriment-oriented" approach dictates a more limited application of the court's remedial powers. Here, the court is minded simply to restrain the legal owner's unconscionable insistence upon his/her strict legal rights and to provide compensation for the detriment sustained by the estoppel claimant arising from the legal owner's assurances. On this basis, on the hypothetical facts posed above, the appropriate award might well be a simple return of the claimant's £200.[33]

The "expectation-oriented" principle of relief has found support in several of the reported cases.[34] Thus, for example, in *Ramsden v. Dyson*,[35] Lord Kingsdown indicated that "a Court of equity will compel the [owner] to give effect to [his] promise or expectation".[36] Similarly, in *E.R. Ives Investment Ltd v. High*,[37] Lord Denning M.R. put the matter in this way[38]:

> "The right arises out of the expense incurred by Mr High in building his garage, as it is now, with access only over the yard: and the Wrights standing by and acquiescing in it, knowing that he believed he had a right of way over the yard. By so doing the Wrights created in Mr High's mind a reasonable expectation that his access over the yard would not be disturbed. That gives rise to an "equity arising out of acquiescence". It is

---

[32] Gray, *Elements of Land Law*, (2nd ed.) at pp. 345–346. See also, S. Moriarty, (1984) 100 L.Q.R. 376, at p. 384: "... the function of the proprietary estoppel doctrine is to enable the informal creation of proprietary interests in land". This thesis has been questioned by J. Dewar, (1986) 49 M.L.R. 741 and M.P. Thompson, [1986] Conv. 406, both supporting the discretinary nature of the jurisdiction.

[33] See, *e.g.* the remarks of Atkinson J. in *Veitch v. Caldicott* (1945) 173 L.T. 30 at 34: "... the mere fact that a man may have acquiesced in some expenditure does not necessarily mean that the fee simple is to vest in the one who has incurred the expenditure".

[34] See further, Chap. 6, pp. 106–108.

[35] (1866) L.R. 1 H.L. 129.

[36] *ibid.* 170.

[37] [1967] 2 Q.B. 379, C.A.

[38] *ibid.* 394–395.

available not only against the Wrights but also their successors in title. The court will not allow that expectation to be defeated when it would be inequitable so to do . . . In this case [the equity] could only be satisfied by allowing Mr High and his successors to have access over the yard so long as the block of flats has its foundations in his land."

It is clear that this passage is couched in the language of expectations. Mr High was awarded a right of access over the land in question on the basis that this would accord with his legitimate expectations arising out of the parties' conduct. Again, in *E. & L. Berg Homes Ltd v. Grey*,[39] Ormrod L.J. suggested that the extent of the remedy "must . . . depend upon the sort of legal rights [the claimants] mistakenly thought they had, or to use Lord Kingsdown's words, 'under an expectation created or encouraged' by the other side."[40] More recently, in *Watson v. Goldsbrough*,[41] Sir Nicolas Browne-Wilkinson V.-C. opined that "the court makes an order securing to the person who establishes the estoppel the rights in expectation of which he incurred the expenditure or did the work."[42] Accordingly, he held that the trial judge had erred in giving the claimant, an angling club, rights greater than that which they could properly have expected to receive when they incurred their expenditure on certain fishing ponds. In this case, a form of lease had been executed by the club but not the owners of the ponds. In holding that the relief given in the trial judge's order was too wide, the Vice-Chancellor was influenced by the terms of the proposed lease, which was expressed to be for an initial period of 10 years with an option for a further renewal of 10 years on the same terms. The lease also contained a tenant's covenant to preserve a sufficient stock of fish in the ponds and to leave such ponds well-stocked at the determination of the lease. Significantly also, the lease provided that it could be determined at any time by either party giving to the other not less than 12 months' notice in writing. On this basis, the judge's award of five years' security of tenure to the club was considered excessive. The order was thus varied by shortening the period of security to one year and safeguarding the preservation of a sufficient stock of fish in the ponds at the end of this period. In the course of his judgment, the Vice-Chancellor said[43]:

"In my judgment, in seeing what is equitable to award to the plaintiff in this case it cannot be right to give the plaintiffs a right greater than that which they themselves expected to receive or thought they were going to receive

---

[39] (1979) 253 EG 473, C.A.
[40] *ibid.* 479.
[41] [1986] 1 EGLR 265, C.A. See also, *Shaida v. Kindlane Ltd*, unreported, June 22, 1982, available on Lexis, where H.H. Judge Baker Q.C. said: "If the promise or representation is that he would obtain the fee simple interest in land, that is how you give effect to it, by transferring that. One does not, on the one hand, give more, so that if the expectation was a personal licence for life, then one canot give such interest that brings in its train the Settled Land Act provisions which would authorise not just a personal licence for life but would enable the licensee actually to sell, as tenant for life, the premises in question and have the money invested in other ways, and so on. If the representation is that one is to have an interest on making certain payments, keeping down mortgage payments, or something of that sort, then one does not give effect to it by giving a free transfer of the interest."
[42] *ibid.* 267.
[43] *ibid.* 267.

when they incurred the expenditure which gave rise to the estoppel. The best evidence of that must be the lease ... "

In the High Court of Australia, however, there has been an emphatic move away from the "expectation-oriented" approach towards a detriment-based philosophy. In *Commonwealth of Australia v. Verwayen*,[44] the High Court held, by a majority, that the Commonwealth was estopped from resiling from its promise not to raise a defence of limitations in a negligence action brought against it by the respondent, a member of the Royal Australian Navy. In the course of his dissenting judgment, Mason C.J. alluded to the theoretical basis of the estoppel doctrine. In his view, all categories of estoppel (*i.e.* promissory estoppel, proprietary estoppel and estoppel by acquiescence) are intended to serve the same fundamental purpose, namely, "protection against the detriment which would flow from a party's change of position if the assumption (or expectation) that led to it were deserted."[45] On this reasoning, the estoppel doctrine permits a court to do what is required in order to avoid detriment to the party who has relied on the assumption induced by the party estopped, but no more. In appropriate cases, this may require that the party estopped be held to the assumption created or encouraged, even if that means the effective enforcement of a voluntary promise. This may be particularly justified if the assumption has been relied upon by the estoppel claimant for a considerable period of time.

In the earlier case of *Waltons Stores (Interstate) Ltd v. Maher*,[46] the High Court of Australia, by a majority, concluded that the doctrine of estoppel entitled a party only to that relief which was necessary to prevent unconscionable conduct and to do justice between the parties. In the course of his judgment, Brennan J. said[47]:

> " ... the better solution of the problem is reached by identifying the unconscionable conduct which gives rise to the equity as the leaving of another to suffer detriment occasioned by the conduct of the party against whom the equity is raised. Then the object of the principle can be seen to be the avoidance of that detriment and the satisfaction of the equity calls for the enforcement of a promise only as a means of avoiding the detriment and only to the extent necessary to achieve that object. So regarded, equitable estoppel does not elevate non-contractual promises to the level of contractual promises and the doctrine of consideration is not blown away by a side wind."

A key feature of the "detriment-based" approach is that there must be a proportionality between the remedy and the detriment which is its purpose to avoid. Thus, it would be "wholly inequitable and unjust to insist upon a disproportionate making good of the relevant assumption."[48] Thus, for

---

[44] (1990) 170 C.L.R. 394, High Court of Australia.

[45] See, *Waltons Stores (Interstate) Ltd v. Maher* (1988) 76 A.L.R. 513 at 534–535, *per* Brennan J.

[46] (1988) 76 A.L.R. 513.

[47] *ibid.* 540. See also, *Silovi Property Ltd v. Barbaro* (1988) 13 N.S.W.L.R. 466 at 472, *per* Priestley J.A. and *Stratulatos v. Stratulatos* [1988] 2 N.Z.L.R. 424 at 438, *per* McGechan J.

[48] *Commonwealth of Australia v. Verwayen* (1990) 170 C.L.R. 394 at 413, *per* Mason C.J.

example, the conveyance of the fee simple to the claimant may be wholly unwarranted in so far as such form of relief would be wholly disproportionate to the detriment suffered by the claimant.[49]

The view that the estoppel remedy is not necessarily designed to enforce the legal owner's assurances is also supported by the modern English caselaw. Thus, in *Crabb v. Arun District Council*[50] the Court of Appeal granted the estoppel claimant a right of access over the defendants' land, this being the "minimum equity"[51] to do justice to the plaintiff. In *Crabb*, Lord Denning M.R. took the opportunity to qualify his language of expectations in the *Ives* case (mentioned above), by stating that the court will prevent a person from insisting on his strict legal rights "when it would be inequitable for him to do so having regard to the dealings which have taken place between the parties."[52] Ultimately, therefore, the remedy required to satisfy the equity will vary according to the circumstances of the case. In the words of Robert Goff J. in *Amalgamated Investment & Property Co. Ltd v. Texas Commerce International Bank Ltd*[53]: "Of all doctrines, equitable estoppel is surely one of the most flexible". Holding the legal owner to his assurances may be merely one way of doing justice between the parties. In some situations, however, the minimum equity will not be satisfied by anything short of enforcing the promise. In the *Amalgamated* case, Lord Denning M.R. referred to the doctrine of estoppel as one of the most flexible in the armoury of the law. In his view, one general principle emerged from the cases, namely, that:

"When the parties to a transaction proceed on the basis of an underlying assumption ... on which they have conducted the dealings between them—neither of them will be allowed to go back on that assumption when it would be unfair or unjust to allow him to do so. If one of them does seek to go back on it, the courts will give the other such remedy as the equity of the case demands."

As a general rule, therefore, the *maximum* extent of the equity is to have made good the expectations of the claimant.[54] The doctrine of estoppel "has never been applied so as to give the person establishing the estoppel any right greater than that which he either mistakenly thought he had or thought he was going to be afforded."[55] Anything beyond this would be oppressive to the legal owner.[56]

---

[49] *Beaton v. McDivitt* (1987) 13 N.S.W.L.R. 162 at 172, *per* Kirby P.
[50] [1976] Ch. 179, C.A.
[51] *ibid.* 198, *per* Scarman L.J. See also, *Pascoe v. Turner* [1979] 1 W.L.R. 431 at 438, C.A., *per* Cumming-Bruce L.J.
[52] *ibid.* 187–188. See also, *Inwards v. Baker* [1965] 2 Q.B. 29 at 37, C.A. where Lord Denning M.R. stated: " ... the court will not allow that expectation to be defeated where it would be inequitable so to do".
[53] [1982] Q.B. 84 at 103.
[54] See, *e.g. Dodsworth v. Dodsworth* (1973) 228 EG 1117, C.A., where Russell L.J. said: "We do not think that it can be right to satisfy such an equity by conferring upon the defendants a greater interest in the property than was envisaged by the parties". See also, *Griffiths v. Williams* (1977) 248 EG 947, at 949, C.A.
[55] *Watson v. Goldsbrough* [1986] 1 EGLR 265 at 267, C.A., *per* Sir Nicolas Browne-Wilkinson V.-C.
[56] See, *e.g. Baker v. Baker & Baker* (1993) 25 H.L.R. 408 at 412, C.A., *per* Dillon L.J. In this case, the trial judge's order to pay the claimant £33,950 with interest was oppressive to the legal owners since they could only satisfy the order by selling the house, and it was the original intention of the

The element of discretion allows the court to "maintain a flexibility in determining the appropriate remedy to satisfy the equity" but, at the same time, "as far as possible ... to take account of the parties expectations."[57] Thus, "if, for example, A's expectation is that he could stay in a house for the rest of his life, this will not be given effect to in such a way as to confer on him the rights of a tenant for life under the Settled Land Act 1925, for that, with its concomitant right of sale, would give him a greater interest than he was entitled to expect."[58]

(C) Range of Remedies

It will be convenient now to examine the various estoppel-based remedies available to the court. It should be remembered that the court retains a very wide discretion in the exercise of its remedial powers and the list given below is not intended to be exhaustive. In a proper case, the equity granted may, by its very nature, be for a limited period,[59] or determinable upon certain conditions,[60] or subject to terms.[61]

(i) Denying the Legal Owner's Claim to Possession

At one extreme, the court, in the exercise of its discretionary jurisdiction, may do no more than is necessary to protect the occupation rights of the claimant by simply denying the legal owner's claim to possession.[62] This was considered to be the appropriate form of relief in *Matharu v. Matharu*.[63] Here, the plaintiff (in 1968) bought a property which became the matrimonial home of the defendant and the plaintiff's son, after their marriage in 1971. During the course of the marriage, the defendant's husband made extensive improvements to the property at his own expense. In 1988, the marriage broke down, and in 1990 the defendant obtained an order excluding the husband from the house. The husband died in 1991. Later that year, the plaintiff emigrated to Canada but returned the following year and sought possession of the property. The Court of Appeal held that the defendant's equity defeated the plaintiff's claim for

---

parties that the house should be bought as a family home, with a granny room to be occupied rent-free by the claimant for life.

[57] R. Pearce and J. Stevens, *The Law of Trusts and Equitable Obligations* at p. 681.

[58] Snell's, *Equity*, (29th ed.) at p. 577, citing *Dodsworth v. Dodsworth* (1973) 228 EG 1115, C.A., discussed in *Griffiths v. Williams* (1977) 248 EG 947, C.A.

[59] See, *Hardwick v. Johnson* [1978] 1 W.L.R. 683, C.A., (licence irrevocable until some event occurred which would justify bringing it to an end). See further, Chap. 7, pp. 145–146.

[60] *Williams v. Staite* [1979] Ch. 291 at 300, *per* Goff L.J., C.A. Thus, in *E.R. Ives Investment Ltd v. High* [1967] 2 Q.B. 379, C.A., the equity was satisfied by granting access over the yard but only so long as the adjoining block of flats' foundations encroached on the claimant's land. See also, *Classic Communications Ltd v. Lascar* (1986) 21 D.L.R. (4th) 579 at 588, (licensee entitled, under doctrine of proprietray estoppel, to maintain cable so long as hydro poles remained).

[61] See, *e.g. Jones (A.E.) v. Jones (F.W.)* [1977] 1 W.L.R. 438, C.A., where the making of a rent payment was canvassed as a condition of granting the equity: *ibid.* 443, *per* Roskill L.J. See also, *Crabb v. Arun District Council* [1976] Ch. 179, C.A.

[62] This may be done by granting the claimant an injunction restraining an action for possession: see *Lord Cawdor v. Lewis* (1835) 1 Y. & C. Ex. 427 at 433; 160 E.R. 174 at 176; *Powell v. Thomas* (1848) 6 Hare 300; 67 E.R. 1180. More typically, the court simply dismisses the plaintif's claim for possession: *Forbes v. Ralli* (1925) L.R. 52 Ind. App. 178. See also, *Steed v. Whitaker* (1740) Barn. Ch. 220; 27 E.R. 621, where a claim to enforce a mortgage was restrained by injunction.

[63] (1994) 68 P. & C.R. 93, C.A. See M. Welstead, [1995] Conv. 61 and G. Battersby, (1995) 7 C.F.L.Q. 59–65.

possession. The defendant did not, however, acquire a beneficial interest in the property on the basis of the estoppel. What was created was a licence for the defendant to remain in the property for life or for such shorter period as she may decide. The form of relief granted to the defendant was, however, to refuse the plaintiff's claim for possession on terms, *inter alia*, that the defendant be responsible for the outgoings on the house (*i.e.* council tax, repayments under the mortgage, insurance premiums, water, electricity and gas), keep the premises in good decorative repair and be responsible for the structural repair of the property.

The nature of the relief granted in this case has been criticised not least because it fails to accord with the claimant's expectations that she was to have a licence to remain in the property for the rest of her life. The court declined to grant such a positive right but merely barred the plaintiff from possession. Another difficulty relates to the defendant's security against any third party seeking to purchase the property from the plaintiff.[64] In *Stevens v. Stevens*,[65] for example, the Court of Appeal felt it inappropriate, in satisfying the defendant's equity, simply to dismiss the plaintiff's action for possession because the parties "would not know where they stood".[66] Instead, it was declared that the claimant had the right to remain in occupation of the plaintiff's house for so long as she wished to live there. These, and other objections, are raised by Welstead[67]:

> "In the context of unregistered land, she has no right capable of registration although the doctrine of notice may possibly ensure that any future purchaser who has actual notice will be bound by the equity. In registered land, her right is also incapable of registration and does not constitute an overriding interest but it is possible that constructive trust theory may come to her rescue if it can be shown that the third party has behaved unconscientiously in acquiring the property. She will be unable to assign her right should she wish to finance the purchase of alternative property. It remains most uncertain in what circumstances the appellant might be allowed to reapply for possession thus revoking the [defendant's] equity. For instance, what if she should wish to remarry and bring a new husband to live with her in the property? The court order made [the defendant] liable for all the outgoings on the house, including mortgage payments, in addition to reimbursing the [plaintiff] for the interim mortgage payments made by him. The [defendant] was made responsible for any structural repairs to the property. The warring parties are thus left in a continuing relationship with each other. The barring of the [plaintiff's] right to possession also raises the issue of a potential claim of possessory title on the part of the [defendants]; they are in occupation adversely to the [plaintiff] and he is unable to assert title to the property to bring that

[64] See generally, Chap. 7.
[65] Unreported, March 3, 1989, C.A., available on Lexis.
[66] *ibid. per* Slade L.J.
[67] [1995] Conv. 61 at pp. 66–67. See also, G. Battersby, (1995) 7 C.F.L.Q. 59 at pp. 64–65, who suggests that a clean break would have been a better solution. Alternatively, the court should have conferred on the claimant a life interest which would enable her to move house since, on any sale, she could request the Settled Land Act trustees to invest the proceeds of sale in a new house for her occupation. In the further alternative, the Settled Land Act 1925 could have been avoided by conferring on the claimant a lease at a nominal rent.

occupation to an end. Furthermore, it remains most unclear to what extent the barring of the [plaintiff's] right to possession extends to the other [defendants] who were the three children of the [defendant] and the grandchildren of the [plaintiff]. Do they all have a secure home for life?"

This last point was briefly addressed by Slade L.J. in *Stevens v. Stevens*,[68] who suggested that "the position of [the claimant's children] is more doubtful". He concluded that the claimant's right to occupy the property "obviously extends to them" but doubted whether any equity "which she may have to live in the property can survive for the benefit of her children after her occupation comes to an end."[69]

A negative form of remedy was also awarded in the case of *Jones (A.E.) v. Jones (F.W.)*,[70] where the Court of Appeal held that the plaintiff was estopped from turning the defendant, her stepson, out of his father's house by reason of the father's conduct which had led the defendant to leave his job and pay money to his father in the belief that the house would be his home for the rest of his life. The court declined to order a life interest to be created in favour of the defendant but simply refused to order a sale of the property: "Even though there is an implied trust for sale, nevertheless, the courts will not allow it to be used so as to defeat the purpose contemplated by the parties."[71]

In *Hopgood v. Brown*,[72] the plaintiff's claim for trespass in respect of the position of a boundary was dismissed on the ground that the plaintiff was estopped from asserting that the boundary was at any other position than was shown on the ground by a garage, wall and fence. The plaintiff's conduct impliedly represented that the defendant could safely proceed to build as he planned. In this case, the defendant was simply given protection from possession without obtaining any proprietary interest in the land.

It will be observed that, in such cases, the equity is given effect as a defence like any other estoppel.

(ii) Licence to Occupy

The leading case is *Inwards v. Baker*,[73] the facts of which may be briefly stated. In 1931, a son wished to build a bungalow as his home and to acquire a piece of land for that purpose. His father, who owned some six acres of land in the district, said to him: "Why don't you build the bungalow on my land and make it a bit bigger?" So encouraged, the son gave up his plan to buy other land and built the bungalow on his father's land, largely by his own labour. The cost was about £300, of which the son provided £150 and the father the balance. The son went into occupation and lived in the bungalow continuously thereafter, in the expectation and belief that he would be allowed to remain there for his lifetime or for so long as he wished. The father died (in 1951) leaving a will under which

---

[68] Unreported, March 3, 1989, C.A., available on Lexis.
[69] He also added that: "It is not for me, however, in these proceedings to say what would happen if the [claimant] were to leave the property at a time whilst her children were still living there". The point remains an open one.
[70] [1977] 1 W.L.R. 438, C.A. See further, J. Alder, (1978) 41 M.L.R. 208.
[71] *ibid.* 442, *per* Lord Denning M.R.
[72] [1955] 1 W.L.R. 213, C.A.
[73] [1965] 2 Q.B. 29, C.A. See also, *Cullen v. Cullen* [1962] I.R. 268.

the land vested in trustees for the benefit of persons other than the son. In 1963, the trustees of the will brought proceedings for possession of the bungalow against the son. The Court of Appeal had no difficulty in satisfying the son's equity by allowing him to remain in occupation of the bungalow for as long as he desired. In effect, the court awarded the son an irrevocable licence to occupy the house rent-free for life. The equity granted in this case was expressly referred to by Danckwerts L.J. as being one "created by estoppel".[74]

A similar result was achieved in the later case of *Greasley v. Cooke*,[75] where the defendant occupant was initially a living-in maid to the legal owner and later a cohabitant to one of his sons. She had looked after the house and, in particular, cared for the owner's daughter who was mentally ill. She claimed that she had been encouraged by members of his family to believe that she could regard the house as her home for the rest of her life and that, therefore, the plaintiffs were estopped from evicting her. The Court of Appeal, in satisfying her equity, granted a declaration that she was entitled to occupy the house rent-free for the rest of her life.

Again, in *Maharaj v. Chand*,[76] a case involving an unmarried couple, the male partner (the plaintiff) told his female cohabitee (the defendant) that the house (on which he had a sublease) would be a permanent home for her and the children. The defendant gave up her own flat, moved into the house and looked after the plaintiff and the children as wife and mother. The plaintiff financed the sublease and the building of the house while the defendant contributed to household expenses from her own earnings. In 1980, the relationship broke down and the plaintiff left the house telling the defendant that she could stay there. The Privy Council, in satisfying the defendant's estoppel equity, held that she had, as against the plaintiff, a permission to reside permanently in the house, on the basis that the children might be with her for as long as they needed a home. This was categorised as a personal right not amounting to a property interest diminishing the rights of the plaintiff's landlord and mortgagee. It appears, however, that a personal licence when coupled with a legal interest (*e.g.* in the nature of a *profit à prendre*) may prevent a later equitable interest of a purchaser, acquired under a contract of sale, from prevailing over the earlier claimant's equitable rights.[77]

It is not unusual for the court to grant an occupational licence upon terms that the claimant maintains the property in reasonable repair and decoration, indemnifies the legal owner in respect of usual outgoings and does not seek payment by him for any outgoings, repairs or decorations.[78] As has been pointed out,[79] the terms of the claimant's licence to occupy must be consistent with the

---

[74] *ibid*. 38.
[75] [1980] 1 W.L.R. 1306, C.A. Contrast earlier "housekeeper" cases, notably, *Maddison v. Alderson* (1883) 8 App. Cas 467, H.L. and *Wakeham v. Mackenzie* [1968] 1 W.L.R. 1175, based on contract principles, which were not cited in *Greasley*. See further, G. Woodman, (1981) 44 M.L.R. 461; M. Thompson, (1981) 125 S.J. 539 and R.E. Annand, [1981] Conv. 154. See also, *Cadman v. Bell* [1988] EGCS 139, where the defendant was awarded an irrevocable licence to reside in the house for life.
[76] [1986] A.C. 898, P.C.
[77] *Silovi Property Ltd v. Barbaro* (1988) 13 N.S.W.L.R. 466 at 475, *per* Priestley JA., (Supreme Court of New South Wales).
[78] See, *e.g. Stevens v. Stevens*, March 3, 1989, unreported, C.A., available on Lexis, *per* Slade L.J.
[79] *ibid. per* Slade L.J.

legal owner's intention that the property should remain in his ownership, but not be an income producing investment.

In an appropriate case, a licence may be granted for the claimant to remain in occupation until a loan is repaid.[80]

(iii) Conveyance of the Fee Simple Without Compensation

This was the nature of the relief granted in *Dillwyn v. Llewelyn.*[81] Here, a father placed one of his sons in possession of land belonging to the father and, at the same time, signed a memorandum (not by deed) that he had presented the land to the son for the purpose of furnishing him with a house. The son, with the assent and approval of the father, built at his own expense (*i.e.* some £14,000) a house on the land and resided there. The father subsequently died leaving a will which left all his real estate upon certain trusts in favour of others. It was held that the son was entitled to call for a conveyance of the fee simple of the house. Lord Westbury concluded[82]:

> "The estate was given as the site of a dwelling-house to be erected by the son. The ownership of the dwelling-house and the ownership of the estate must be considered as intended to be co-extensive and co-equal. No one builds a house for his own life only, and it is absurd to suppose that it was intended by either party that the house, at the death of the son, should become the property of the father. If, therefore, I am right in the conclusion of law that the subsequent expenditure by the son, with the approbation of the father, supplied a valuable consideration originally wanting, the memorandum signed by the father and son must be thenceforth regarded as an agreement for the soil extending to the fee-simple of the land".

The decision has been criticised[83] on the grounds that it is inconsistent with the rule that a gratuitous promise is not enforceable and that an incomplete gift will not be completed in favour of a volunteer. Although regarded by some[84] as the origin of the doctrine of proprietary estoppel, it is evident that Lord Westbury did not have any such principle in mind. It is apparent that the Lord Chancellor found consideration in the detrimental reliance of the son upon his father's promise. The difficulty with this approach is that detrimental reliance does not furnish consideration at law.

A more extreme example of the application of a proprietary-based remedy is to be found in *Pascoe v. Turner,*[85] where the Court of Appeal held that the "minimum equity" to do justice to the female claimant in that case was to

---

[80] *Re Sharpe, (A Bankrupt)* [1980] 1 W.L.R. 219.
[81] (1862) 4 De G.F. & J. 517; 45 E.R. 1285. See also, *Cameron v. Cameron* (1892) 11 N.Z.L.R. 642 at 659; *Eagleson v. Public Trustee* [1922] N.Z.L.R. 1054 at 1057; *Thomas v. Thomas* [1956] N.Z.L.R. 785, Supreme Court of Wellington and *Raffaele v. Raffaele* [1962] W.A.R. 29, Supreme Court of Western Australia, and D.E. Allan, (1963) 79 L.Q.R. 238. In *Riches v. Hogben* [1986] 1 Qd R. 315, the Queensland Supreme Court ordered a transfer of the legal title to the claimant subject to an equitable life interest in favour of the legal owner so as to enable the latter to reside in a granny flat associated with the property.
[82] *ibid.* 522; 1287.
[83] See, *e.g. Hanbury and Martin, Modern Equity,* (14th ed.) at p. 883.
[84] See, *e.g. Sen v. Headley* [1991] Ch. 425 at 439, C.A., *per* Nourse L.J.
[85] [1979] 1 W.L.R. 431, C.A.

compel the legal owner to give effect to his promises by ordering him to execute a conveyance of the property to her. Essentially, the court was perfecting the imperfect gift as was done in *Dillwyn v. Llewelyn*. The practical result, however, was to award the claimant the fee simple in the house where she had expended only £230 on improving the property. Even though the claimant never sought to establish that she had spent more money on the house than she would have done had she believed that she only had a licence to live there for life, the court felt that protection for her lifetime was insecure without an outright conveyance of the house. The court was influenced by a number of factors. First, the claimant was a widow in her middle-fifties. Her capital had been reduced considerably during the period that she lived with the plaintiff. She devoted a quarter of her remaining capital upon the house and fixtures. Secondly, the court was anxious to grant a remedy which assured to the defendant security of tenure, quiet enjoyment, and freedom of action in respect of repairs and improvements without interference from the plaintiff. In this connection, the history of the plaintiff's conduct lead to the conclusion that he was determined to pursue his purpose of evicting her from the house by any legal means at his disposal. The court was, thus, determined to grant a remedy to protect the defendant against any future manifestations of the plaintiff's harrassing conduct. Thirdly, it had been conceded that, if the defendant was granted a licence to occupy for life, such a licence could not be registered as a land charge so that she could find herself ousted by a purchaser for value without notice. Fourthly, if the defendant was minded in the future to do further repairs, she would only be able to finance them by a loan, but as a mere licensee she would be unable to charge the house. In all these circumstances, therefore, the court concluded that the defendant's equity could only be satisfied by compelling the plaintiff to give effect to his promise and her expectations. The decision must, it is submitted, be treated as somewhat exceptional. For example, in *Inwards v. Baker*,[86] discussed above, it does not appear to have been suggested anywhere that it was necessary or appropriate to satisfy the equity in that case by allowing the claimant more than a right of occupation of the property in question for as long as he wished.

In the more recent case of *Voyce v. Voyce*,[87] however, the court was, once again, compelled to order an outright conveyance of the property. In this case, the defendant's mother had said that he could take her cottage as a gift provided that he did it up to her satisfaction, which it was agreed he subsequently did do, at considerable expense. The gift was never executed by deed. The mother (some 10 years later) made a gift of her farm and the cottage, duly executed by deed of gift, to her younger son, the plaintiff. He was aware, at all material times, that his brother was living at the cottage. The mother then died and the defendant (in 1984) began to build an extension onto the cottage to which the plaintiff took exception on the grounds that it would interfere with light to the farmhouse and that it was being built on his land. The plaintiff claimed to be the owner of the whole farm (including the cottage) and sought an order that the defendant should vacate the land except for the cottage itself and should remove the foundations for the extension carried out on the land. The trial judge found

---

[86] [1965] 2 Q.B. 29, C.A.
[87] (1991) 62 P. & C.R. 290, C.A.

that the mother had intended to give the cottage and garden (which included the site of the extension) to the defendant, that he had done considerable work upon the cottage in reliance on this, and that he had lived there for 32 years. He considered that justice could only be done by ordering that the freehold of the cottage and garden be transferred to the defendant, even though this would have the effect of perfecting an imperfect gift. On appeal, the plaintiff's contention that it would have been sufficient for the judge to declare that the defendant and his wife had the right to remain in the cottage during their lives, was dismissed. Since the defendant had spent a substantial sum of money on the cottage in reliance upon his mother's promise that if he did this the cottage would be his, his mother would have been estopped from asserting that the cottage belonged to her. The plaintiff's position as a volunteer could be no better than that of his mother. Dillon L.J., who gave the leading judgment of the court, cited[88] the following passage from the judgment of Sir Terence Donovan in *Chalmers v. Pardoe*[89] as being applicable to the issue before him:

> "Where an owner of land has invited or expressly encouraged another to expend money upon part of his land upon the faith of an assurance or promise that that part of the land will be made over to the person so expending his money, a court of equity will prima facie require the owner by appopriate conveyance to fulfil his obligation".

In *Voyce*, there was a promise of a gift of the cottage if work of modernisation of a substantial nature was carried out on the property. That work was, indeed, carried out to the donor's satisfaction by 1972 with continued and undisturbed occupation by the donee ever since. In these circumstances, the appropriate form of relief was to perfect the donor's imperfect gift.

Again, in *Re Basham (dec'd)*,[90] the plaintiff's mother married the deceased when she was 15 years old. The plaintiff helped them run their business and was never paid, but understood that she would inherit the deceased's property when he died. In 1947, the plaintiff's husband was offered a job with a tied house but the deceased opposed that, purchasing instead for her future use a tenanted cottage with money largely provided by the plaintiff's mother. She died in 1976 and the deceased moved into the cottage which had become vacant. The deceased told the plaintiff that the cottage belonged to her. The plaintiff and her husband helped the deceased with the day to day running of the cottage, and she was told by him that she would lose nothing by it. A few days before his death, he said to her that she was to have the cottage. He died intestate and the plaintiff claimed a declaration that she was absolutely and beneficially entitled to the cottage, the furniture, and other property owned by the deceased. In granting the declaration, Mr Edward Nugee Q.C. (sitting as a High Court judge) said[91]:

> "The question then arises in what manner effect should be given to the equity which has arisen in the plaintiff's favour. The extent of the equity is

---

[88] *ibid.* 293.
[89] [1963] 1 W.L.R. 677 at 681–682, P.C.
[90] [1986] 1 W.L.R. 1498. See also, *Wayling v. Jones* (1995) 69 P. & C.R. 170, C.A., (proceeds of sale awarded to claimant). See further, p. 95 below.
[91] *ibid.* 1510.

to have made good, so far as may fairly be done between the parties, the expectations which the deceased encouraged . . . Prima facie, therefore, the plaintiff is entitled to a declaration that the defendants, as personal representatives of the deceased, hold the whole of his net estate on trust for the plaintiff".

Similarly, in *Durant v. Heritage*,[92] the deceased's niece successfully claimed that, by virtue of proprietary estoppel, she was entitled to have the deceased's house and garden (Holme Farm) transferred to her. Mr Andrew Park Q.C. (sitting as a deputy judge of the High Court) held, on the facts, that the claimant's expectation or belief was the actual extent of the equity as well as its maximum extent. Her expectation or belief was that she would become the owner of Holme Farm after her uncle's death and that was the extent of her equity. This could only be achieved by an outright transfer of the freehold ownership of the property to the claimant. In this case, a question arose also as to the extent of the property that should be comprised in the transfer. On this point, the deputy judge held that the uncle had indicated (or meant to indicate) that he would leave to the claimant the ownership of what in his lifetime he was letting to her as tenant. On this basis, the claimant was held entitled to a transfer of the house and garden (but not the fields, yard and outbuildings) forming Holme Farm including two garages, together with a right of access across the yard to enable her to use the same.

In *Plimmer v. Wellington Corporation*,[93] the plaintiff erected a wharf on public land with the permission of the Crown and subsequently added a jetty which was later extended at the request of the Provincial Government. When the Government took over the jetty under statutory powers, the plaintiff claimed compensation under the Public Works Act 1882, which only applied if he had "any estate or interest in" the jetty. The Privy Council held that the plaintiff had acquired an equitable right which constituted an "estate or interest in, to or out of the land" within the meaning of the 1882 Act entitling him to compensation under the statute. Essentially, the plaintiff's revocable licence to use the jetty was rendered irrevocable by reason of the expenditure on the extension which had been specifically requested by the Government. The reasonable expectation created in the mind of the plaintiff was that his occupation would not be disturbed and, consequently, he was held to have acquired an indefinite (*i.e.* perpetual) right to the jetty for the purposes of his original licence.

In an appropriate case,[94] a landlord may be compelled to grant his tenant licence to assign the lease.

The form of the court order will usually be in terms that the legal owner do, within a specified time from the date of the order, execute a proper transfer/conveyance of the property to the claimant.[95]

---

[92] [1994] EGCS 134.
[93] (1884) 9 App. Cas. 699. See also, *Ahmed Yar Khan v. Secretary of State for India* (1901) L.R. 28 I.R. 21.
[94] See, *e.g. Willmott v. Barber* (1880) 15 Ch.D. 96, where the claim failed.
[95] See, *e.g. Thomas v. Thomas* [1956] N.Z.L.R. 785, where Gresson J. ordered that "the respondent within fourteen days of the date of service upon him of this order execute a proper transfer of the property to which the application relates (subject to the existing mortgage) from the joint names of the applicant and the respondent into the name of the applicant": *ibid.* 794. The costs of the transfer were ordered to be borne by the applicant.

(iv) Conveyance of the Fee Simple With Compensation

In some cases, a more appropriate solution is to order a conveyance of the fee simple but only on payment of the site value of the land. This was the form of order made in *Duke of Beaufort v. Patrick*,[96] where nothing but perpetual retention of the improved land in question would satisfy the equity raised in favour of those who spent money on it, but subject to the payment of fair compensation based on its agricultural value.

An alternative approach, canvassed by the Privy Council in *Lim Teng Huan v. Ang Swee Chuan*,[97] is to order the transfer of the property to the estoppel claimant but only on payment of a reasonable purchase price after deducting the amount expended on improvements.

In this case, the plaintiff was held entitled to recover by way of compensation the value of the land as a site excluding such part of its value as was attributable to the improvement works. Since there had been no agreement by the parties as to the amount of compensation payable by the claimant, an inquiry was ordered to determine the value of the land improved at the date of the inquiry on the assumption that no works had been carried out by the claimant on the land. Following such inquiry, the claimant was required to pay to the plaintiff a sum equal to half this amount (since the parties were joint owners) and that, on such payment being made, the plaintiff would be ordered to transfer his one-half share of the land to the claimant absolutely.

In some cases, it may be appropriate, in the exercise of the court's equitable jurisdiction, to allow the claimant to purchase the subject property at a discount in order to satisfy the estoppel equity. This may be the correct solution where the representation relied on by the claimant is to the effect that he would be entitled to acquire the property at a discount on the market price.[98]

Another solution is to compel the legal owner to hold the land on trust for sale and to hold the net proceeds after discharge of the respective expenditure of the parties to divide the residue between them.[99]

(v) Grant of Incorporeal Interests

In *Crabb v. Arun District Council*,[1] the equity was held to be satisfied by granting the plaintiff a right of way along the defendants' road without paying anything for it. The decision not to give the defendants any compensation for the plaintiff's right of way was influenced by the defendants' conduct in rendering the plaintiff's land landlocked and sterile for over five years. In the words of Scarman L.J.[2]:

---

[96] (1853) 17 Beav. 60; 51 E.R. 954. See also, *Mold v. Wheatcroft* (1859) 27 Beav. 510; 54 E.R. 202.

[97] [1992] 1 W.L.R. 113 at 118, P.C.

[98] *Cameron v. Murdoch* (1986) 63 A.L.R. 575 at 594–595, P.C.

[99] See, *Holiday Inns Inc. v. Broadhead* (1974) 232 EG 951, (proposed joint venture to build and operate hotel on the representor's land).

[1] [1976] Ch. 179, C.A. See also, *Soames-Forsythe Properties Ltd v. Tesco Stores Ltd* [1991] EGCS 22, where, by reason of permitting a supermarket tenant to improve the premises on the assumption that it had the right to stack trolleys on the walkway, the landlords were held estopped from asserting that the tenant had no right of stacking. Effect was given to the equity by conferring on the tenant the right in the nature of an easement of stacking. See further, P. Jackson, (1969) 33 Conv. 135; P.S. Atiyah, (1976) 92 L.Q.R. 174; P.J. Millett, (1976) 92 L.Q.R. 342.

[2] *ibid.* 199.

"[The defendants' conduct] has involved [the plaintiff] in loss, which has not been measured; but, since it amounted to sterilisation of an industrial estate for a very considerable period of time, it must surpass any sort of sum of money which the plaintiff ought reasonably, before it was done, to have paid the defendants in order to obtain an enforceable legal right."

Similarly, in the earlier case of *E.R. Ives Investment Ltd v. High,*[3] the Court of Appeal held that the defendant had a good right of way across the plaintiffs' yard, arising by virtue of estoppel, which (according to Lord Denning M.R. and Danckerts L.J.) did not need to be registered under the Land Charges Act 1925 so as to bind the plaintiffs as successors in title to the yard.[4] Again, in *Ward v. Kirkland,*[5] it was held that the claimant was entitled to an equitable right to keep certain drains permanently in position in the farmyard of his neighbouring owner (the defendant) for the purpose of draining off bath-water from his premises. Moreover, he was granted an injunction restraining the defendant from interfering with that right.

(vi) Award of Compensation

In *Inwards v. Baker,*[6] the Court of Appeal seems to have overlooked the possibility that the grant of a *de facto* life interest to the claimant may make the property settled land and give much more extensive rights than the parties contemplated.[7] The point was referred to in *Dodsworth v. Dodsworth,*[8] where the Court of Appeal held that the proper way to satisfy the equity was to declare that possession could only be obtained against the estoppel claimants if they were repaid their outlay (£711) on improvements they had made to the bungalow in question. Russell L.J. pointed out[9]:

"The defendants would necessarily become joint tenants for life. As such they could sell the property, or quit and let it. In the one case, they would be entitled to the income of the invested proceeds of sale for life and the life of the survivor: in the other, they would be entitled to the net rents. None of these possibilities could conceivably have been embodied in the expectations giving rise to the equity in question, and we do not think that it can be right to satisfy such an equity by conferring upon the defendants a greater interest in the property than was envisaged by the parties".

---

[3] [1967] 2 Q.B. 379, C.A.

[4] Winn L.J., the third member of the court, held that the estoppel was not registrable under the Land Charges Act 1925, although it prevented the plaintiffs from denying the defendant's user of the right of way. See further, Chap. 7, pp. 132–134.

[5] [1967] Ch. 194.

[6] [1965] 2 Q.B. 29, C.A.

[7] In *Binions v. Evans* [1972] Ch. 359, C.A., Lord Denning M.R. suggested that the Settled Land Act 1925 had no application because the estate is not necesarily limited in trust for persons by way of succession in this type of case. Contrast, *Bannister v. Bannister* [1948] 2 All E.R. 133, C.A. and *Ungurian v. Lesnoff* [1990] Ch. 206 at 224–226, *per* Vinelott J. See S. Moriarty, (1984) 100 L.Q.R. 376 at 408–411.

[8] (1973) 228 EG 1115, C.A. In *Re Sharpe, (A Bankrupt)* [1980] 1 W.L.R. 219, the court refused to make an order for possession until a loan made in reliance upon a promise of accommodation had been repaid. See also, *Mayes v. Mayes* (1969) 210 EG 935 at 938, *per* Goff J.

[9] *ibid.* 1115.

In this case, it was inexpedient to give effect to the parties' expectations in full, because it was not possible to enforce a sharing arrangement without introducing the complications of the Settled Land Act, so some lesser interest was given instead which took the form of a repayment of the money expended.[10]

Where there is family discord, an award of compensation *simpliciter* may provide the only solution in order to achieve a clean break between the parties. In this sense, the award of monetary compensation may be categorised as a "default remedy"[11] given where the reasonable expectation of shared occupation between owner and claimant is no longer a realistic possibility. In effect, the equity may have to be satisfied in a way wholly different from what was intended when the parties were on good terms. Thus, in *Burrows & Burrows v. Sharp*[12] the equity, at the time of the trial, could have been satisfied either by an order giving the claimants a right to live in the property or by an order for the refund to them of their expenditure on the premises. In reality, however, the former type of order (for which the trial judge opted) was quite unworkable in view of the breakdown in relations in the family. The Court of Appeal, therefore, had no choice but to order that the claimants give up possession of the premises (within an appropriate period) and award them compensation representing their expenditure on the property (comprising mortgage instalments, conveyancing costs, planning application fees and cost of appliances and fixtures) with interest thereon at 9 per cent.[13] The court felt considerable sympathy for the claimants (in so far as their expectations had not been realised) but, in view of the breakdown in the relationship between the parties, the only "proper and fair solution to the problem"[14] was to make a clean break. Dillon L.J., giving the leading judgment of the court, said[15] that the appropriate remedy had to be decided "in the light of the circumstances at the date of the hearing, taking into account if appropriate conduct of the parties up to that date, including any high-handed conduct of any party". Generally speaking, it was appropriate to satisfy the equity by granting the claimant the interest he or she was intended to have but, if that was not practicable, the court had to do the best it could. It would, however, seek to avoid giving the claimant more than his or her expectation.

A compensation-based approach was also taken in *Baker v. Baker & Baker*,[16] where the plaintiff was a 75-year-old man with a secure tenancy of a

---

[10] The point was alluded to by H.H. Judge Baker Q.C. in *Shaida v. Kindlane Ltd*, unreported, June 22, 1982, available on Lexis. See also, S. Moriarty, (1984) 100 L.Q.R. 376 at 412, where it is suggested that "normally ... a remedy will be chosen which gives the party precisley what he has been led to expect, but occasionally, where joint rights to land have been represented, he may get money instead".

[11] R. Pearce and J. Stevens, *The Law of Trusts and Equitable Obligations*, (Butterworths) at p.678.

[12] (1991) 23 H.L.R. 82, C.A. See further, J. Martin, [1992] Conv. 54; S. Jones, (1992) 142 New L.J. 320. See also, *Charlton v. Lester* (1976) 238 EG 115.

[13] Compensation based on the actual cost of improvements plus interest thereon was adopted in *Morris v. Morris* [1982] 1 N.S.W.L.R. 61, 64, *per* McLelland J. No interest was awarded in *Re Whitehead* [1948] N.Z.L.R. 1066, 1071.

[14] *ibid.* 94, *per* Glidewell L.J.

[15] *ibid.* 92.

[16] (1993) 25 H.L.R. 408, C.A. See also, *Raffaele v. Raffaele* [1962] W.A.R. 29, Supreme Court of Western Australia, where, in the particular circumstances of the case, an order for specific performance was considered unsuitable, and an award of damages assessed on the market value of the constructed house exclusive of the land was made.

council house in Finchley. The defendants were his son and daughter-in-law who lived in privately rented accommodation, with their two children, in Bath. In 1987, the plaintiff and the defendants agreed that the plaintiff should provide capital towards the purchase of a house for the defendants and that he should have a right to reside in a room rent-free for the rest of his life. A house was found in Torquay—the plaintiff providing £33,950 towards the purchase price and the defendants securing a mortgage for the balance. The plaintiff duly lived in the house rent free but contributed to the housekeeping expenses. In 1988, the relationship between the parties broke down and the plaintiff left the house and was rehoused as a secure tenant by the Plymouth City Council. He was awarded housing benefit for his rent. The plaintiff then took proceedings against the defendants claiming a beneficial interest by way of a resulting trust and, alternatively, claimed that, by reason of proprietary estoppel, he was entitled to compensation. At first instance, the judge dismissed the claim in respect of the beneficial interest but found for the plaintiff on estoppel and awarded him £33,950 (*i.e.* the return of his capital outlay) with interest from the date of his departure from the house. On appeal, this approach was held to be wrong. The plaintiff had not lost the whole of the £33,950 (which he had contributed to the purchase price) but merely the right to rent-free occupation of his room in a family home from the date of his departure, for the rest of his life (*i.e.* the value of the interest he expected). In the present case, the appropriate relief, in the circumstances, was to order that the defendants pay to the plaintiff a sum of money commensurate with the extent of the plaintiff's equity, subject to adjustment appropriate in the light of the behaviour of the parties and other material circumstances of the case. As the value of the plaintiff's interest fell to be assessed at the date when he left the property, the fact that he had since obtained other accommodation, whether paid for out of his own means, by other relatives or by public funds, was irrelevant.[17] As in the *Burrows* case, mentioned above, an award of compensation was, in the circumstances, the only appropriate form of relief—the plaintiff would not return to live in the defendants' house nor would the defendants agree to his returning. As to how the plaintiff's equity should be assessed, Beldam L.J. observed[18]:

> "A practical starting point for the valuation of the plaintiff's interest is the annual value of the accommodation he enjoyed capitalised for the remainder of his life ... Some reduction in the normal expectation should be made for his frail state of health and the sum awarded should be discounted as an award of a capital sum ... "

Some compensation for disturbance and the removal from the defendants' house to temporary accommodation (and then from temporary accommodation to the plaintiff's permanent accommodation in Plymouth) was also to be included.[19]

Awards of compensation have also been made on the basis of the amount of the enhanced value of the land by reason of the improvements carried out by the

---

[17] Since the court did not have any evidence on which it could found an answer to the question of the extent of the equity, the case was remitted for a further hearing before the judge.

[18] *ibid.* 415.

[19] *ibid.* 419, *per* Beldam L.J.

estoppel claimant.[20] This provides an alternative to the "actual cost" basis of assessment.

Awards of compensation in the estoppel context have also been made by the New Zealand courts. In *Stratulatos v. Stratulatos*,[21] the plaintiff and her husband, in reliance on the defendant's (her mother-in-law's) statement that they could have permanent occupation of her house until the defendant's death, proceeded to expend considerable sums of money on renovating and upgrading the property and enhancing its capital and rental value. The court considered it would be unconscionable to require the defendant to transfer the property or a share in the same *in specie* to the plaintiff. It would offend conscience to order a conveyance of the family home to a former wife now remarried and a stranger to the family. Conversely, restricting the plaintiff's recovery to a mere reimbursement to the plaintiff of their expenditure and effort would offend conscience. In the result, an order was made determining entitlement to the plaintiff in respect of a fractional interest in the property assessed on the basis of the respective capital inputs made by the parties. Such an approach gave each side the benefit of capital growth attributable to the capital of each side and prevented unjust windfall gains. As against this fractional interest, an appropriate *contra* allowance was made for use and occupation by the plaintiff of the defendant's remaining interest. On this approach, the plaintiff's interest was fixed at $34,950 with payment to be made on a fixed date when the plaintiff was also to vacate the property. Here again, a clean break was considered appropriate in the light of the parties' bitterness towards each other: "The plaintiff and the defendant should not remain locked together as co-owners, the plaintiff being a minority owner but having actual occupation. It is a matter which should be finalised forthwith, with a parting of the ways."[22]

If the claimant is no longer in occupation of the property, the most appropriate way of satisfying the equity may be to award the claimant reimbursement of moneys expended on improvements to the property. In *Cushley v. Seale*,[23] the defendant had spent a considerable sum of money on fitting out and improving shop premises in the expectation of a substantial tenancy which, ultimately, was not granted to her. The defendant had already given up possession of the shop at the date of the trial so the appropriate form of relief was held to be restitution of the funds she had laid out in improving the premises.

Reference may also be made to the case of *Holiday Inns Inc. v. Broadhead*,[24] where the plaintiff hotel company and a financier entered into a joint venture with respect to a hotel development. The company incurred expenses and used its name and reputation to obtain permission for the development which might not otherwise have been granted. It was encouraged to do so by the belief that the financier would enter into an agreement with it for a lease in its usual terms.

---

[20] *McBride v. McNeil* (1912) 9 D.L.R. 503 at 504–505, Ontario High Court; *Montreuil v. Ontario Asphalt Co and Caldwell Sand and Gravel Co.* (1922) 69 D.L.R. 313, Supreme Court of Canada; *Van den Berg v. Giles* [1979] 2 N.Z.L.R. 111, Supreme Court of Wellington; *The Queen v. Smith* (1981) 113 D.L.R. (3d) 522 at 583, Federal Court of Appeal.

[21] [1988] 2 N.Z.L.R. 424, High Court of Wellington.

[22] *ibid*. 440.

[23] Unreported, October 28, 1986, C.A., available on Lexis.

[24] (1974) 232 EG 951 and 1087.

The financier subsequently granted a lease to another hotel company. Goff J. held that the plaintiff company had an equity which gave it the right to participate in the profits made from exploitation of the site by the other hotel company. The plaintiff was effectively awarded damages for loss of expectation by the award of a beneficial interest under a trust for sale. The grant of a lease was not practicable because a lease had already been granted to a third party (*i.e.* the other hotel company). The return of the plaintiff's expenditure was considered to be inadequate. The only sensible course was to allow the plaintiff the value of the lost interest but, since this would prove very difficult to calculate, the plaintiff was awarded half of the value of the reversion.

In *Wayling v. Jones*,[25] the Court of Appeal awarded the plaintiff the net proceeds of sale of an hotel (£72,386,65) plus interest thereon, which he had been led to believe he would inherit following the death of his male partner. It is interesting to note that, in this case, a claim of proprietary estoppel was allowed against the executors of the deceased at a time when they no longer had the property forming the basis of the claim. It has been suggested[26] that this case has "expanded the availability of the doctrine of proprietary estoppel from claiming an interest in land, to claiming compensation for the loss of an interest in land that the court would have awarded if the defendant had still owned the land."[27]

(vii) Grant of a Lease

An alternative method of avoiding the Settled Land Act difficulties raised by the *Inwards v. Baker* case is to award the claimant a lease for a fixed term of years[28] or for life at a nominal rent. The latter solution was adopted in *Griffiths v. Williams*.[29] Here, the daughter had lived in her mother's house for most of her life and had been assured by her mother that it was her home for life. The daughter spent money on improvements to the house in reliance on this assurance. The mother subsequently died leaving the house to her granddaughter. The daughter had a clear equitable right but what was the best way of implementing her equity? In fact, the parties consented to an order granting the daughter a lease of the house determinable on her death at a nominal rent. This had the effect of giving her a right of occupation for life (thus giving effect to her mother's assurance) but without attracting the statutory powers under the Settled Land Act 1925.[30] Although the payment of a nominal rent would have been an obligation not contemplated by the parties, the court accepted that in such cases "perfect equity is seldom possible".[31] Two other objections were raised to the form of order. First, the daughter might assign the lease but that could be dealt with by including in the lease an absolute covenant against assignment and by an undertaking on the part of the daughter not to assign.

---

[25] (1995) 69 P. & C.R. 170, C.A. See, C.J. Davis [1995] Conv. 409.
[26] C.J. Davis, [1995] Conv. 409 at pp. 413–414.
[27] *ibid.* 414.
[28] See F.R. Crane, (1967) 31 Conv. (N.S.) 332 at p. 342.
[29] (1978) 248 EG 947, C.A.
[30] The grant of a lease for life creates a term of no less than 90 years determinable by notice following the death: s.149(6) of the Law of Property Act 1925. See further, [1978] Conv. 250 at pp. 251–252.
[31] *ibid.* 950.

Secondly, if the daughter were to marry again, her husband might be able to claim statutory protection under the landlord and tenant legislation. This potential difficulty was resolved by the court directing that the nominal rent should fall below two-thirds of the rateable value of the property on the relevant date, thereby taking the tenancy outside Rent Act protection. The case provides a good example of the broad exercise of the court's jurisdiction and also of a solution which avoids the complications which follow from the award of a life interest in the property.

In *Siew Soon Wah v. Yong Tong Hong*,[32] a tenant, who went into possession and paid rent on the faith of an agreement that, in return for a lump sum, the landlord would not evict him, was held entitled to a lease for so long as the landlord had power to grant (*i.e.* 30 years, under the local legislation). The tenant was protected by equitable estoppel until the end of the 30-year term. Similarly, in *Andrews v. Colonial Mutual Life Assurance Society Ltd*,[33] the tenant believed it had a renewal of its lease for six years and spent a large sum of money on refurbishing the demised premises. When the landlord learnt of the refurbishing work, it did nothing to disabuse the tenant of the fact that the lease, in its view, expired in 16 months' time. In fact, it agreed to alter the entrance step to the property thereby encouraging the tenant to spend money. It was held that the landlord's conduct gave rise to an action based on proprietary estoppel and the tenant was entitled to a new lease.

Where it is impossible or impracticable to order specific performance of a lease arising by virtue of proprieraty estoppel principles, the court may be minded to granted the estoppel claimant an award of damages instead.[34]

(viii) Grant of a Beneficial Interest

In an appropriate case, the court may satisfy the equity by granting a beneficial interest to the estoppel claimant as in *Hussey v. Palmer*.[35] In this case, the plaintiff, an elderly widow, was invited to live with her daughter and son-in-law, the defendant, in the house where they lived with their family. A bedroom was built on as an extension for the plaintiff. The plaintiff paid £607 for the cost of the extension herself. After living there for 15 months, differences arose and the plaintiff left claiming the return of her outlay on the extension. The majority[36] of the Court of Appeal concluded that the plaintiff had an equitable interest[37] in the defendant's property proportionate to the £607 which she put into it. In the course of his judgment, Lord Denning M.R. alluded to the possibility of using the constructive trust as a mechanism for satisfying the estoppel-based equity. He said[38]:

---

[32] [1973] A.C. 836, P.C.

[33] [1982] 2 N.Z.L.R. 556, High Court of Auckland. See also, *Stiles v. Cowper* (1748) 3 Atk. 692; 26 E.R. 1198; *Gregory v. Mighell* (1811) 18 Ves. 328; 34 E.R. 341.

[34] This was done in *Brownlee v. Duggan* (1976) 27 N.I.L.Q. 291.

[35] [1972] 1 W.L.R. 1286, C.A. See also, *Ungurian v. Lesnoff* [1990] Ch. 206, C.A.

[36] Lord Denning M.R. and Phillimore L.J. The other member of the court, Cairns L.J., held that the plaintiff had paid the £607 as a loan.

[37] In *Re Sharpe (A Bankrupt)* [1980] 1 W.L.R. 219 at 222–223, Browne-Wilkinson J. referred to the "equitable interest" in *Hussey* as being "not apparently a share of the proceeds of sale but something akin to a lien for the moneys advanced".

[38] *ibid.* 1290, approved in *Pearce v. Pearce* [1977] 1 N.S.W.L.R. 170 at 177, *per* Helsham C.J., Supreme Court of New South Wales. See also, *Re Basham, (dec'd)* [1986] 1 W.L.R. 1498, where

"In those [proprietary estoppel] cases it was emphasised that the court must look at the circumstances of each case to decide in what way the equity can be satisfied. In some by an equitable lien. In others by a constructive trust".

He concluded that the court should impose or impute a constructive trust by which the property was to be held by the defendant on terms that the plaintiff had an interest in it proportionate to the £607 which she had contributed. Phillimore L.J., on the other hand, preferred to treat it as an example of a resulting trust.[39] The significance of adopting constructive trust doctrine in the context of proprietary estoppel claims is that this may lead to a general widening of the circumstances in which it would be possible for the court to grant an equitable interest in matrimonial or quasi-matrimonial property.[40] At present, the House of Lords decision in *Lloyds Bank plc v. Rosset*[41] dictates that the claimant must show either an express or inferred common intention to share beneficially. In relation to the latter category, only direct contributions to the purchase price will suffice. If, however, the constructive trust is adopted as a remedy in proprietary estoppel claims, the lesser requirements of assurance, reliance and detriment will apply for the purpose of establishing a proprietary claim in the property. This "remedial" form of constructive trust falls to be distinguished from the "substantive" (common/inferred intention) constructive trust exemplified by the *Rosset* decision in that being remedial, imposed in order to satisfy the estoppel-based equity, it would have only prospective (as opposed to retrospective) effect from the date of the court order creating it.[42]

The award of a beneficial interest may have important legal consequences for the estoppel claimant. Thus, in *Preston and Henderson v. St Helen's Metropolitan Borough Council*,[43] the question at issue was whether the owner-occupier's supplement was payable upon the compulsory purchase of a long leasehold interest in a house, in accordance with schedule 24 to the Housing Act 1985. The Lands Tribunal held that, since the claimant had established an equitable interest in the property by virtue of proprietary estoppel, she was entitled to the supplement. The case is particularly interesting because the claimant had already acquired a half-share in the house by way of a common intention constructive trust since she had paid all the mortgage instalments and other expenses relating to the property. Her husband, who was the legal owner, had left the property stating that the property was hers. She continued to pay the outgoings in reliance on this assurance. The Lands Tribunal held that, in these circumstances, she was entitled to the other half of the beneficial interest by virtue of proprietary estoppel. Thus, by a combination of common intention constructive trust principles and estoppel doctrine, she was held entitled to the whole beneficial ownership of the property.

Mr Edward Nugee Q.C. opined that a constructive trust was an appropriate remedy in proprietary estoppel cases "at all events where the belief is that A is going to be given a right in the future": *ibid.* 1504, and *Re Sharpe, (A Bankrupt)* [1980] 1 W.L.R. 219.

[39] *ibid.* 1291.

[40] See generally, Chap. 8.

[41] [1991] 1 A.C. 107, H.L.

[42] See further, Chap. 1, pp. 10–16.

[43] (1989) 58 P. & C.R. 500, Lands Tribunal.

(ix) Lien Or Charge On Property

Instead of granting an equitable interest in the premises, the court may be minded to grant the claimant a lien or charge on the property for his expenditure[44] or for the value of his or her improvements.[45] This was alluded to by Lord Denning M.R. in the *Hussey* case, mentioned above. It also formed the basis of relief in *Unity Joint Stock Mutual Banking Association v. King*,[46] where a father had land on which he built a granary. His two sons built two other granaries on it at a cost of £1,200. Sir John Romilly M.R. held that the father did not intend to part with his land to his sons and considered that their equity would be satisfied by granting them a lien or charge on the land for their outlay as against the father, and any person claiming through him.

In *Mayes v. Mayes*,[47] a husband was entitled to a lien for the money and time he had spent on works of improvement and repair to a flat (the matrimonial home) and for mortgage interest for the period after his wife had left the home. As Oliver L.J. observed in *Savva v. Costa and Harymode Investments Ltd*[48]:

> "The expenditure gives rise to an equity to which the court will give effect in such way as may be appropriate in the circumstances of the individual case. It may be by injunction, it may be by declaring a trust of the beneficial interest or it may be by a declaration of lien for monies expended".

The award of a lien on the land may sometimes be coupled with a right to occupy the property until such time as the lien is discharged.[49]

(x) Injunctive Relief

In *Ward v. Kirkland*,[50] certain drains in a farmyard had been laid at the plaintiff's expense in reliance on the permission given by the legal owner without any stipulation as to period. In these circumstances, the plaintiff was held to have an equitable right to keep the drains in position permanently for the purpose of draining off bathwater from his cottage and, accordingly, was

---

[44] *Unity Joint Stock Mutual Banking Asociation v. King* (1858) 25 Beav. 72; 53 E.R. 563 (land); *Re Foster, Hudson v. Foster (No. 2)* [1938] 3 All E.R. 610 (life insurance policy).

[45] *Raffaele v. Raffaele* [1962] W.A.R. 238. See further, D.E. Allan, (1963) 79 L.Q.R. 238.

[46] (1858) 25 Beav. 72; 53 E.R. 563, applied in *Chalmers v. Pardoe* [1963] 1 W.L.R. 677 at 681–682, P.C., where it was suggested that an equitable charge or lien may be appropriate when, for reasons of title, a conveyance of the subject property cannot effectively be made. See also, *Lee-Parker v. Izzet (No. 2)* [1972] 2 All E.R. 800 at 804–805, (where the court made a *contra* allowance against expenditure for improvements by way of effecting a rent for possession) and *Avondale Printers & Stationers Ltd v. Haggie* [1979] 2 N.Z.L.R. 124 at 143, *per* Mahon J. In *Re Whitehead* [1948] N.Z.L.R. 1066, the Court of Appeal allowed a sum equivalent to expenditure on materials plus the claimant's own labour in building a cottage (though not the greater value of the cottage structure itself). See also, *Taylor v. Taylor* [1956] N.Z.L.R. 99.

[47] (1969) 210 EG 935.

[48] (1981) 131 New L.J. 1114, C.A.

[49] In *Re Sharpe (A Bankrupt)* [1980] 1 W.L.R. 219, 224, *per* Browne-Wilkinson J. See also, *Dodsworth v. Dodsworth* (1973) 228 EG 115 at 117, C.A.

[50] [1967] Ch. 194. See also, *Savage v. Foster* (1723) 9 Mod. 35; 88 E.R. 299; *East India Co v. Vincent* (1740) 2 Atk. 83; 26 E.R. 451, where the plaintiff was granted a perpetual injunction to protect his possession of the land, which he had improved; *Jackson v. Cator* (1800) Ves. 688; 31 E.R. 806; *Cotching v. Bassett* (1862) 32 Beav. 101; 55 E.R. 40; *Crabb v. Arun District Council* [1976] Ch. 179, C.A.; *Lim Teng Huan v. Ang Swee Chuan* [1992] 1 W.L.R. 113 at 119, P.C.

entitled to an injunction restraining the defendant from interfering with that right.

In *Lim Teng Huan v. Ang Swee Chuan*,[51] the estoppel claimant was held entitled *inter alia* to an injunction restraining the plaintiff from entering or dealing with the land upon which he had built a house in reliance on an agreement between the parties that he would become sole owner thereof.

According to Snell's *Equity*,[52] the representor may be restrained by injunction from:

" . . . interfering with possession of land,[53] or from exercising a right to cut down trees and so destroy the beauty of the improvements made by A in which he has acquiesced,[54] or from obstructing ancient lights altered by A with O's acquiescence.[55] Further, the injunction may be granted subject to an undertaking by A, *e.g.* to exercise compulsory purchase powers of acquisition."[56]

(xi) Specific Performance

In *Taylor Fashions Ltd v. Liverpool Victoria Trustees Co Ltd*,[57] Oliver J. ordered specific performance of the renewal option in the lease in order to satisfy the equity.

(D) Bars to Relief

We have already seen[58] that the estoppel claimant's misconduct towards the legal owner may affect his/her entitlement to relief. An estoppel claim may thus be barred for "want of clean hands". Also, there may be a *quid pro quo* for the claimant's outlay on improvements to the land which cancels out any detriment suffered.[59] In *Appleby v. Cowley*,[60] for example, Sir Robert Megarry V.-C. held that the plaintiffs had had "sufficient satisfaction" for their expenditure by virtue of the legal owner's forebearance to charge them a full economic rent.

If the improvement is prohibited by statute, this will also bar relief. In *Chalmers v. Pardoe*,[61] section 12 of the Native Land Trust Ordinance of Fiji

---

[51] [1992] 1 W.L.R. 113, P.C.
[52] (29th ed.) at p. 577.
[53] Citing *Duke of Devonshire v. Eglin* (1851) 14 Beav. 530; 51 E.R. 389.
[54] Citing *Jackson v. Cator* (1800) 5 Ves. 688; 31 E.R. 806.
[55] Citing *Cotching v. Bassett* (1862) 32 Beav. 101; 55 E.R. 40.
[56] Citing *Somersetshire Coal Canal Co. v. Harcourt* (1858) 2 De G. & J. 596; 44 E.R. 1120.
[57] [1982] Q.B. 133.
[58] See above, pp. 74–76.
[59] See further, Chap. 4, pp. 58–60.
[60] *The Times*, April 14, 1982; [1982] C.L.Y. 1150, available on Lexis. See also, *Att.-Gen. v. Balliol College Oxford* (1744) 9 Mod. 407 at 412; 88 E.R. 538 at 541, *per* Lord Hardwicke, L.C.
[61] [1963] 1 W.L.R. 677, P.C. Contrast, *Maharaj v. Chand* [1986] A.C. 898, P.C., where it was held that an equitable estoppel, being a purely personal right not amounting to a property interest, was not a dealing with the land for the purposes of s.12 of the Native Land Trust Act and so was not defeated by that section. The decision in *Chalmers* was distinguished, relying principally on *Kulamma v. Manadan* [1968] 2 W.L.R. 1074 P.C. See also, *Ward v. Kirkland* [1967] Ch. 194, where Ungoed-Thomas J. held that the permission given by the legal owner to lay drains in the farmyard at the plaintiff's expense was not invalid as being a "disposition" made by a rector without the necessary consent of the Ecclesiastical Commissioners under the Ecclesiastical Leasing

rendered it unlawful for a tenant under the Ordinance to "alienate or deal with" land comprised in a lease without the consent of the Native Land Trust Board. The appellant, with the consent of his friend, the respondent, who held such a lease, built a house on part of the leased land without the Board's consent, the respondent saying that he would apply to the Board to allow an underlease or the grant of a new lease to the appellant. Later, the respondent changed his mind and the appellant sued him for a declaration of a charge or lien on the land for the amount expended. The Privy Council held that, although equity would normally intervene to prevent the respondent from going back on his word and taking the building for nothing, nevertheless, a "dealing" with the land had taken place, and since prior consent of the Board was not obtained, that dealing (under section 12 of the Ordinace) was unlawful and equity could not lend its aid to the appellant. Accordingly, the appellant was not entitled to an equitable lien or charge for the amount expended. Similarly, in Dewhirst v. Edwards,[62] Powell J. would have refused an equity "upon the basis of a discretionary defence of want of clean hands"[63] since the building of a carport by the claimant in that case was done in breach of local government legislation. It was evident that the contravention of the statute would have had "an immediate and necessary relation to the equity sued for".[64]

It has been held that no estoppel will arise if the legal owner's assurance relied on by the estoppel claimant has been procured by the latter's false representations. In Ildebrando de Franco v. Stengold Ltd,[65] the plaintiff contended that he was the tenant of a flat owned by the defendants. The defendants wanted to find a company tenant for the flat, which would then license the plaintiff to occupy it. This was made known to the plaintiff, who produced a company which the defendants considered unsatisfactory as it had just recently been formed. The plaintiff then put forward another company, Mia Carla Ltd, and represented to the defendants that it was to be the tenant knowing that this company was only to be used by the defendants for the purpose of obtaining a reference. In reliance on this false representation, the plaintiff was let into possession of the flat. Subsequently, the defendants discovered that

---

Act 1858, or without the consent of their successors in title for that purpose, the Ministry of Agriculture (under the Glebe Lands Act 1858), notwithstanding that the plaintiff had acquired an interest in land as a result of the equity which arose out of the permission: ibid. 241–242. The learned judge said: "It is true . . . that such an equity may, in effect, take effect as an interest in property, but that is merely the consequence of the court's action in recognising an equity arising by reason of its being unconscionable in the circumstances to do otherwise. I, therefore, for my part, do not consider that this submission prevents the equity arising."

[62] [1983] 1 N.S.W.L.R. 34, Supreme Court of New South Wales. See also, Beaton v. McDivitt [1985] 13 N.S.W.L.R. 134 at 157–159, Supreme Court of New South Wales, where Young J. rejected the suggestion that the illegality could be cured by the court making an appropriate order for relief in terms that the defendant applies for the necessary statutory consent for the improvements. He said: "I do not believe it is consistent with authority to say that the court's order creates the right so as to fill a void where the right created by the parties is void because it is contrary to statute": ibid. 159. But see, Silovi Property Limited v. Barbaro [1988] 13 N.S.W.L.R. 466, Court of Appeal of New South Wales, where it was held that the provisions of the Local Government Act 1919 did not prevent an estoppel equity from coming into existence and could not prevent orders permitting satisfaction of the equity if the orders were so framed as not to breach the sections.

[63] ibid. 51.

[64] Moody v. Cox and Hatt [1917] 2 Ch. 71 at 88, per Scrutton L.J.

[65] Unreported, May 14, 1985, Court of Appeal, available on Lexis.

there was, in fact, no relationship between the plaintiff and this (second) company. Parker L.J. said:

"Insofar as any conduct of the defendants is relied on, it was conduct which was procured by the false representation of the plaintiff, and it does not therefore lie in his mouth to try and set up any form of estoppel, or agreement by conduct, when such conduct can only have been produced ... by the misrepresentations of the plaintiff."

It is also evident that an estoppel cannot be raised to prevent a statutory body exercising its statutory discretion or performing its statutory duty. In *Western Fish Products Ltd v. Penwith District Council*,[66] the plaintiffs alleged that a letter written by the defendant council's planning officer, in reply to letters from the plaintiffs, constituted a representation that the plaintiffs had an existing use right in respect of certain property and that planning permission would be granted for the development. The plaintiffs subsequently spent money on the premises and, when they applied for planning permission, it was refused. The Court of Appeal held *inter alia* that, even if the defendant's planning officer had purported to determine the plaintiffs' planning applications, this was not binding on the defendant council as the council alone had power to do so. Moreover, while a local authority might be bound if the power to decide had been (or appeared to be) delegated to a planning officer, for an estoppel to arise in such circumstances there had to be something over and above the officer's position which justified the applicant in believing that the officer would bind the authority. Since in the instant case there was nothing, apart from the position held by the planning officer, on which the plaintiffs could have assumed that the officer could bind the council, the council was not estopped by anything the planning officer had said from refusing the plaintiffs' applications for planning consent.

Finally, it is possible[67] that excessive delay in seeking relief may provide a bar to a proprietary estoppel claim. In *Voyce v. Voyce*,[68] the estoppel claimant had for many years remained in occupation of the subject property without taking any positive steps to perfect his title. It was argued that this delay in coming to court should be taken into account by the court. Dillon L.J., having cited a passage from Snell's *Equity*[69] that mere delay will not prevent a plaintiff with an equitable interest in land from claiming specific performance by seeking a conveyance of the legal estate, said[70]:

"I find it difficult to see why the defendant should be prejudiced in the

[66] [1981] 2 All E.R. 204, C.A. See, P. Jackson, [1982] Conv. 450 and A.W. Bradley, [1981] 34 C.L.P. 1. See also, *Rootkin v. Kent County Council* [1981] 1 W.L.R. 1186, C.A., where the Court of Appeal confirmed the general principle that the doctrine of estoppel could not be used against a local authority for the purpose of preventing it from exercising a statutory discretion. The decision is noted at (1981) 40 C.L.J. 198.
[67] See *Beaton v. McDivitt* [1987] 13 N.S.W.L.R. 162 at 172–173, Court of Appeal of New South Wales, where Kirby P. suggested that "delay on the part of the appellant in seeking relief despite the passing of so many years and the appellant's failure to take any earlier step at all to enforce his alleged interest in the land" might provide a bar to relief.
[68] (1991) 62 P. & C.R. 290, C.A.
[69] (1991) 29th ed. at p. 610.
[70] *ibid.* 293.

present case by delay in taking steps to perfect his title when his possession
of Coles Cottage and the garden . . . was not being challenged".

In this case, the defendant's mother had said that he could take the cottage
and garden as a gift provided that he refurbished it to her satisfaction, which he
subsequently did do at considerable expense. The gift was never executed by
deed. The case is, therefore, one where the claimant had simply delayed in
perfecting an imperfect gift of title and Dillon L.J.'s observations on the
question of delay were, clearly, confined to this type of case.

It is apparent that no equity will arise if the representor was a minor at the
time when the expenditure was incurred.[71] An equity will arise, however, if after
the representor attains majority, there is prolonged acquiescence by him in the
use of the improvements by the representee.[72]

Neither the Crown[73] nor a limited company[74] is exempted from the equity.

---

[71] *Somersetshire Coal Canal Co. v. Harcourt* (1858) 2 De G. & J. 596; 44 E.R. 1120.

[72] In *Somersetshire Coal Canal Co v. Harcourt* (1858) 2 De G. & J. 596; 44 E.R. 1120, the period of
acquiescence was over 40 years.

[73] See *Att.-Gen. to the Prince of Wales v. Collom* [1916] 2 K.B. 193.

[74] See *Laird v. Birkenhead Railway Co* (1859) Johns. 500; 70 E.R. 519.

6. THE ORTHODOX CATEGORIES

In this Chapter, it is proposed to examine three broad categories of cases underlying proprietary estoppel. Although the modern judicial trend,[1] albeit not consistent,[2] is to seek to rationalise the caselaw under one unified doctrine,[3] it is apparent that the rigid application of a given set of criteria is not appropriate to the varied circumstances giving rise to an estoppel-based equity. As indicated by Gray,[4] "the response of the courts to estoppel claims seems in some respects to be graded with reference to the criteria which differentiate between [three] broad categories", namely:

> (A) imperfect gift cases; (B) common expectation cases and (C) unilateral mistake cases.

It is to these that we now turn.

(A) Imperfect Gifts[5]

In *Milroy v. Lord*,[6] Turner L.J. formulated the now well-known principle that "there is no equity to perfect an imperfect gift". Thus, the general rule is that a gift of an estate or interest in land must be executed using the appropriate legal formalities. In the absence of such formalities, the gift is normally unenforceable both at law and in equity. There are, of course, a number of exceptions to this well-recognised principle.[7] Most notably, in the present context, the doctrine of proprietary estoppel may be invoked, in appropriate cases, to complete an imperfect gift.[8]

The leading case is *Dillwyn v. Llewelyn*,[9] where a father placed one of his sons in possession of land belonging to the father, and at the same time signed a memorandum that he had presented the land to the son for the purpose of

---

[1] See, *Taylor Fashions Ltd v. Liverpool Victoria Trustees Co. Ltd* [1982] Q.B. 133 and *Re Basham (dec'd)* [1986] 1 W.L.R. 1498.

[2] See, *e.g. Coombes v. Smith* [1986] 1 W.L.R. 808 and *Matharu v. Matharu* (1994) 68 P. & C.R. 93, C.A.

[3] See, Chap. 10.

[4] Gray, *Elements of Land Law*, (2nd ed.) at p.316.

[5] See, generally, S. Stoljar, (1989) 12 Sydney L. R. 17; M.Garner, (1990) 10 Ox. J.L.S. 42 at pp. 52–62.

[6] (1862) 4 De G.F. & J. 264 at 274; 45 E.R. 1185 at 1189.

[7] See, *e.g.* the rule in *Strong v. Bird* (1874) L.R. 18 Eq. 315; the doctrine of *donatio mortis causa* as applied in *Sen v. Headley* [1991] Ch. 425, C.A.; ss. 9 and 27 of the Settled Land Act 1925.

[8] See, L. Bentley and P. Coughlan, (1988) 23 Ir. Jur. 38, where the authors consider the inter-relationship between proprietary estoppel and the related doctrine of part performance. See also, C. Davis, (1993) 13 Ox. J.L.S. 99.

[9] (1862) 4 De G.F. & J. 517; 45 E.R. 1285. See also, *Crampton v. Varna Railway Co* (1872) L.R. 7 Ch. App. 562 at 568, *per* Hatherley L.C.; *Re Barker's Estate, Jones v. Bygott* (1875) 44 L.J. Ch. 487 at 490, *per* Lord Jessel M.R.

furnishing him with a house, but no formal conveyance was ever executed. The son, with the approval of the father, built at his own expense (*i.e.* some £14,000) a house on the land and resided there. The father later died leaving a will which left all his real estate upon certain trusts in favour of others. Lord Westbury, after reciting the principle that equity will not complete an imperfect gift,[10] held that subsequent acts of the donor of a gift might give the donee a right or ground of claim which he did not have under the original gift. In the words of Lord Westbury[11]:

> "So if A puts B in possession of a piece of land, and tells him, 'I give it to you that you may build a house on it', and B on the strength of that promise, with the knowledge of A, expends a large sum of money in building a house accordingly, I cannot doubt that the donee acquires a right from the subsequent transaction to call on the donor to perform that contract and complete the imperfect donation which was made."

In declaring that the son was entitled to a conveyance of the house from the trustees of the father's will, Lord Westbury held that the son's expenditure on the faith of his father's assurances supplied a valuable consideration and created a binding obligation on the father. It appears, therefore, that the Lord Chancellor rested his decision, not on estoppel as such, but on analogy with the equitable doctrine of part-performance of an unenforceable contract. Thus, in the course of his judgment, he said[12]:

> "The case is somewhat analogous to that of a verbal agreement not binding originally for the want of the memorandum in writing signed by the party to be charged, but which becomes binding by virtue of the subsequent part-performance."

Although the basis of the decision has been judicially categorised as contractual,[13] it is submitted that the better view[14] is to admit the case as an exception to the rule that equity will not perfect an imperfect gift. In the Irish case of *Cullen v. Cullen*,[15] for example, Kenny J. categorised *Dillwyn* as an authority for the proposition that[16]:

> "... a person claiming under a voluntary agreement will not be assisted by a Court of Equity but that the subsequent acts of the donor may give the donee a ground of claim which he did not acquire from the original gift".

---

[10] "A voluntary agreement will not be completed or assisted by a Court of Equity, in cases of mere gift. If anything be wanting to complete the title of the donee, a Court of Equity will not assist him in obtaining it; for a mere donee can have no right to claim more than he has received": *ibid.* 521; 1286.

[11] *ibid.* 521; 1286.

[12] *ibid.* 521–522; 1286.

[13] *Re Diplock* [1947] Ch. 716 at 784, *per* Wynn-Parry J.

[14] See, D.E. Allan, (1963) 79 L.Q.R. 238.

[15] [1962] I.R. 268.

[16] *ibid.* 282.

The *Dillwyn* principle was followed and applied in *Thomas v. Thomas*,[17] where a husband and wife had bought land as joint tenants, contributing equally to the price. A house was built on the land from monies largely contributed by the wife. The husband later deserted the wife informing her that she could have the house in her name. Applying *Dillwyn v. Llewelyn*, the court held that the exclusive possession by the wife, the expenditure of money by her on the faith of the husband's abandonment of his interest in the property and the husband standing by and allowing the wife's expenditure, gave the wife a right in equity to compel the husband to perfect the gift so that she became entitled to the whole beneficial ownership. Gresson J. said[18]:

> "I think the position in this case amounts to an unconditional gift of land followed by possession and expenditure on the land pursuant to the gift and in the belief that the donee was the owner of the land, the donor standing by and allowing such expenditure to be made. Although the gift was verbal only, it gives the donee a right in equity to call upon the donor to complete the imperfect gift."

Similar reasoning was applied by the Supreme Court of Western Australia in *Raffaele v. Raffaele*.[19] In this case, the defendants owned lots 1–4 in South Street, Freemantle. Their son married the plaintiff in 1947. In 1952, he purchased land in Smith Street, Fremantle, and began to construct a house on it. Shortly thereafter, he sold the Smith Street land and erected a house instead on a portion of the South Street land owned by the defendants, where he lived with the plaintiff until his death in 1959. It was established that the son had moved to South Street in pursuance of an agreement with the defendants that, if he would sell the Smith Street land and build instead on a portion of the South Street land, the defendants would divide the South Street land into three lots and would transfer one lot to the son. This agreement was, apparently, brought about by a desire of the defendants to have their son living near them. In addition to finding an express contract between the parties, the court held that there was also a "notional contract" created by the conduct of the defendants in putting the son into possession of their land and acquiescing in his building a house thereon. In these circumstances, the son was held to have acquired an equity to compel the defendants to perfect their promise to transfer the land. As in *Dillwyn v. Llewelyn*, the expenditure of money by the son with the approval of the defendants supplied a valuable consideration for the defendants' promise. In the particular circumstances of the case, however, specific performance of the agreement was not ordered but an award of damages (assessed on the market value of the house exclusive of the land) was made instead. In *Chalmers v. Pardoe*,[20] the Privy Council has since asserted that[21]:

---

[17] [1956] N.Z.L.R. 785, Supreme Court of Wellington. See also, *Taylor v. Taylor* [1957] N.Z.L.R. 99, Supreme Court of Wellington, where the claimant was granted a right of reimbursement for his expenses in improving the land.
[18] *ibid.* 794.
[19] [1962] W.A.R. 29. See further, D.E. Allan, (1963) 79 L.Q.R. 238.
[20] [1963] 1 W.L.R. 677, P.C.
[21] *ibid.* 681.

"There can be no doubt upon the authorities that where an owner of land has invited or expressly encouraged another to expend money upon part of his land upon the faith of an assurance or promise that that part of the land will be made over to the person so expending his money, a court of equity will prima facie require the owner by appropriate conveyance to fulfil his obligation."

A striking example of the operation of this principle is to be found in the case of *Pascoe v. Turner*,[22] involving an unmarried couple. Here, the plaintiff moved into the defendant's house as his housekeeper but later became his mistress. They lived together as man and wife until in 1973 the defendant left the house for another woman. Before leaving, the defendant assured the plaintiff that the house was hers and everything in it. The defendant stayed on in the house and, in reliance upon the plaintiff's declaration that he had given her the house and its contents, she spent money (approximately £230) on redecorations, improvements and repairs. The plaintiff knew that she was improving what she thought to be her property. Although the plaintiff said that he had put the transfer of the house into his solicitor's hands, he never did so. There was no conveyance and nothing in writing. In 1976, the plaintiff wrote to the defendant giving her two months' notice to determine her licence to occupy the house. When the defendant refused to leave, the plaintiff commenced an action for possession. The Court of Appeal held that, since there were no documents supporting the plaintiff's statement that he had given the house to the defendant, the gift had not been perfected[23] and, in 1973, the defendant occupied the house under a licence revocable at will. However, the circumstances from 1973 to 1976, when the plaintiff encouraged or acquiesced in the defendant improving the house in the belief that the property belonged to her, gave rise to an estoppel and the "minimum equity"[24] to do justice to the defendant was to compel the plaintiff to give effect to his promises by ordering him to execute a conveyance of the house to the defendant.[25]

More recently, in *Voyce v. Voyce*,[26] the Court of Appeal re-affirmed the principle that an intention to make a gift, coupled with conduct which makes it inequitable for the donor to continue to assert legal ownership, can give rise to an estoppel. In this case, the defendant's mother gave him a cottage and land as a gift provided that he "did it up", which he did do. The work involved considerable expense. The gift was never executed by deed and subsequently the mother made a gift of the cottage to the plaintiff, her younger son. This second gift was executed by deed. Later, the defendant began to build an extension onto the cottage to which the plaintiff objected as it interfered with light to his property. The Court of Appeal ordered the freehold in the cottage and land to be transferred to the defendant, thereby perfecting the imperfect gift. Dillon L.J., who gave the leading judgment of the court, after noting the

---

[22] [1979] 1 W.L.R. 431, C.A. Interestingly, the case has not been followed in the Irish High Court: *McGill v. S* [1979] I.R. 283 at 293, *per* Gannon J. See also, B. Surfin, (1979) M.L.R. 574; F.R. Crane, [1979] Conv. 379; R.D. Oughten, (1979) 129 New L.J. 1193. See further, Chap. 8.
[23] There had been no compliance with s.53 of the Law of Property Act 1925.
[24] *ibid.* 438, *per* Cumming-Bruce L.J., giving the judgment of the court.
[25] See further, Chap. 5, pp. 86–87.
[26] (1991) 62 P. & C.R. 290, C.A.

above-cited passage from *Chalmers v. Pardoe*,[27] considered that the defendant's claim to an estoppel-based equity was unaffected by his delay in taking steps to perfect his title throughout the time when his possession of the cottage was not being challenged.[28] Reliance was placed on a passage from Snell's *Equity*[29] that, in considering delay by a plaintiff in a claim for specific performance under a contract, where the plaintiff had been let into possession under the contract and has obtained the equitable interest (so that all is required is a conveyance of the legal estate), even many years' delay in enforcing his claim will not prejudice him.

It has been suggested by Moriarty,[30] in an influential article, that the device of estoppel is simply a mechanism by which the law sanctions the informal creation of proprietary rights in land. For example, in all the above cases it is the lack of legal formality that creates the problem and proprietary estoppel is used simply to make up for its absence. In the words of Moriarty[31]:

> " ... the role of proprietary estoppel seems self-evident: it provides for the informal creation of interests in land whenever a person has acted detrimentally in reliance upon an oral assurance that he has such an interest. Oral grants of interests by themselves, therefore, are insufficient; but an act in reliance upon some such assurance, and proprietary estoppel will validate what the Law of Property Act 1925 says has no effect".

On this basis, the award of the fee simple in *Pascoe v. Turner*[32] appears eminently correct because this is, in fact, what was intended to be gifted to the claimant. The value of Mrs Turner's contribution (*i.e.* £230) is irrelevant since the fairness of the gift does not, on this analysis, fall to be measured by how much the recipient has done in return for it. The function of proprietary estoppel is to give effect to the informal gift of land, not to question whether the value of the expenditure proferred by the donee is in some way proportionate to the value of the land which has to be conveyed. The remedy granted is governed by the nature of the representation to which it gives effect. The emphasis is on the form of the donor's assurance. This, argues Moriarty,[33] explains why the freehold estate was granted in *Dillwyn* and *Pascoe* but not in other cases.[34] He also points out that, whilst in most cases a remedy is selected which best gives effect to what the claimant was told he (or she) could have, this may not always be possible, especially where joint occupation arrangements were intended,[35] and a monetary award is made instead.

This view of the cases, although illuminating, is not without its critics. It has been pointed out,[36] for example, that the courts have consistently emphasised

---

[27] [1963] 1 W.L.R. 677 at 681, *per* Sir Terence Donovan.
[28] *ibid.* 293.
[29] (1991), 29th ed., at p. 610.
[30] S. Moriarty, (1984) 100 L.Q.R. 376.
[31] *ibid.* 381.
[32] [1979] 1 W.L.R. 431, C.A.
[33] *ibid.* p. 383.
[34] *i.e. Inwards v. Baker* [1965] 2 Q.B. 29, C.A. and *Williams v. Staite* [1979] Ch. 291, C.A.
[35] See, *e.g. Dodsworth v. Dodsworth* (1973) 228 E.G. 117, C.A.; *Hussey v. Palmer* [1972] 1 W.L.R. 1286, C.A.; *Re Sharpe, (A Bankrupt)* [1980] 1 W.L.R. 219, all cited by Moriarty: *ibid.* 384–388.

[36] See, J. Dewar, (1986) 49 M.L.R. 741 at p. 745, and M.P. Thompson, [1986] Conv. 406 at pp.

the discretionary nature of the choice of remedy in estoppel cases and, thus, even in *Pascoe* itself, the Court of Appeal was faced with two alternative options, namely, a licence for life or a conveyance of the fee simple, and was ultimately guided in its choice by a range of factors[37] intended to ensure Mrs Turner's security of tenure, quiet enjoyment and freedom of action in respect of repairs and improvements without interference from the plaintiff. Moreover, not all the cases fit neatly into Moriarty's categorisation. In *Jones (A.E.) v. Jones (F.W.)*,[38] for example, the son moved into a house owned by his father and incurred a detriment in reliance on his father's assurance that "as far as I am concerned, it's yours". However, the son was not awarded the house but merely a one-quarter share in it and a protected right to possession. In this case, however, there was no claim by the son for the fee simple and, in any event, the court was bound by a previous decision which had awarded the mother a three-quarter interest in the house. This may explain the outcome. The case of *Griffiths v. Williams*,[39] however, provides a more striking illustration. Here, the defendant had lived for many years with her mother (in the latter's house) and had often been told that the house would be her home for life. The defendant spent money on improving it but the mother left the house to the defendant's daughter, who, as co-executor of the will, sought possession. The Court of Appeal held that, as a result of the mother's conduct, an equity had arisen in the defendant's favour, which would be satisfied by the grant to her of a long lease determinable upon her death. Although the court recognised that the defendant had "an equity to have made good, so far as may fairly be done between the parties, the representation that [she] should be entitled to live in the house rent-free for the rest of her life",[40] it recognised that if such an equity were implemented the result would be to create a tenancy for life within the meaning of the Settled Land Act 1925 with all the statutory powers of sale and leasing associated with a tenant for life under the Act. In order to avoid this difficulty, therefore, the defendant was awarded a lease determinable upon her death subject to the payment of a nominal rent on the basis that this was the fairest way of dealing with the matter. The court recognised that "perfect equity is seldom possible".[41]

It may not always be possible to identify precisely the expectation engendered in the mind of the estoppel claimant. In the typical case, the assurance is vaguely expressed given the informal circumstances in which it is usually made. The expectation may not have been sufficiently defined to

---

406–412. The reality is that there are numerous judicial statements which emphasise the court's discretionary power in arriving at the appropriate remedy: See, *e.g. Plimmer v. The Mayor, Councillors and Citizens of the City of Wellington* (1884) 9 App. Cas. 699 at 714, *per* Sir Arthur Hobhouse. See further, Chap. 5, p. 73, n. 4. See also, *Crabb v. Arun District Council* [1976] Ch. 179 at 188, C.A., *per* Lord Denning M.R.; *Greasley v. Cooke* [1980] 1 W.L.R. 1306 at 1312, C.A., *per* Lord Denning M.R.; *Griffiths v. Williams* (1977) 248 EG 947 at 949, C.A., *per* Goff L.J.; *Morris v. Morris* [1982] 1 N.S.W.L.R. 61 at 64, Supreme Court of New South Wales, *per* McLelland J.; *Denny v. Jensen* [1977] 1 N.Z.L.R. 635 at 638, Supreme Court of Dunedin, *per* White J.

[37] See, Chap. 5, pp. 86–88.

[38] [1977] 1 W.L.R. 438, C.A.

[39] (1977) 248 EG 947, C.A. See, R.D. Oughten, (1979) 129 New L.J. 1193.

[40] *ibid.* 949, *per* Goff L.J.

[41] *ibid.* 950, *per* Goff L.J.

determine the appropriate remedy. A good example is *Inwards v. Baker*,[42] where the father's assurance to his son was: "Why don't you build the bungalow on my land and make it a bit bigger". What was the son's expectation in this case? Was it a right to remain on the land or a right to own it? The fact that the son built a house on his father's land, in reliance on this assurance, suggested that something more than just a mere right of occupation was intended. This has led to the comment that "to some extent the court is engaged in the business of rationalising the expectation and so the element of discretion is simply built into that process".[43]

Finally, it may be asked whether there is a minimum which must be spent on the land before the equity is raised. In the words of one academic commentator[44]:

> "Supposing [Mrs Turner] had spent only £50 on improvements and all the rest on refurbishing? Or £20? Or £10? In *Pascoe v. Turner* the court said that 'in reliance on the plaintiff's declaration of gift, encouragement and acquiescence she arranged her affairs on the basis that the house and contents belonged to her' and seems almost to be moving towards a doctrine of 'change of position' in which the requirement of expenditure *on the land* is not important so long as ill-afforded money has been spent by one party in a mistaken belief, encouraged by the other, as to his rights in the land."

(B) Common Expectation

In this category of case, referred to frequently as "estoppel by encouragement",[45] emphasis is placed by the courts on the claimant's reliance on a shared expectation with the legal owner that he will acquire rights in the latter's property. Unlike the imperfect gift cases, the situation is not that A has attempted to make a gift of land to B, but rather that the parties have dealt with each other on a common supposition that B would acquire some interest in A's land. The underlying principle was formulated by Lord Kingsdown in his dissenting speech in *Ramsden v. Dyson*[46] as follows:

> "If a man, under a verbal agreement with a landlord for a certain interest in land, or, what amounts to the same thing, under an expectation, created or encouraged by the landlord, that he shall have a certain interest, takes possession of such land, with the consent of the landlord, and upon the faith of such promise or expectation, with the knoweldge of the landlord, and without objection by him, lays out money upon the land, a Court of equity will compel the landlord to give effect to such promise or expectation."

---

[42] [1965] 2 Q.B. 29, C.A.
[43] R. Pearce and J. Stevens, *The Law of Trusts and Equitable Obligations* at p. 679.
[44] B. Sufrin, (1979) 42 M.L.R. 574 at p. 576.
[45] See, *e.g. Amalgamated Investment & Property Co Ltd v. Texas Commerce International Bank Ltd* [1982] Q.B. 84 at 103, C.A., *per* Robert Goff J., at first instance.
[46] (1866) L.R. 1 H.L. 129 at 170. The point of dissent was on the facts, not on the law applicable.

In the earlier case of *Gregory v. Mighell*,[47] upon which Lord Kingsdown relied, Sir William Grant M.R. alluded to the fact that the defendant in that case had "permitted the plaintiff to remain in possession, and to make expenditure upon the land for eight years, before he brought an ejectment. He must have known, that the expenditure was made upon the faith of the agreement; and I cannot now permit him to turn around, and say, the plaintiff has been possessing merely as a trespasser; as he must be, if his possession is not to be referred to the agreement."[48]

Although put into the language of landlord and tenant (since it was a landlord and tenant situation with which Lord Kingsdown was concerned), Lord Kingsdown's formulation has been held to be of general application.[49] It was expressly affirmed by the Privy Council in *Plimmer v. Wellington Corporation*,[50] where the plaintiff had erected a wharf on public land with the permission of the Crown and subsequently added a jetty which was later extended at the request of the Provincial Government. The case was held to fall squarely within Lord Kingsdown's principle in that it was difficult to suppose that "a person who is so using the seabed, and the Government who are its owners, can go on dealing with one another in the way stated . . . for a series of years, except with a sense in the minds of both that the occupant has something more than a merely precarious tenure."[51] The additional factor in this case was that the government landlord had done more than just encourage the plaintiff's expenditure—it had actually taken the initiative in requesting the improvements. The plaintiff's equity, arising from the expenditure, was held to constitute a perpetual right to the jetty for the purposes of his original licence.

It has also been observed[52] that the five *probanda* postulated by Fry J. in *Willmott v. Barber*,[53] whilst forming an appropriate test in cases of silent acquiescence, are not necessarily appropriate in cases where the conduct relied on has gone beyond mere silence and amounts to active encouragement. In the latter type of case, exemplified by Lord Kingsdown's example in *Ramsden*, "there is no room for the literal application of the *probanda*, for the circumstances there postulated do not presuppose a 'mistake' on anybody's part, but merely the fostering of an expectation in the minds of *both* parties at the time but from which, once it has been acted upon, it would be unconscionable to permit the landlord to depart."[54] For this reason, the requirement of mistake on the claimant's part as to his legal rights (*i.e.* the first *probandum* cited by Fry J. in *Willmott*) has little relevance in the context of the common expectation cases. In *Griffiths v. Williams*,[55] for example, Goff L.J. said[56]:

---

[47] (1811) 18 Ves. Jun. 328; 34 E.R. 341. See also, *Pilling v. Armitage* 12 Ves. Jun. 78; 33 E.R. 31, where the claim failed for lack of any encouragement on the part of the landlord in the tenant's expenditure.

[48] *ibid.* 333; 343.

[49] *Crabb v. Arun District Council* [1976] Ch. 179 at 194, *per* Scarman L.J.

[50] (1884) 9 App. Cas. 699 at 710–711, P.C.

[51] *ibid.* 712.

[52] *Taylors Fashions Ltd v. Liverpool Victoria Trustees Co Ltd* [1982] Q.B. 133 at 147, *per* Oliver J. See further, below, pp. 124–127.

[53] (1880) 15 Ch.D. 96. See below, pp. 117–118.

[54] [1982] Q.B. 133 at 147, *per* Oliver J.

[55] (1977) 248 EG 947, C.A.

[56] *ibid.* 949. Goff L.J. relied on the judgment of Lord Denning M.R. in *Inwards v. Baker* [1965] 2 Q.B. 29, C.A.

"In so far as it is necessary, to prove that Mrs Williams made a mistake, I think the mistake is to be found in her belief that she would be allowed to live in the house for the whole of her life. But I do not myself think that it really depends upon mistake. The equity is based upon the fact that where one has made a representation on the faith of which another party has expended his money, then the man who made the representation will not, to the prejudice of the other, be allowed to go back on it and assert his strict legal rights if to do so would be unconscionable."

Similarly, in *Holiday Inns Inc v. Broadhead*,[57] Goff J. observed[58] that "mistake is not an essential element of a claim to relief of this nature". It is apparently sufficient, in the context of a common expectation case, for the claimant to prove that there was a belief on his or her part, induced by the legal owner, that he or she would receive "a sufficient interest in the land to justify the expenditure"[59] or other detriment suffered by the claimant. The exact nature of the right or interest need not be specified at this time—it is sufficient if "there is an expectation of some future entitlement of some recognisable kind, and that the disadvantage incurred by the claimant is 'referable' to his belief that he would acquire some interest in or over the land."[60] It is apparent, therefore, that this type of claim will fail if there is insufficient evidence of some "belief or expectation that [the claimant] was being offered an interest in the house of the nature which [he] now claims."[61] It is necessary, in the words of May L.J.[62]:

" . . . to show that the work had been [done] in the belief that [the claimant] did in truth own a sufficient interest in [the property] to justify the expenditure; in other words, that the work . . . was referable to [the claimant's] belief that [he] had a beneficial interest in the house as justified by that expenditure; alternatively, that [he] would not have ordered the work to be done if [he] had not believed [he] had had a sufficient interest to justify it."

Thus, in *Warnes v. Hedley*,[63] from which the above-cited passage is taken, the house was bought as a family home for a young married couple by the husband's generous mother. The claimant and her husband did work on the house but this was just as consistent with a belief that they had a licence to occupy as it was with the suggestion that they had been given or acquired a beneficial interest in it. There was insufficient evidence to conclude that the

[57] (1974) 232 EG 951.
[58] *ibid.* 1087.
[59] *ibid.* 1089.
[60] Gray, *Elements of Land Law*, (2nd ed.) at p. 340, citing *Cameron v. Murdoch* [1983] W.A.R. 321 at 354, 360, for the proposition that it is enough that the claimant merely believed that he would become entitled "in due course of time . . . in some way".
[61] *Warnes v. Hedley*, January 31, 1984, C.A., unreported, available on Lexis, *per* Slade L.J. In this case, the claimant's reasonable expectation or belief did not go beyond the expectation that her mother-in-law was generously offering her and her husband a licence to occupy the house terminable on reasonable notice. In other words, there was nothing to suggest that the claimant and her husband would not have done the improvement work if they had been told that they only had a licence to occupy the property.
[62] *Warnes v. Hedley*, January 31, 1984, C.A., unreported, available on Lexis.
[63] Unreported, January 31, 1984, C.A., available on Lexis.

claimant and her husband would not have done the work if they had been told that they only had a licence to occupy terminable on reasonable notice. On this basis, therefore, their claim based on proprietary estoppel failed. Similarly, in *Philip Lowe (Chinese Restaurant) Ltd v. Sau Man Lee*,[64] it was held that the female claimant had undertaken various works of repair and redecoration at the house, not on the basis of acquiring any interest in it, but simply because she was part of the legal owner's family. Again, in *Clayton v. Singh*,[65] the Court of Appeal dismissed the plaintiff's claim based on proprietary estoppel on the ground that there was no evidence establishing that the work carried out by the plaintiff was referable to a genuine belief that he was entitled to legal ownership of the land in dispute. On the contrary, the facts pointed the other way, namely, that the plaintiff knew perfectly well that he was not being given the land.

The *Ramsden* principle has been considered and applied in a number of cases. In *Inwards v. Baker*,[66] a son was planning to buy land and build a bungalow on it when his father said: "Why don't you build the bungalow on my land and make it a bit bigger". The son did so, paying £150 of the cost of the bungalow, the father supplying the balance. In an action by the trustee of the father's will for possession of the land and bungalow, the Court of Appeal held that the son's expenditure of his money on the land of his father, in the expectation, induced and encouraged by his father, that he would be allowed to remain in occupation for as long as he desired, created an equity which, having regard to all the circumstances, would be satisfied by allowing him to remain in occupation of the bungalow for as long as he desired. It was stressed that it was unnecessary for the claimant to point to an expectation of some precise period of occupation or legal term. In this connection, it is evident from the decision in *Plimmer* that the equity arising from the expenditure need not fail "merely on the ground that the interest to be secured has not been expressly indicated".[67] The correct approach is to look at the circumstances in each case in order to determine how best to satisfy the equity.[68]

In *E.R. Ives Investment Ltd v. High*,[69] the defendant (High), a builder, bought the site of a bombed house in Norwich and proceeded to build a house on it. About the same time, a Russell Westgate (Westgate) bought an adjoining double site and started to build a block of flats there. Westgate encroached on High's site, putting the foundations of the flats a foot over the boundary into High's land a feet below ground level. High objected to the trespass and, at a meeting, it was orally agreed that Westgate was to be allowed to keep the foundations of the flats on High's land and that High was to have a right of way from the back of his house across the yard of Westgate's flats so as to give access to a side road. Letters passed between the parties evidencing the agreement which was acted on by both sides. Subsequently, Westgate sold his site to Mr and Mrs Wright, who knew of the agreement. Soon afterwards, both

---

[64] Unreported July 9, 1985, C.A., available on Lexis.
[65] Unreported April 12, 1984, C.A., available on Lexis.
[66] [1965] 2 Q.B. 29, C.A. See further, R.H. Maudsley, (1965) 81 L.Q.R. 183. See also, *Siew Soon Wah v. Yong Tong Hong* [1973] A.C. 836, P.C. and *Bank Negara Indonesia v. Hoalim* [1973] 2 Mal. L.J. 3, P.C.
[67] (1884) 9 App. Cas. 699 at 713, P.C.
[68] *ibid.* 714. See further, Chap. 5, pp. 76–77.
[69] [1967] 2 Q.B. 379, C.A. See further, F.R. Crane, (1967) 31 Conv. (N.S.) 332.

High's house and the block of flats were finished. High used the way across the yard and, relying on it, built a garage which was so constructed that it could only be used by means of the yard. Mr and Mrs Wright raised no objection to the building of the garage or to High's use of the yard for access to it. In fact, at one point Mr and Mrs Wright got High to resurface the yard and he paid one-fifth of the cost of this work. Later, the block of flats was sold by auction to the plaintiffs. The particulars of sale referred to High's right of way over the yard and the conveyance of the block of flats to the plaintiffs stated that the property was conveyed subject to the right of way. On these facts, the Court of Appeal had no difficulty in concluding that High had, in equity, a good right of way across the yard which (according to Lord Denning M.R. and Danckwerts L.J.[70]) did not require registration under the Land Charges Act 1925. In the words of Lord Denning M.R.[71]:

"The right arises out of the expense incurred by Mr High in building his garage, as it is now, with access only over the yard: and the Wrights standing by and acquiescing in it, knowing that he believed he had a right of way over the yard. By so doing the Wrights created in Mr High's mind a reasonable expectation that his access over the yard would not be disturbed. That gives rise to an 'equity arising out of acquiescence'. It is available not only against the Wrights but also their successors in title."[72]

A similar approach was taken by the Court of Appeal in *Crabb v. Arun District Council*.[73] In this case, the plaintiff owned a piece of land which had access at point A on to a road owned by the defendants and a right of way from A along the road. To enable him to sell his land in two parts, the plaintiff sought from the defendants a second point of access, at point B, and a further right of way along the road. At a site meeting, the additional access point was agreed. Subsequently, the defendants fenced the boundary between their road and the plaintiff's land, erecting gates at both points A and B. After the plaintiff had sold part of his land (together with the right of access at point A and easement over the road), without reserving any right in favour of the land retained, the defendants removed the gates at point B and fenced the gap, thereby leaving the retained part of the plaintiff's land landlocked. It was held that the defendants, knowing of the plaintiff's intention to sell his land in separate parts, had led the plaintiff to believe that he would be granted a right of access at point B and, by erecting the gates and failing to disabuse him of his belief, encouraged the plaintiff to act to his detriment in selling part of his land without reservation over it of any right of way, thereby giving rise to an equity in the plaintiff's favour. In the circumstances, the equity was satisfied by granting the plaintiff a right of access at point B and a right of way along the road.

---

[70] Winn L.J., the third member of the court, held that the estoppel was not registrable under the Land Charges Act 1925, although it prevented the plaintiffs from denying the defendant's user of the right of way. See, further, Chap. 7 at pp. 132–135.

[71] *ibid.* 394. See also Danckwerts and Winn L.JJ. at 399 and 404–405, respectively.

[72] For a discussion of the effect of Mr High's equity on third party rights: see, Chap. 7, pp. 132–135.

[73] [1976] Ch. 179, C.A. See further, F.R. Crane, (1976) 40 Conv. (N.S.) 156; P.S. Atiyah, (1976) 92 L.Q.R. 174; P.J. Millett, (1976) 92 L.Q.R. 342; M. Vitoria, (1976) 126 New L.J. 772; J.D. Davies, (1979) 8 Sydney L.R. 578.

It was argued, on behalf of the defendants, that in order to establish such an equity there must be a belief in the *existence* of a right created or encouraged by the words or actions of the defendant, and that a belief that a right will be granted *in the future* was insufficient.[74] This argument was firmly rejected by the Court of Appeal as not correctly stating the law as laid down by Lord Kingsdown in *Ramsden v. Dyson*[75] who spoke of a verbal agreement "or what amounts to the same thing, an expectation, created or encouraged".[76] Another point raised in argument was that the defendants had no notice of the sale of part of the plaintiff's land and, therefore, no opportunity to disabuse or correct the plaintiff in his belief that he had rights of access over the road. In this connection, it was conceded by the plaintiff that there was no previous case where the fact known to the defendant was an intention and not the realisation of that intention. Scarman L.J., careful to avoid generalisation, felt that there may well be cases where such an argument would succeed—where, for example, the defendant could say to the plaintiff, "If you had told me before you acted, I could have put you straight." However, on the facts of the instant case, he had no hesitation in rejecting this argument since, in his view, it was far too late for the defendants, having regard to the length of period of abstension and the installation of the gates, to place upon the plaintiff the duty of referring back to the defendants before binding himself to a sale of the land.[77]

The decision in *Ward v. Kirkland*[78] is also illustrative of the application of Lord Kingsdown's principle. Here, the plaintiff wished to install a bathroom and toilets in his cottage. He asked for, and was given, permission by the defendant to lay drains and also advised the owner of an adjoining farm (a rector) of his plans and asked for permission to lay drains through the farmyard to connect with a septic tank on his own premises. The rector gave permission for the bath water to be so drained without imposing any limit on the time that the drains might remain there. Nothing was said about the effluent from the toilets. The plaintiff did the work, laying drains for both effluent and bath water and constructing his septic tank to take both and also surface water, which had come from the defendant's land onto his. Ungoed-Thomas J, held[79] on this point that the drains had been laid at the plaintiff's expense in reliance on the permission given by the rector without any stipulation as to period and, in those circumstances, the plaintiff had an equitable right to keep the drains in position permanently for the purpose of draining off the bath water enforceable by means of an injunction. Although the plaintiff's equity was held not to extend to the drainage of effluent, nevertheless, the defendant's claim for an injunction to restrain such drainage failed because she had herself given consent to the

---

[74] See also, *Re Basham (dec'd)* [1986] 1 W.L.R. 1498. See further, Chap. 2, pp. 36–39.
[75] (1866) L.R. 1 H.L. 129 at 170.
[76] *ibid.* 170.
[77] *ibid.* 197–198. See also, *J.T. Developments Ltd v. Quinn* (1991) 62 P. & C.R. 33 at 52–53, C.A., *per* Ralph Gibson L.J., who confirmed that the principles of estoppel did not require the claimant to give further notice to the legal owner that he was about to carry out the improvement works. It is interesting to observe that in *E.R.Ives Investment Ltd v. High* [1967] 2 Q.B. 379, C.A., the point did not arise since in that case the party, who was found to be estopped, did have notice of what the other party was doing at the time he was doing it.
[78] [1967] Ch. 194.
[79] *ibid.* 242–243.

insertion of the drains and had stood by while they were put in, not making objection until much later.

It may be convenient, at this point, to refer also to the case of *Matharu v. Matharu*,[80] where the Court of Appeal applied the five probanda promulgated by Fry J. in *Willmott v. Barber*[81] to a defendant wife in respect of the matrimonial home owned by her father-in-law. The decision has been criticised on a number of grounds, not least because the Court sought to force the facts into the straitjacket of a unilateral mistake case, to which it was eminently unsuited. The better view[82] is that there is a clear distinction between common expectation cases and unilateral mistake cases and that *Matharu* lies more easily within the former category. The facts of this case have already been rehearsed elsewhere,[83] but suffice it to say here that this was not a situation where one party was mistaken as to the nature of his (or her) rights in the property but where there was an expectation common to both parties as to the creation of rights in the land. As between the defendant's husband and his father (the legal owner), they both shared an assumption that the former and his family would be allowed to live in the house and, in reliance on that assumption, the defendant's husband made considerable improvements to the house at his own expense with the knowledge of his father. On this basis, it has been suggested[84] that the broader approach established by Oliver J. in *Taylor's Fashions Ltd v. Liverpool Victoria Trustees Co Ltd*[85] should have been applied, rendering it unconscionable, as between the father and the defendant's husband, for the former to obtain possession of the improved house.

(C) Unilateral Mistake

In this category of case, often referred to as "estoppel by acquiescence",[86] the situation is that one party is mistaken as to the nature of his rights in the land. Here, equity intervenes so as to prevent one party from fraudulently taking advantage of the other party's error. This is in sharp contrast to the "common expectation" category, where there is an assumption common to *both* parties as to the creation of rights in the property. In cases of unilateral mistake, the courts place greater emphasis on the element of detriment which is suffered by the estoppel claimant who innocently relies on his mistaken supposition that he has rights in the land. As Gray[87] puts it: "This branch of the doctrine of proprietary estoppel regards it as unconscionable that the owner of the land should wilfully stand by and allow such a person to incur 'detriment' by relying on his own uncorrected misapprehension of the true legal position".

---

[80] (1994) 68 P. & C.R. 93, C.A.
[81] (1880) 15 Ch.D. 96, C.A.
[82] See, G. Battersby, (1995) 7 C.F.L.Q. 59 at p. 61. See also, M. Wesltead, [1995] Conv. 61.
[83] See below, pp. 122–124. See also Chap. 8, pp. 154–155.
[84] G. Battersby, (1995) 7 C.F.L.Q. 59 at p. 62.
[85] [1982] Q.B. 133.
[86] See, *e.g. Amalgamated Investment & Property Co Ltd v. Texas Commerce International Bank Ltd* [1982] Q.B. 84 at 103, C.A., *per* Robert Goff J., at first instance.
[87] Gray, *Elements of Land Law*, (2nd ed.) at p. 320.

An early example of the formulation of the principle is to be found in the speech of Lord Cranworth L.C. in *Ramsden v. Dyson*[88]:

"If a stranger begins to build on my land supposing it to be his own, and I, perceiving his mistake, abstain from setting him right, and leave him to persevere in his error, a Court of Equity will not allow me afterwards to assert my title to the land on which he had expended money on the supposition that the land was his own. It considers that, when I saw the mistake into which he had fallen, it was my duty to be active and to state my adverse title; and that it would be dishonest in me to remain wilfully passive on such an occasion, in order afterwards to profit by the mistake which I might have prevented."

It is to be observed that to raise such an equity, essentially two things are required, namely (1) that the person making the expenditure believes himself to be building on his own land and (2) that the legal owner, at the time of the expenditure, knows that the land belongs to him and not to the person expending the money in the belief that he is the owner.[89] The principle forms an exception to the general rule that services rendered voluntarily without encouragement or reward do not give rise to any claim to compensation[90] or to any proprietary interest in the property improved. As Lord Cranworth L.C. went on to observe[91]:

"For if a stranger builds on my land knowing it to be mine, there is no principle of equity which would prevent my claiming the land with the benefit of all the expenditure made on it. There would be nothing in my conduct, active or passive, making it inequitable in me to assert my legal rights".

An early example of the operation of the doctrine of acquiescence is to be found in *Huning v. Ferrers*,[92] where the plaintiff successfully brought a bill

---

[88] (1866) L.R. 1 H.L. 129 at 140–141. See also, *De Bussche v. Alt* [1878] 8 Ch.D. 286 at 314, C.A., *per* Thesiger L.J.

[89] See, *e.g. Proctor v. Bennis* [1887] 36 Ch. D. 740 at 760, *per* Cotton L.J.

[90] See, *e.g. Falcke v. Scottish Imperial Insurance Co* (1886) 34 Ch.D. 234 at 248, where Bowen L.J. said: "The general principle is, beyond all question, that work and labour done or money expended by one man to preserve or benefit the property of another do not according to English law create any lien upon the property saved or benefited, nor, if standing alone, create any obligation to repay the expenditure. Liabilities are not to be forced upon people behind their backs any more than you can confer a benefit upon a man against his will". See also, *Pettit v. Pettit* [1970] A.C. 777 at 818, H.L., where Lord Diplock said: "It has been well settled ... that if A expends money on the property of B, prima facie he has no claim on such property". See further, *Re Vandervell's Trusts (No. 2)* [1974] Ch. 269 at 299, *per* Megarry J. In *Bennet v. Bennett*, May 18, 1990, C.A., unreported, available on Lexis, Slade L.J. said: "[proprietary estoppel] is one of the qualifications of the general rule that a person who spends money on improving the property of another has no claim to reimbursement or to any proprietary interest in the property".

[91] *ibid.* 141. See also, *Ezekiel v. Orakpo and Scott*, unreported, February 20, 1980, C.A., available on Lexis. In this case, the tenant, who had been granted an option to purchase the freehold, had "spent his money on that basis with his eyes open. His plans went awry, not because he was under any mistake or was misled by [the landlord], but because he ran out of money ... Simply put, he was a speculator and his speculation did not pay off": *per* Brightman L.J.

[92] (1711) Gilb. Eq. 85; 25 E.R. 59. See also, *Edlin v. Battaly* (1668) 2 Lev. 152; 83 E.R. 494, *Hobbs v. Norton* (1682) 1 Vern. 136; 23 E.R. 370, *Bath and Mountague's Case* (1693) 3 Chan. Cas. 55 at 104; 22 E.R. 963, *Savage v. Foster* (1723) 9 Mod. 35; 88 E.R. 299, *East India Co. v. Vincent*

against the defendant who had acquiesced in an improvement to his land. The plaintiff had spent some £2,800 on improvements to the land in the mistaken belief that he had a valid lease granted by the tenant for life. The defendant, who was the remainderman, stood by and encouraged him to do so even though he knew that the tenant for life had no power to make the grant. Lord Hardwicke decreed that the plaintiff should enjoy the land during the residue of the lease, commenting that this was "such a fraud and practice in him [the defendant] as ought to be discountenanced in this court".[93]

In *Ramsden* itself, the requisite pre-conditions formulated by Lord Cranworth L.C. to raise an equity were not satisfied on the facts. The tenant had improved the leasehold property knowing that he had no more than a yearly tenancy but he mistakenly believed that by building on the land he would become entitled to a long lease. The House of Lords held on the facts that he was not so entitled and that there was no equitable jurisdiction either to prevent the landlord from ejecting him or to grant him compensation for the value of his work. In the words of Lord Cranworth L.C.[94]:

" ... if my tenant builds on land which he holds under me, he does not thereby, in the absence of special circumstances, acquire any right to prevent me from taking possession of the land and buildings when the tenancy has determined. He knew the extent of his interest, and it was his folly to expend money upon a title which he knew would or might soon come to an end".

By contrast, in *Attorney-General to H.R.H. Prince of Wales v. Collom*,[95] involving the Duchy of Cornwall's claim to a house, the defendant was able to establish a good equitable defence based on estoppel, her expenditure on the house having been made to the knowledge of the agent to the Duchy and on property which the defendant reasonably believed to be her own. The estoppel was held to bind the Crown.

The leading case is *Willmott v. Barber*[96] where the facts were as follows. The tenant of three acres of land agreed to let one acre to the plaintiff for the residue of his term, and he also agreed to sell to the plaintiff his interest in the whole three acres at any time within five years from the date of the agreement. The tenant's lease contained a qualified covenant against assignment, of which the plaintiff was unaware. He was let into possession of the one acre and laid out money on it (and also on adjoining property of his own) with the view of occupying the two together. The landlord was aware of this expenditure. Later, the tenant, without the plaintiff's knowledge, surrendered the lease to the landlord in exchange for a new lease for a longer term of the three acres (together with other property). The new lease contained a similar covenant by the tenant against assignment. Subsequently, the plaintiff gave the tenant notice

---

(1740) 2 Atk. 83; 26 E.R. 451, *Att.-Gen. v. Balliol College Oxford* (1744) 9 Mod. 407; 88 E.R. 538, *Stiles v. Cowper* (1748) 3 Atk. 692; 26 E.R. 1198, *Hardcastle v. Shafto* (1794) 1 Anst. 184; 145 E.R. 802 at 805, 839, *Jackson v. Cator* (1800) 5 Ves. 688; 31 E.R. 806, *Gregory v. Mighell* (1811) 18 Ves. 328; 34 E.R. 341.

[93] *ibid.* 86; 60.

[94] (1866) L.R. 1 H.L. 129 at 141.

[95] [1916] 2 K.B. 193.

[96] (1880) 15 Ch.D. 96.

of his desire to to exercise his option to purchase his interest under the original lease in the three acres. The tenant declined on the ground that the landlord refused to give his licence to an assignment. The plaintiff then brought an action against both the tenant and landlord claiming specific performance of the agreement by the tenant, and to compel the landlord to give his licence on the ground that he had acquiesced in the plaintiff's expenditure. The claim failed. The tenant could not be compelled to perform his agreement since this would involve a breach of his covenant not to assign without licence. Moreover, in as much as the landlord was unaware of the existence of the tenant's covenant against assignment (and, therefore, ignorant of his own rights) and did not know that the plaintiff had been acting in ignorance of his legal rights, he could not be said to have acquiesced. In the course of his judgment, Fry J. put forward the following (now classic) formulation[97]:

> "It has been said that the acquiescence which will deprive a man of his legal rights must amount to fraud, and in my view that is an abbreviated statement of a very true proposition. A man is not to be deprived of his legal rights unless he has acted in such a way as would make it fraudulent for him to set up those rights. What, then, are the elements or requisites necessary to constitute fraud of that description? In the first place the plaintiff must have made a mistake as to his legal rights. Secondly, the plaintiff must have expended some money or must have done some act (not necessarily upon the defendant's land) on the faith of his mistaken belief. Thirdly, the defendant, the possessor of the legal right, must know of the existence of his own right which is inconsistent with the right claimed by the plaintiff. If he does not know of it he is in the same position as the plaintiff, and the doctrine of acquiescence is founded upon conduct with a knowledge of your legal rights. Fourthly, the defendant, the possessor of the legal right, must know of the plaintiff's mistaken belief of his rights. If he does not, there is nothing which calls upon him to assert his own rights. Lastly, the defendant, the possessor of the legal right, must have encouraged the plaintiff in his expenditure of money or in the other acts which he has done, either directly or by abstaining from asserting his legal right. Where all these elements exist, there is fraud of such a nature as will entitle the Court to restrain the possessor of the legal right from exercising it, but, in my judgment, nothing short of this will do".

In *Willmott*, all the requisite elements (bar the first) were held to be lacking. Similarly, in *Lala Beni Ram v. Kundan Lal*,[98] the claim failed since the tenants knew that their title to the land, upon which they had constructed a number of

---

[97] *ibid.* 105–106.
[98] (1899) 15 T.L.R. 258, P.C. See also, *Ezekiel v. Orakpo*, February 20, 1980, C.A., unreported, available on Lexis, where there was no evidence that the claimant was, at any time, under any misapprehension as to his legal rights. The claimant was a tenant under a seven-year lease of part of the property, and he was in possession of the remainder for the period of an option term. In the words of Brightman L.J.: "He spent his money on that basis with his eyes open. He spent the money in the knowledge that he was improving a property which he could make his own and in the expectation that he would make it his own and reap a handsome profit . . . His plans went awry, not because he was under any mistake or was misled by [the legal owner], but because he ran out of money . . . Simply put, he was a speculator and his speculation did not pay off."

houses, was limited to their occupation as tenants upon the terms provided by their lease. Moreover, they had failed to show that the conduct of the legal owners had amounted to acquiescence. The claim also did not succeed in *E. & L. Berg Homes Ltd v. Grey*,[99] where the occupiers, who had lived in a caravan on the plaintiff's land for 24 years as bare licensees, failed to satisfy the requirements that they had mistaken their legal rights and had been encouraged by the owners to spend money and take other action on the faith of such encouragement. The claim was also rejected in *Stilwell v. Simpson*,[1] where the plaintiff held a tenancy of part of a house from the defendant. He carried out repairs and improvements to the property, which was in bad condition. His claim, based on proprietary estoppel, failed for a number of reasons. First, it was held that the plaintiff had carried out the work for his own benefit and had done so because he knew that the defendant could not afford to pay for it to be done. Secondly, if there had been encouragement or acquiescence by the defendant, this was limited to the plaintiff's right of a first option to buy the house which had been granted by the defendant. Thirdly, the plaintiff was unable to identify what precisely he had been led to expect from the defendant in carrying out the work. Finally, he had failed to show that he had made any mistake as to his legal rights. Accordingly, none of Fry J.'s probanada had been satisfied.

In *Kammins Ballrooms Co. Ltd v. Zenith Investments (Torquay) Ltd*,[2] Lord Diplock, in relation to the five *probanda*, concluded that the party estopped must, at the time of the encouragement, know of the existence of his legal right and of the other party's mistaken belief in his own inconsistent legal right. For these purposes, it was not enough that he should know of the *facts* which gave rise to his legal right. What was also required was a knowledge of the *entitlement* to the legal right to which those facts gave rise. In *Kammins*, there was insufficient evidence pointing to the landlords' knowledge of the existence of their own legal right to object to the tenants' application seeking the grant of a new business tenancy as being out of time, prior to the last day upon which the tenants could have made a fresh application to the court. Accordingly, the tenants' claim based on estoppel was not made out.

In *Crabb v. Arun District Council*,[3] Scarman L.J. applied Fry J.'s five *probanda* as a valuable guide as to the matters of fact which had to be established in order to raise an estoppel equity. He pointed out, however, that what Fry J. called "fraud" in 1880 should today be called taking advantage of a person in a way which was "unconscionable, inequitable or unjust". He also alluded to the fact that the fraud or injustice does not take place during the course of negotiation but only when the defendant decides to refuse to allow the plaintiff to set up his claim against the defendant's undoubted right. Thus, "the fraud, if it be such, arises after the event, when the defendant seeks by relying on his right to defeat the expectation which he by his conduct encouraged the plaintiff to have".[4] On this basis, there need not be anything fraudulent or unjust in the initial conduct of the actual transaction by the owner. Applying the five

---

[99] (1979) 253 EG 473, C.A.
[1] (1983) 133 New L.J. 894.
[2] [1971] A.C. 850, H.L.
[3] [1976] Ch. 179, C.A.
[4] *ibid.* 195.

probanda to the facts of the case before him, Scarman L.J. had no doubt that the first four elements existed. As to the fifth element, had the defendants, as possessors of the legal right, encouraged the plaintiff in the expenditure of money or in the other acts which he had done, either directly or by abstaining from asserting their legal rights? The answer was clearly in the affirmative in so far as the defendants had agreed in principle that there should be access and a right of way over the road in question and this was subsequently re-affirmed by the defendants' conduct in installing gates at the relevant access points.

The principle that the owner of a legal right is only to be deprived of the benefit of that right, on the ground of acquiescence on his part, when it would be unconscionable of him to set it up, was applied in *Shaw v. Applegate*.[5] In this case, the defendant purchased a yard and tea-room covenanting not to use the premises as an amusement arcade. Despite the covenant, he started installing amusement machines and added more in subsequent years. The plaintiffs, the assignees of the benefit of the covenant, brought an action seeking an injunction to restrain the defendant from using his property as an amusement arcade in breach of covenant. They also claimed damages. At first instance, Blackett-Ord V.-C. found that there had been a continuing breach of covenant but dismissed the action on the ground that the plaintiffs had acquiesced in the breach and that damages were incapable of assessment. The Court of Appeal, however, allowing the plaintiffs' appeal, held that to deprive the possessor of a legal right of that right on the ground of his acquiescence, the situation must have become such that it would be dishonest or unconscionable for him to continue to seek to enforce it. In the present case, since the plaintiffs, during the period in question, were confused as to whether the defendant's activities in law constituted a breach of covenant, it could not be said that they would be acting dishonestly or unconscionably in seeking to enforce their rights under the covenant because of their failure to sue earlier. Accordingly, the court concluded that there was insufficient acquiescence to bar the plaintiffs from all remedy in respect of the covenant. In the circumstances, the appropriate remedy was held to be an award of damages. Buckley L.J. intimated[6] that, in order to establish dishonesty or unconscionability, it may not be necessary to comply strictly with all five tests put forward by Fry J. in *Willmott* in every particular case on acquiescence. Goff L.J. also intimated[7] that it might be easier to establish a case of acquiescence where the right was equitable only.

Despite these judicial suggestions of a wider principle underlying the proprietary estoppel doctrine, Fry J.'s five *probanda* have been applied with full rigour in several cases involving claims by cohabitees. In *Coombes v. Smith*,[8] the plaintiff and defendant were both married to other partners when they became on intimate terms. The defendant told the plaintiff that he wished them to live together and they discussed having a child. The defendant bought a house and, when the plaintiff became pregnant by the defendant, she left her husband and moved into the house, giving up her job two months before the birth of the

---

[5] [1977] 1 W.L.R. 970, C.A.

[6] *ibid.* 978, and Goff L.J. (at 980) expressed similar doubts. See also, *Electrolux Ltd v. Electrix Ltd* (1954) 71 R.P.C. 23 at 33, *per* Sir Raymond Evershed M.R. and *Taylors Fashions Ltd v. Liverpool Victoria Trustsees Co. Ltd* [1982] Q.B. 133 at 147, *per* Oliver J.

[7] *ibid.* 980, citing *Osborne v. Bradley* [1903] 2 Ch. 446.

[8] [1986] 1 W.L.R. 808.

child. The defendant did not move in with the plaintiff but visited her regularly, paid all bills including the mortgage instalments, and gave the plaintiff an allowance for herself and the child. The arrangement continued when the defendant bought another house nearer his work into which the plaintiff moved with the child. The plaintiff redecorated the house several times, installed decorative beams and improved the garden. She twice asked the defendant if he would put the house into their joint names, but he refused, though during the course of the relationship he assured her that he would always provide for her and that she would always have a roof over her head. The relationship ended after 10 years. On her claim based on proprietary estoppel,[9] it was held there was nothing on the evidence to show that the plaintiff had held a mistaken belief that she would have the right to remain in the house indefinitely against the defendant's wishes. The parties had not discussed what was to happen in the event of their relationship breaking down and a belief that the defendant would always provide a roof over her head was not sufficient. Moreover, the plaintiff had not acted to her detriment in becoming pregnant, leaving her husband, looking after the house and child, improving the house or in not looking for a job. Accordingly, the plaintiff had failed to establish the five elements necessary to give rise to an equity in her favour. On the latter point, the court concluded that it was implicit in Fry J.'s analysis that the act or acts done by the plaintiff on the faith of his mistaken belief, the doing of which has been encouraged by the defendant, must be acts by which the plaintiff had prejudiced himself or acted to his detriment.[10] The court considered it wholly unrealistic to assume that the plaintiff had allowed herself to become pregnant by the defendant in reliance on some mistaken belief as to her legal right. She had allowed herself to become pregnant because she wished to live with the defendant and to bear his child. Even if this was done in reliance on the defendant's assurances, the court refused to admit that this could constitute detriment in the context of the doctrine of proprietary estoppel. The act of leaving her husband was also discounted as a sufficient act of reliance on the defendant's assurance that he would provide for her if and when their relationship came to an end. The reality was that the plaintiff decided to move to the defendant's house because she preferred to have a relationship with, and child by, him rather than continuing to live with her husband. The third act relied on by the plaintiff as detriment was giving birth to the child, which was treated by the court as no more than a repetition of the first act (*i.e.* becoming pregnant). The acts of looking after the defendant's house, being ready for the defendant's visits, and looking after the child were also rejected as being done by the plaintiff as occupier of the property, as the defendant's mistress, and as the child's mother, in the context of a continuing relationship with the defendant. Moreover, no detriment flowed from them. The same observations were held to apply to redecorating the property and installing the decorative beams. Forebearance to look for a job was also dismissed by the court on the

---

[9] The plaintiff also unsuccessfully argued on the basis of a contractual licence. She did nothing that amounted to providing consideration for, and it was impossible to infer, a contract between the parties that the defendant would provide her with a house for the rest of her life.
[10] Relying on the remarks of Dunn L.J. in *Greasley v. Cooke* [1980] 1 W.L.R. 1306 at 1313, C.A.

grounds of lack of evidence and lack of detriment. As to the other elements in Fry J.'s list, these were also held not to be made out[11]:

"Elements (3) and (4) both involve knowledge on the part of the defendant. I am certainly prepared to infer that the defendant knew that he had a legal right to recover possession of the property, but I have no evidence from which I could infer that he was aware of any relevant mistaken belief on the part of the plaintiff. As I have already indicated, a statement by the defendant to the effect that he would always provide a roof over the plaintiff's head does not, in my judgment, amount to a representation that the plaintiff had a legal right to remain in the property contrary to his wishes. Lastly, element (5), the defendant must have encouraged the plaintiff to act on her mistaken belief. Such encouragement may either be direct, or it may take the form of acquiescence, by the defendant standing back and allowing the plaintiff to act to her detriment. On the evidence, the most that the defendant did, as I see it, was to lead the plaintiff to believe, at least until towards the end of 1983, that he was intending to join her at [the property]. The fact that he did not do so cannot, in my judgment, be sufficient to found a proprietary estoppel."

The case illustrates that strict adherence to Fry J.'s five *probanda* and, in particular, that the estoppel claimant should have made a positive mistake as to his or her existing rights, will inevitably lead to a denial of equitable entitlement in circumstances where the parties' arrangement is informal and based on a "vague and ill-defined expectation of future entitlement".[12] By contrast, reference may be made to the recent decision in *Matharu v. Matharu*,[13] where the majority of the Court of Appeal applied Fry J.'s five elements with considerable liberality so as to afford the female claimant an equity in her father-in-law's house. In this case, the plaintiff bought a property which became the matrimonial home of the defendant and the plaintiff's son, after their marriage in 1971. During the course of the marriage, the defendant's husband made extensive improvements[14] to the property at his own expense. The marriage broke down and later the defendant obtained an order excluding the husband from the house. He died in 1991. Later that year, the plaintiff emigrated to Canada but returned the following year demanding that the defendant vacate the property. The leading majority judgment was given by Roch L.J., who concluded that all five *probanda* had been satisfied by the defendant and, accordingly, she had an equity which barred the plaintiff's claim for possession. First, he concluded that the various alterations and improvemensts to the house and the making of mortgage repayments by the defendant's husband to the plaintiff were money expended and acts done of which the defendant was entitled to take advantage. On this aspect, his Lordship said[15]:

---

[11] *ibid.* 821, *per* Mr Jonathan Parker Q.C., sitting as a deputy High Court Judge.

[12] Gray, *Elements of Land Law*, (2nd ed.), at p. 322.

[13] (1994) 68 P. & C.R. 93, C.A.

[14] The work involved the construction of a through lounge and kitchen/diner, installation of central heating, replacement of an old staircase, refurbishment of the cellar, removal of two chimney breasts, and the replacement of all doors and the bathroom.

[15] *ibid.* 102.

"Although the [defendant] did not know that her husband was making mortgage repayments to the [plaintiff], she nevertheless knew that [her husband] was paying the mortgage and other outgoings on the house when the improvements were made. The [defendant] was married to and living with [her husband] at the relevant time, and the expenditure of those sums by [her husband] meant that the amount of his income available to benefit the [defendant] and their children was less than it otherwise would have been. Although the money would have been earned by [the husband], it would be wrong in my view to consider that it was money solely belonging to him".

This reasoning has been the subject of academic criticism. Battersby[16] has pointed out that the premise underlying the above-cited passage must be that, since the money expended by the son on the improvements was co-owned by himself and his wife, then any estoppel arising out of that expenditure must benefit both of them. The trouble with this approach is that there was no evidence to suggest that the plaintiff's son had ever agreed or intended to share his money with his wife.

As to the requirement of mistake on the part of the defendant as to her legal rights, Roch L.J. held that there could be little doubt that, when the defendant agreed to resume cohabitation with her husband (in 1981), she had done so in the belief that she was going to a house which he owned on the basis that the house would be as much hers as it was his. Although this assurance had come from the defendant's husband, and not the plaintiff as legal owner of the property, Roch L.J. accepted that, in the context of an Indian family (and the life of this Indian family in particular), anything said by the plaintiff's son to the defendant was to be taken as said with the authority of the plaintiff. Moreover, although the defendant's expenditure on a new kitchen, using money (£4,000) borrowed from her family, being made *after* the defendant knew that the plaintiff owned the house, could not be money expended on the faith of her mistaken belief, nevertheless, it was treated as conduct confirming that the defendant had gone to live at the property under a mistaken belief as to her rights and that the plaintiff had by his conduct (between 1981 and 1990) lead the defendant to believe (once she had learned that he was the legal owner) that he would abstain from asserting his legal rights. As to the second requirement, namely, detrimental reliance, the defendant relied on a number of factors.

Firstly she had abandoned her divorce proceedings in order to resume her relationship with her husband in reliance on her mistaken belief that the house was as much hers as his. Secondly she had abandoned also the possibility, at that time, of claiming local authority accommodation as a homeless person with a priority need. Thirdly the expenditure by the defendant's husband on substantial improvements to the property, and fourthly the defendant's own expenditure on the installation of a new kitchen.

---

[16] [1995] 7 C.F.L.Q. 59 at 62. He suggests that, apart from agency, the only other method by which the defendant could have become entitled to take advantage of the estoppel was to argue that her husband had transferred to her, either during his lifetime or on his death, the benefit of the arrangements which he had made with his father: *ibid.* 63. The crucial question, however, would be whether the inchoate equity arising out of proprietary estoppel has a sufficiently proprietary character capable of assignment. See further, Chap. 7.

The third requirement was also satisfied because the plaintiff knew at all material times that he was the owner of the property. Further, in relation to the fourth requirement, it was considered inconceivable that the plaintiff did not know the basis on which his son had been successful in persuading the defendant to drop her divorce proceedings against him and to resume cohabitation with him at the property. Lastly, with regard to the fifth requirement, Roch L.J. felt that there was clear evidence that the plaintiff and his wife created and encouraged the defendant's mistaken understanding of the basis on which she and her husband occupied the property.

A strong dissenting judgment was given by Dillon L.J. who dismissed the defendant's claim to an equity on a number of grounds. The fact that no steps were taken by the plaintiff to evict the defendant after the latter's exclusion from the property could not, in his view, give rise to any legitimate expectation in the defendant that she would be allowed to live in the property for the rest of her life (or as long as she liked). On this point, Dillon L.J. accepted the observations of Ormrod L.J. in *E. & L. Berg Homes Ltd v. Grey*[17] that people were not liable to be penalised for not enforcing their strict legal rights. As to the installation of the new kitchen, the defendant knew at the time that the house belonged to the plaintiff and not her husband. Although incurring the expense was a detriment to the defendant, there was nothing to suggest that the plaintiff had stood by while she was having the work done, and tacitly encouraged her in the expenditure. Further, the fact that she had abandoned other possible alternatives and was reconciled to her husband and went back to live with him at the property (when that house was made available to them by the plaintiff) could not have given her an equity to live in the house for the rest of her life. At most, this would afford her a licence not to be evicted without reasonable notice. What of the husband's improvement works? According to Dillon L.J., the plaintiff was dealing only with his son and was making the house available for his son and family. Thus, at best, the improvement works would have prevented the plaintiff obtaining possession against the wishes of his son during the latter's lifetime. The equity could not extend to the defendant after his son's death.

The strict adherence to the *Willmott* formulation of proprietary estoppel by the majority in *Matharu* is somewhat surprising given that the modern trend is not to treat Fry J.'s criteria as being of universal application.[18] In *Taylor Fashions Ltd v. Liverpool Victoria Trustees Co Ltd*,[19] Oliver J. drew a clear distinction between common expectation and unilateral mistake cases[20] and suggested that, whilst all five *probanda* may be relevant to a unilateral mistake case, not all would necessarily be appropriate to a common expectation case.

---

[17] (1979) 253 EG 473 at 479, C.A.

[18] See, however, the speech of Lord Diplock in *Kammins Ballrooms Co. Ltd v. Zenith Investments (Torquay) Ltd* [1971] A.C. 850 at 884, which appears to support as essential the application of all five *probanda* to all cases of proprietary estoppel.

[19] [1982] Q.B. 133. Oliver J. had occasion to repeat his formulation (and adding the authority of the Court of Appeal to it) in *Habib Bank Ltd v. Habib Bank A.G. Zurich* [1981] 1 W.L.R. 1265 at 1285, C.A. The other members of the Court of Appeal, Watkins and Stephenson L.JJ., concurred with Oliver L.J.'s statement in *Taylor Fashions*.

[20] The same distinction was drawn by the Privy Council in *Plimmer v. Wellington Corporation* (1884) 9 App. Cas. 699, where Sir Arthur Hobhouse noted that, in the present case, "the equity is not claimed because the landowner has stood by in silence while his tenant has spent money on his land": *ibid*. 712.

Moreover, he suggested that all the *probanda* may[21] still have to be satisfied if the defendant has simply stood by without protest (*i.e.* silently acquiesced) while his rights have been infringed.[22] In cases of mere passivity, it seems logical that there should be shown a duty to speak, protest or interfere which cannot normally arise in the absence of knowledge or, at least, a suspicion of the true position. Thus, "for a landowner to stand by while a neighbour lays drains in land which the landowner does not believe that he owns (*Armstrong v. Sheppard & Short Ltd*)[23] or for a remainderman not to protest at a lease by a tenant for life which he believes he has no right to challenge (*Svenson v. Payne*)[24] does not create an estoppel".[25] On the other hand, if the defendant has *actively encouraged* the plaintiff to act as he did, then it may be immaterial whether the defendant knew of his own legal rights and that the plaintiff was acting in the mistaken belief that they will not be enforced against him. It is to be observed, in this connection, that Lord Cranworth's speech (forming the basis of the unilateral mistake doctrine) in *Ramsden v. Dyson*[26] makes specific reference to these criteria whilst the (common expectation) formulation presented by Lord Kingsdown in the same case omits any mention of them. As Oliver J. observed[27]:

> "In Lord Kingsdown's example ... there is no room for the literal application of the *probanda*, for the circumstances there postulated do not presuppose a 'mistake' on anybody's part, but merely the fostering of an expectation in the minds of *both* parties at the time but from which, once it has been acted upon, it would be unconscionable to permit the landlord to depart."

In cases where all the *probanda* were not relevant, Oliver J. identified a much broader approach involving an enquiry as to whether "in the particular individual circumstances, it would be unconscionable for a party to be permitted to deny that which, knowingly or unkowingly, he has allowed or encouraged another to assume to his detriment" rather than "whether the circumstances can be fitted within the confines of some preconceived formula serving as a universal yardstick for every form of unconscionable behaviour".[28]

---

[21] Interestingly, Oliver J. prefaced this statement with the proviso that strict adherence to the five *probanda* "must now be considered open to doubt" in the silent acquiescence cases: *ibid.* 147.

[22] *ibid.* 147. It is to be observed that *Willmott v. Barber* (1880) 15 Ch.D. 96 was a case of simple acquiescence by standing by without protest.

[23] [1959] 2 Q.B. 384.

[24] (1945) 71 C.L.R. 531.

[25] [1982] Q.B. 133 at 147, *per* Oliver J.

[26] (1866) L.R. 1 H.L. 129.

[27] [1982] Q.B. 133 at 147. Oliver J. also concluded that it was unclear from the earlier authorities that the courts considered it in all cases an essential element of the estoppel that the party estopped, although he must have known of the other party's belief, necessarily knew that that belief was mistaken. In *Stiles v. Cowper* (1748) 3 Atk. 692; 26 E.R. 1198, there was nothing to suggest that, at the time of the expenditure and receipt of rent, the remainderman knew that the lease, granted by the life tenant in excess of his powers, was invalid. In *Jackson v. Cator* (1800) 5 Ves Jun. 688; 31 E.R. 806, it does not appear that either party was under any misapprehension as to the legal position, although the case may have been decided on the basis of promissory estoppel. Similarly, in *Gregory v. Mighell* (1811) 18 Ves. Jun. 328; 34 E.R. 341, there does not appear to have been a unilateral misapprehension as to what was the legal position.

[28] *ibid.* 151–152.

On this analysis, knowledge of the true position by the party alleged to be estopped falls to be treated "as merely one of the factors—it may even be a determining factor in certain cases—in the overall inquiry".[29] In support of this broader approach, Oliver J. relied on several of the common expectation cases[30] where, it will be recalled, the courts have accepted a much wider jurisdiction to intervene in cases where the assertion of strict legal rights is found to be unconscionable. In *Crabb v. Arun District Council*,[31] for example, both Lord Denning M.R. and Scarman L.J. emphasised the flexibility of the estoppel doctrine, although Scarman L.J. ultimately adopted and applied the five *probanda* in *Willmott* describing them as a "valuable guide"[32] as to the matters of fact which had to be established for this type of equity.[33]

In *Taylor Fashions* itself, one of the plaintiffs was granted a lease for 42 years of a shop, No. 21, subject to the defendants' right to determine the lease if an adjoining tenant did not exercise his option to renew his lease of shop No. 22 for a further 14 years. Subsequently, the plaintiff also took a lease of shop No. 20 and spent some £12,000 to combine No. 20 and No. 21 into a single shop. The lease of No. 20 was for 14 years with an option to renew for a further 14 years, but, once again, subject to the defendants' right to determine the lease if the tenant of No. 22 did not exercise his option to renew. The tenant of No. 22 claimed to exercise his option. All the parties thought that an option to renew a lease was not registrable as an estate contract under the Land Charges Act 1925 and that the particular options were valid and binding. In fact, they were mistaken since the options were registrable and were void for non-registration against the defendants. Oliver J. held, however, that the doctrine of estoppel (by encouragment) was not restricted to cases where the representor was aware of his rights and the representee acted in the belief that those rights would not be enforced against him. Applying the broader test of unconscionability (referred to above), the learned judge held that the defendants were estopped from asserting that the tenant of shop No. 22 had not effectively exercised his option and from relying on a ground of invalidity existing at the date when they represented the option to be valid. They had represented in the lease granted to the plaintiff that the option granted to the third party, the tenant of No. 22, was valid and encouraged him to spend large sums on improvements and to alter his legal position by acquiring the lease of the adjacent premises. Accordingly, the plaintiff was granted specific performance of the renewal options in its leases.

The approach taken by Oliver J. in *Taylor Fashions* was adopted by Robert Goff J in *Amalgamated Investment & Property Co Ltd v. Texas Commerce International Bank Ltd*,[34] who also rejected any rigid classification of equitable

---

[29] *ibid.* 152.

[30] *Inwards v. Baker* [1965] 2 Q.B. 29, C.A.; *E.R. Ives Investment Ltd v. High* [1967] 2 Q.B. 379, C.A. and *Crabb v. Arun District Council* [1976] Ch. 179, C.A.

[31] [1976] Ch. 179, C.A.

[32] *ibid.* 194. Oliver J., in *Taylor Fashions*, inferred that Scarman L.J. had applied the fourth *probandum*, namely, that the possessor of the legal right must know of the other party's mistaken belief, as meaning that the defendant must know merely of the plaintiff's belief which, in the event, turns out to be mistaken: *ibid.* 153.

[33] The five *probanda* were adopted as a valuable guide in *Salvation Army Trustee Co. Ltd v. West Yorkshire Metropolitan County Council* (1981) 41 P. & C.R. 179 at 194, *per* Woolf J.

[34] [1982] Q.B. 84 at 103–104, C.A. and Lord Denning M.R., at 122. The decision at first instance was given by Robert Goff J. See also, *Appleby v. Cowley, The Times*, April 14, 1982; [1982] C.L.Y. 1150, where the plaintiff, the present head of a set of barristers' chambers, claimed that

estoppel into exclusive and defined categories. Like Oliver J., he concluded that the inquiry which he had to make was simply whether, in all the circumstances of the case, it would be unconscionable for the party asserting his strict legal rights to seek to take advantage of the mistake which, at the material time, all parties shared. Again, in *Re Basham (dec'd)*,[35] Mr Edward Nugee Q.C., sitting as a High Court judge, accepted the "broadening process"[36] initiated by Oliver J.'s consideration of the authorities, and concluded that the principle of proprietary estoppel, at least where the relevant belief is that the claimant is going to be given a right in the future, fell properly to be regarded as giving rise to a species of constructive trust—this being "the concept employed by a court of equity to prevent a person from relying on his legal rights where it would be unconscionable for him to do so."[37]

It has been commented by Wesltead[38] that the elements of proprietary estoppel have now been condensed into essentially:

"two interlinked requirements distilled from Oliver J.'s broad test of unconscionability postulated in *Taylor's Fashions*. First, there must be conduct, express or tacit, on the part of the landowner, relating to the acquisition of rights in or over his or her property. Secondly, the claimant of the equity must prove a detrimental alteration of position in reliance on a belief engendered by the landowner's conduct."

To Welstead and other commentators,[39] the majority reasoning of the Court of Appeal in *Matharu*, which ignored the unconscionability test promulgated by Oliver J., provides a retrograde step in the development of proprietary estoppel doctrine.

In Chapter 10, we examine in more detail whether the English caselaw now supports a trend towards an underlying concept of "unconscionability" as the basis for proprietary estoppel claims.

---

the defendants, a former head of chambers and a family company associated with him, held the chambers on trust for the present members of the set. The plaintiff claimed, in the alternative, that the members' expectation and expenditure resulted in an equity based on proprietary estoppel. Sir Robert Megarry V.-C. held that (1) such fiduciary relationship as existed between the parties was insufficient to establish the obligations of trusteeship and (2) the assertion of legal rights would not in any way be unconscionable. In *Andrews v. Colonial Mutual Life Assurance Society Ltd* [1982] 2 N.Z.L.R. 556, High Court of Auckland, Barker J. canvassed "the flexible approach which does not rely so heavily on the ... five *probanda*": *ibid.* 568.

[35] [1986] 1 W.L.R. 1498.
[36] *ibid.* 1508.
[37] *ibid.* 1504. See further, Chap. 10, pp. 181–189.
[38] [1995] Conv. 61 at p. 63.
[39] See G. Battersby, [1995] 7 C.F.L.Q. 59.

7. AN INCHOATE EQUITY

(A) Distinction Between Right and Remedy

It has been said that "in order to provide a remedy the court must first find a right which has been infringed".[1] Thus, in the context of a proprietary estoppel claim, a distinction needs to be drawn between the granting of a remedy by the court necessary to satisfy the "equity" and the equity (or right) itself which arises as soon as the conscience of the legal owner is affected by the parties' transaction. Thus, in *Re Sharpe (A Bankrupt)*,[2] Browne-Wilkinson J. observed[3]:

> "The right must have arisen at the time of the transaction in order for the plaintiff to have any right the breach of which can be remedied . . . . the equity predates any order of the court."

The equity arises as soon as the legal owner attempts to go back upon the basic assumptions which underlay the transaction of the parties. The matter was put succinctly by Scarman L.J. in *Crabb v. Arun District Council*[4] in the following terms[5]:

> " . . . the plaintiff has to establish as a fact that the defendant, by setting up his right, is taking advantage of him in a way which is unconscionable, inequitable or unjust. It is to be observed . . . that the fraud or injustice alleged does not take place during the course of negotiation, but only when the defendant decides to refuse to allow the plaintiff to set up his claim against the defendants' undoubted right. The fraud, if it be such, arises after the event, when the defendant seeks by relying on his right to defeat the expectation which he by his conduct encouraged the plaintiff to have."

It is evident from this passage that there need not be anything fraudulent or unjust in the conduct of the actual negotiations—the element of unconscionability arises when the legal owner seeks to depart from the assumption which he permitted the claimant to make[6] and it is this unconscionable insistence upon strict legal rights which brings the equity into play.

---

[1] *Re Sharpe (A Bankrupt)* [1980] 1 W.L.R. 219 at 225, *per* Browne-Wilkinson J.
[2] [1980] 1 W.L.R. 219.
[3] *ibid.* 225.
[4] [1976] Ch. 179, C.A.
[5] *ibid.* 195.
[6] *Lim Teng Huan v. Ang Swee Chuan* [1992] 1 W.L.R. 113 at 117, P.C., *per* Lord Browne-Wilkinson.

(B) What is the Nature of the Equity?

The equity which arises from the unconscionable conduct of the legal owner "after the act of incomplete gift"[7] is the right of the claimant to be heard in court and, if appropriate, to have his claim enforced by means of a proprietary (or compensatory) award. As such, the equity merely attracts the discretion of the court -it remains "inchoate" until such time as the court actually decrees a specific interest or award in favour of the estoppel claimant. It is at this point that the equity may crystallise into a full property right. Thus, according to Hayton,[8] the estoppel claim (prior to the court's decree) is not sufficiently certain or stable to qualify as a property interest—the estoppel claimant "is really a suitor for discretionary equitable relief".[9] The "equity" is simply "a right of an exclusively personal nature to pursue an equitable remedy".[10] In the words of Ferguson[11]:

> "In estoppel cases, the claimant's rights and remedies are at the discretion of the court, which will only confer 'the minimum equity to do justice' on the facts of the case. Any remedy given will be prospective only, and any rights granted to the claimant originate only in the court's order ... "

In the strict conveyancing sense,[12] therefore, the equity is unable to mature into an interest in land until such time as the court, in the exercise of its equitable jurisdiction, grants the claimant a remedy equivalent to a full property right. On this basis, because of the "inchoate and uncertain nature"[13] of the claimant's rights, a third party will not be bound by the equity even if he has notice of the circumstances giving rise to the estoppel claim.[14] This orthodox view is

---

[7] *Olsson v. Dyson* (1969) 120 C.L.R. 365 at 379, *per* Kitto J.

[8] D. Hayton, (1990) 106 L.Q.R. 87 at p. 97, n.26.

[9] D. Hayton, [1990] Conv. 370 at p. 381. The concept of "an equity" has been described as "a grey and murky fog, consistent in depth of colour, the boundaries hazy and ill-defined": A. Everton, (1976) 40 Conv. (N.S.) 209, who suggests that the equity arising from proprietary estoppel is "naked and alone" as opposed to "ancillary or dependent upon an interest in land": *ibid.* 212, n. 16.

[10] A. Everton, (1976) 40 Conv. (N.S.) 209 at 220, who talks in terms of "an equitable right to raise the defence": *ibid.* 220, n. 42. On this basis, of course, the estoppel equity, prior to its satisfaction in court, lacks any proprietary element.

[11] P. Ferguson, (1993) 109 L.Q.R. 114 at p. 121. See also, P. Clarke, (1992) 22 Fam. Law 72 at p. 75.

[12] It should be noted that for certain *specific* purposes the inchoate equity has been recognised as creating an interest in land: *Pennine Raceway Ltd v. Kirkless Metropolitan Borough Council* [1983] 1 Q.B. 382, C.A., where a licensee was held to be a "person interested in the land" within s.164 of the Town and Country Planning Act 1971 so as to be entitled to claim compensation for loss of work rendered abortive by the revocation of planning permission; *Plimmer v. Wellington Corporation* (1884) 9 App. Cas. 699, P.C., where the equitable right was held to constitute an "estate or interest in, to or out of the land" within the meaning of the Public Works Act 1882 entitling the licensee to compensation thereunder.

[13] D. Hayton, [1990] Conv. 370 at p. 384.

[14] Battersby, on the other hand, in a recent article, suggests that a purchaser with notice of the circumstances giving rise to the inchoate equity would be bound. Although he recognises that "there are problems here, since at the inchoate stage it is not known whether the court will decree the creation of a proprietary right or, indeed, any right at all", nevertheless, draws an analogy with a pending land action where "*ex hypothesi*, it is not known whether the action will be successful, but a purchaser with notice of the action (protected as necessary by registration) will take, subject to any resulting proprietary interest: (1995) 58 M.L.R. 637 at p. 642.

illustrated in the following passage from the judgment of Lord Upjohn in *National Provincial Bank Ltd v. Ainsworth*[15]:

> "I myself cannot see how it is possible for a "mere equity" to bind a purchaser unless such an equity is ancillary to or dependent upon an equitable estate or interest in land ... a mere "equity" naked and alone is, in my opinion, incapable of binding successors in title even with notice; it is personal to the parties".

There is, however, growing acceptance for the proposition that the estoppel-based equity generates a form of beneficial entitlement under a constructive trust at a much earlier date (*i.e.* from the moment of its inception). This is the view put forward by Gray, *Elements of Land Law*,[16] where the author cites examples from both the English and Commonwealth jurisdictions. In *Voyce v. Voyce*,[17] for example, the defendant had spent a substantial sum of money on a cottage in reliance upon his mother's promise that, if he did this, the cottage would be his. The Court of Appeal held that the intention to make a gift coupled with conduct which would make it inequitable to assert continuing legal ownership gave rise to an estoppel. Dillon L.J. regarded the defendant's equitable rights as having accrued long before the court hearing so that, whilst he remained in occupation of the cottage "under the equitable rights which were ultimately satisfied by the direction for a conveyance he was, as is now recognised, the equitable owner".[18] This meant that a claim to restrain an infringement of an easement of light could have been made against him. Similarly, in *Re Sharpe (A Bankrupt)*[19] Browne-Wilkinson J. observed[20] that "... it cannot be that the interest in property arises for the first time when the court declares it to exist". It has been suggested,[21] however, that where the claimant's expectation does not relate to specific property (but a mere expectancy), there cannot be any proprietary interest before the court order.

Gray also cites the case of *Sen v. Headley*,[22] where Nourse L.J. observed[23] that where the application of the doctrine of proprietary estoppel gave the promisee a right to call for a conveyance of the land, it could be said that "that right is the consequence of an implied or constructive trust which arises once all the requirements of the doctrine have been satisfied". A similar view has been expressed by the High Court of Australia in *Commonwealth v. Verwayen*,[24] where it has been suggested that the claimant's cause of action in such cases is essentially that of a beneficiary against a trustee for breach of trust. These

---

[15] [1965] A.C. 1175 at 1288, H.L.
[16] Gray, *Elements of Land Law*, (2nd ed.) at pp. 360–361.
[17] (1991) 62 P. & C.R. 290.
[18] *ibid*. 294.
[19] [1980] 1 W.L.R. 219. See also, *Ward v. Kirkland* [1986] 1 W.L.R. 601 at 631–632, *per* Ungoed-Thomas J. and Dawson & Pearce, *Licences Relating to the Occupation or Use of Land*, (1979) at pp. 162–163.
[20] *ibid*. 225.
[21] J. Martin, [1992] Conv. 57, citing *Re Basham (dec'd)* [1986] 1 W.L.R. 1498, where the estoppel claimant had a mere expectation of inheritance of the legal owner's estate.
[22] [1991] Ch. 425, C.A.
[23] *ibid*. 440.
[24] (1990) 170 C.L.R. 394 at 437, *per* Deane J.

developments have led Gray to suggest[25] that the doctrine of proprietary estoppel "generates anticipatory beneficial rights behind a trust which then provides the basis for the court's subsequent order of either specific performance or compensatory damages for breach".

(C) Does the Equity Bind Third Parties?

There is considerable debate[26] as to whether the equity (in its inchoate form) can bind third parties. There is also some controversy as to the effect of the equity on third parties once it has crystallised into a concrete judicial remedy. It will, therefore, be convenient to consider the question under these two separate headings.

(i) The Inchoate Equity

In relation to unregistered land, it seems settled that the equity raised by a proprietary estoppel does not constitute a land charge for the purposes of the Land Charges Act 1972. Thus, in *Pascoe v. Turner*,[27] it was conceded that if the claimant was granted a licence by the court to occupy the house, such a licence could not be registered as a land charge. This seems to accord with principle since it is difficult to envisage such an equity being registrable given that it arises informally without legal advice. To render such informal rights registrable would place too heavy a burden on potential claimants to register. Failure to register, would, of course, mean that the equity was void against purchasers of the legal estate.

An important case which merits consideration in this context is *E.R. Ives Investment Ltd v. High*.[28] In this case, one Russell Westgate built a block of flats whose foundations encroached onto the defendant's land. In 1949, an agreement was reached between them that the defendant would allow the foundations to remain in return for a right of way across the yard at the back of the block. In 1950, Westgate sold his land and the block to the Wrights. In 1959, the defendant, in reliance upon the agreement, built himself a garage which could only be entered over the Wrights' land. The Wrights raised no objection to the building of the garage or to the defendant's use of the yard for access to it. In 1960, he contributed one-fifth to the cost of re-surfacing the yard. That same year, the flats were sold to the plaintiffs expressly subject to the right of way, which was never registered as a land charge. The plaintiffs claimed that, as it was not registered under Class C(IV) as an estate contract or under Class D(III) as an equitable easement, it was void against them under section 13 of the Land Charges Act 1925. The Court of Appeal, however, dismissed the plaintiffs' claim for damages for trespass and an injunction restraining the defendant from trespassing on the yard. According to Lord Denning M.R. and Danckwerts L.J.,

---

[25] *ibid.* p. 361.

[26] G Battersby, [1991] Conv. 36; J. Hill, (1988) 51 M.L.R. 226; S. Moriarty, (1984) 100 L.Q.R. 376; P.N. Todd, (1981) Conv. 347; A. Briggs, [1983] Conv. 285 and [1981] Conv. 212.

[27] [1979] 1 W.L.R. 431 at 439, C.A. See also, generally, *Shilo Spinners Ltd v. Harding* [1973] A.C. 691, H.L.

[28] [1967] 2 Q.B. 379, C.A. See further, F.R. Crane, (1967) 31 Conv. (N.S.) 332; H.W. Wilkinson, (1967) 30 M.L.R. 580; R.E. Poole, (1968) 32 Conv. 96; J.F. Garner, (1967) 31 Conv. (N.S.) 394; G. Battersby, (1995) 58 B.L.R. 637 at pp. 643–652.

by reason of the mutual benefit and burden under the 1949 agreement and the acquiescence of the plaintiffs' predecessors in the rights thereby acquired, the defendant had in equity a good right of way across the yard which did not need to be registered under the Land Charges Act 1925. According to Winn L.J., (the other member of the Court), the plaintiffs' predecessors, by licensing the defendant to use the yard, encouraging him to build a garage and accepting from him part of the cost of resurfacing the yard, had represented to him that he had a right to use the yard which created an estoppel, not registrable under the 1925 Act, preventing the plaintiffs from denying the defendant's user of the right of way.

Lord Denning M.R. was able to avoid the Land Charges Act by holding that the equitable easements required to be registered as land charges are those which before 1926 would have been capable of being created at law but which since 1925 can exist only in equity.[29] Danckwerts L.J. was more dismissive stating simply that the defendant's right of way was not a registrable charge without further analysis of the question.[30] Winn L.J., on the other hand, appears to have accepted that the defendant's right of way was void for non-registration against the Wrights, but concluded that the estoppel arising against them (in the form of an equitable easement), although not capable of registration, nevertheless bound the plaintiffs who had notice of it.[31] In his Lordship's words[32]:

"In my opinion the plaintiffs as successors in title are bound by that estoppel. I do not regard myself as thereby saying anything contradictory of the proposition submitted to the court that the said equity or equitable easement, as distinct from the estoppel, was rendered void as against the plaintiffs by the statutes to which I have referred. Estoppels arising from representations made by owners of land that rights exist affecting their land will, unless in form they are limited to the duration of the interest of the representor, bind successors to his title . . . I cannot see that the statute has any impact upon an estoppel, nor do I think that an estoppel could be registrable under its provisions."

The inherent difficulty with applying this sort of reasoning today is that it appears to fly in the face of the Court of Appeal ruling in *Ashburn Anstalt v. Arnold*[33] to the effect that a contractual licence (save in exceptional circumstances) creates no proprietary interest in land capable of binding third parties. This has led Battersby[34] to observe that "if a contractually created licence to occupy land is personal only, how can a licence to use arising by estoppel be proprietary?" According to Battersby, the decision in *Ives* can be explained on

---

[29] *ibid.* 395–396. He also concluded that the agreement was not an "estate contract" within a Class C(iv) land charge because "there was no contract by Mr Westgate to convey a legal estate of any kind": *ibid.* 395. The reasoning is considered "deeply unconvincing" by G. Battersby: see, (1995) 58 M.L.R. 637, at pp. 646–647.

[30] *ibid.* 400. G. Battersby finds this approach equally "unconvicning": (1995) 58 M.L.R. 637, at p. 647.

[31] G. Battersby finds this analysis "more penetrating and persuasive" but ultimtately concludes that it also "ultimately fails to convince": (1995) 58 M.L.R. 637, at p. 648.

[32] *ibid.* 405.

[33] [1989] Ch. 1, C.A.

[34] G. Battersby, [1991] Conv. 36 at p. 41.

the basis that the plaintiffs were estopped by their conduct from asserting the defendant's failure to register because they could not take the benefit of the 1949 agreement (by leaving their foundations in place), while denying the other half of the agreement (the defendant's right of way). Such right of way should, accordingly, be capable of retrospective registration as a Class D(III) land charge against the original grantor, Westgate. In the case of registered land, the matter could be dealt with in the same way by simple rectification of the register. Other difficult cases,[35] such as *Inwards v. Baker*[36] and *Greasley v. Cooke*,[37] can be explained on the basis that the declarations therein made were sufficient merely to provide a defence to any future possession proceedings without amounting to the creation of full proprietary rights. Alternatively, that they conferred a life interest on the claimant.[38] In a recent article,[39] Battersby has provided a further explanation of the *Ives* decision. In his view, the facts of *Ives* appear to fall within the principle enunciated in *Taylor Fashions Ltd v. Liverpool Victoria Trustees Co. Ltd*[40] that a land charge which has already become void against a purchaser by reason of non-registration may become valid again when subsequently the purchaser acts in such a way as to estop himself from asserting non-registration. Thus, in *Ives* "the Wrights defeated the right of way when they bought Francis Court, but they subsequently accepted the benefit of the agreement and thus became subject to its burden, *i.e.* they became estopped from relying on the failure to register".[41] Battersby suggests that retrospective registration against the original grantor, Westgate, would bind any successor in title of the plaintiffs who was prepared to abandon the agreement in its entirety. He suggests[42] that a similar "estoppel against asserting non-registration" argument can be made in the context of registered land save that here the court would have jurisdiction to rectify the register under section 82(1)(h) or (3)(c) of the Land Registration Act 1925. On this reasoning, Battersby concludes[43] that the *Ives* decision:

"... is not a case where the proprietary interest arose by proprietary estoppel. The interest arose by express agreement and the effect of the estoppel is to prevent the ultimate purchasers (the plaintiffs) from relying on the failure to register. Thus explained, the case fits perfectly well within the registration systems established under both the Land Charges Act and the Land Registration Act."

Despite this rationale for the decision, what does seem to emerge from *Ives* is that an estoppel-based (inchoate) equity will be binding on a purchaser of the

---

[35] In *Williams v. Staite* [1979] Ch. 291, C.A., it was assumed without argument that an equitable licence to occupy a cottage for life was binding on a subsequent purchaser of the legal estate. See also, *J.T. Developments Ltd v. Quinn* (1991) 62 P. & C.R. 33, C.A., where the purchaser was bound without the point being argued.

[36] [1965] 2 Q.B. 29, C.A.

[37] [1980] 3 All E.R. 710, C.A.

[38] G. Battersby, [1991] Conv. 36 at p. 44. But note the difficulties that this may give rise to in terms of the Settled Land Act 1925: *Dodsworth v. Dodsworth* (1973) 228 EG 115, C.A.

[39] (1995) 58 M.L.R. 637 at pp. 648–650.

[40] [1982] Q.B. 133.

[41] *ibid.* 649.

[42] *ibid.* 650.

[43] *ibid.* 652.

legal estate who takes with notice of the circumstances giving rise to the equity.[44] In *Ives*, the purchaser had *actual* notice of the right of way in question (*i.e.* the contract and conveyance specifically made reference to the fact that the land was being sold subject to the defendant's right of way). There is also support for the view that *constructive* notice will suffice for this purpose.[45] Thus, in *Duke of Beaufort v. Patrick*[46] an Act of Parliament authorised the making of a public canal through lands of which A was the owner and B his lessee, and upon payment of compensation the land was to vest in the canal company. An arrangement was made in respect of compensation with B, but not with A, who had consented to the making of the canal through his land. The persons claiming under the will of John Calland, who bought the land from A, failed in a claim to retake possession of the land used by the canal, but they were held entitled to fair compensation based on the agricultural value of the land taken for the canal. It was also held that John Calland (as purchaser) who had bought A's land with notice in the conditions of sale as to the canal was bound by the same equity that "he who stands by and encourages an act, cannot afterwards complain of it, or interfere with the enjoyment of that which he has permitted to be done".[47] In the course of his judgment, Sir John Romilly M.R. stated[48]:

> "[John Calland] bought under particulars of sale, which expressly stated the intention to make [the canal]; he bought at a time when it had actually been completed, and when, therefore, he knew, or, according to the rules of this Court, *must be taken to have known*, that the canal was in existence. I am of the opinion that he bought with the knowledge, and subject to the implied condition, that the canal was to remain, and was to be used for the benefit of the public for ever thereafter; and that neither he, nor his devises, nor those who represent them, can prevent the enjoyment of this easement in future." (Emphasis supplied).

Although, on the facts, John Calland had express notice of the making of the canal, nevertheless, it is evident from the above-cited passage that constructive notice would also have been sufficient to impose the estoppel equity on him. Would it, thus, really have made any difference to the *Ives* decision if the contract and conveyance had been silent as to the defendant's right of way but the same was, nevertheless, readily apparent on inspection of the land?

Professor R.H. Maudsley[49] has sought to distinguish licences conferring possession and other licences. His view is that licences conferring possession,

---

[44] See also, *Inwards v. Baker* [1965] 2 Q.B. 29 at 37, C.A., *per* Lord Denning M.R.; *Voyce v. Voyce* (1991) 62 P. & C.R. 290 at 295, *per* Dillon L.J.; *The Duke of Beaufort v. Patrick* [1853] 17 Beav. 60 at 78–79; 51 E.R. 954 at 961, *per* Sir John Romilly M.R.; *Hopgood v. Brown* [1955] 1 W.L.R. 213 at 225, 231, *per* Lord Evershed M.R. and Morris L.J., respectively. In the *Hopgood* case, however, reliance was placed on the judgment of Mansfield C.J. in *Taylor v. Needham* (1810) 2 Taunt 278, relating to the doctrine of privity of estate. The view that the "equity" is capable of binding purchasers with actual notice is supported by J. Warburton, (1991) 5 Trust Law International 9.
[45] See, F.R. Crane, (1967) 31 Conv. (NS) 332 at p. 339.
[46] (1853) 17 Beav. 60; 51 E.R. 954.
[47] *ibid.* 75; 960.
[48] *ibid.* 78; 961.
[49] R.H. Maudsley, (1956) 20 Conv. (NS) 281 at p. 301.

whether created by contract or estoppel, should bind everyone except a purchaser for value without actual or constructive notice. Non-possessory contractual licences, on the other hand, should not bind successors in title and non-possessory estoppel licences should bind volunteers and purchasers with actual notice, but not purchasers with constructive notice. Professor Maudsley argues for this distinction (between possessory and non-possessory licences) on the basis that a purchaser investigating title can more easily identify the fact of possession but not other types of licence. The *Ives* decision appears to confirm the second and third Maudsley propositions.

As yet, there has been no case expressly dealing with the situation of an estoppel licensee claimant seeking to enforce an equity against a purchaser of the legal estate who does not have express notice of the circumstances giving rise to the equity.[50] Reference, however, may be made to the decision in *Unity Joint Stock Mutual Banking Association v. King.*[51] In this case, a father built a granary on a piece of land of which he was the equitable owner. Later, he allowed his two sons to use and occupy the granary, and they subsequently erected other buildings on the land at considerable expense, as a result of which they acquired a lien over it. One of the sons secured an equitable mortgage from a bank. Before this, the father had become a surety for his sons. The sons became bankrupt and the issue arose as to whether the bank, or those claiming under the surety agreement, had priority over the sons' lien over the land. Sir John Romilly M.R. held that the bank, as a purchaser for value without notice of the surety agreement, had priority.

Although not constituting a land charge, it has been suggested[52] that an estoppel-based claim may be capable of registration as a *lis pendens* under the Land Charges Act 1972. Section 17(1) of the Land Charges Act 1972 defines a "pending land action" as any action "relating to land or any interest in or charge on land". Thus, two pre-conditions appear to present themselves: (1) that litigation has commenced in respect of the claim and (2) that the claim itself is to an interest in the land.

There is clear authority for the proposition that the inchoate estoppel-equity does not qualify as an equitable interest capable of being overreached under s.2(1) of the Law of Property Act 1925. The point was specifically addressed by Lord Wilberforce in *Shiloh Spinners Ltd v. Harding*[53] who, in referring to the *Ives* case, had no hesitation in concluding that an estoppel equity was not an equitable interest capable of being overreached. The overreaching provisions of section 2(1) are designed to override only existing equitable interests. An equitable interest which does not exist at the time of purchase cannot be overreached by that purchase.[54] Moreover, an estoppel licensee's right of

---

[50] But see, *Re Sharpe (A Bankrupt)* [1980] 1 W.L.R. 219 at 226, where Browne-Wilkinson J. expressed the tentative view that the rights of the purchaser (who had purchased without express notice) might prevail over the claimant's equity. See further, J. Martin, [1980] Conv. 207 at pp. 214–215: *Holiday Inns Inc. v. Broadhead* (1974) 232 EG 951 at 961.

[51] (1858) 25 Beav. 72; 53 E.R. 563.

[52] [1983] Conv. 69, 70, (JEM), relying upon *dicta* in *Haslemere Estates Ltd v. Baker* [1982] 1 W.L.R. 1109 at 1119–1120, *per* Sir Robert Megarry V.-C.

[53] [1973] A.C. 691 at 721, H.L.

[54] P.T. Evans, [1989] Conv. 418 at p. 427.

occupation will not derive from a beneficial interest behind a trust for sale and so will not, in any event, be overreachable by two trustees.[55]

Despite these limitations, an inchoate estoppel equity has been held to be binding on a volunteer successor in title from a donor who has notice of the circumstances from which the equity has arisen and notice that the claimant to the equity is, and was at the time of the gift of land to him, in occupation of the property. Thus, in *Voyce v. Voyce*[56] the defendant's mother said he could take a cottage (of which she was the legal owner) as a gift provided that he did it up to her satisfaction, which he subsequently did at considerable expense. The gift was never executed by deed. Later, the mother made a gift of the cottage, duly executed by a deed of gift, to her younger son, the plaintiff. He gave no consideration for this, but he was aware that his brother (the defendant) was living in the cottage. The mother subsequently died. The Court of Appeal held that, since the defendant had spent a substantial sum of money on the cottage in reliance upon his mother's promise that if he did this the cottage would be his, his mother would have been estopped from asserting that the cottage belonged to her. Moreover, the plaintiff's position as a volunteer was held to be no better than that of his mother.

The equity has also been held binding on the legal owner's trustee in bankruptcy. In *Re Sharpe (A Bankrupt)*,[57] a receiving order was made against a bankrupt. He and his wife and his aunt, Mrs Johnson, aged 82, were living together in a maisonette, which (with a shop) formed leasehold premises purchased by the bankrupt in 1975 for £17,000. Mrs Johnson had provided £12,000 of the purchase price, the remainder having been raised on mortgage. In providing the money, Mrs Johnson had been told that she would be able to stay in the premises for as long as she liked, and that she would be looked after by the bankrupt and his wife. Mrs Johnson also spent a considerable sum on decorations and fittings for the property. In 1979, the trustee in bankruptcy contracted to sell the premises to a purchaser with vacant possession. After the date of this contract, Mrs Johnson for the first time put forward a claim to an interest in the maisonette. The Court of Appeal held that Mrs Johnson had provided the £12,000 by way of loan (and not as a gift) and, accordingly, no interest in her favour was created under a resulting trust but, since it was an essential feature of the loan that she was to make her home in the maisonette, she had, as against the bankrupt, the right to occupy the premises for as long as she liked while the loan remained unpaid. The decision is based on the notion that, as between the bankrupt and Mrs Johnson, she had an irrevocable contractual (equitable) licence (arising under a constructive trust) to remain in the property which gave her an interest in the property before the bankruptcy so that the trustee took the property subject to that interest. In the words of Browne-Wilkinson J.,[58] "the mere intervention of the bankruptcy by itself cannot alter Mrs Johnson's property interest". This reasoning, based as it is on a number of pre-*Ashburn Anstalt* Denning authorities,[59] is open to question.

---

[55] *City of London Building Society v. Flegg* [1988] A.C. 54, H.L. See, M.P. Thompson [1988] Conv. 108 at p. 120.

[56] (1991) 62 P. & C.R. 290, C.A.

[57] [1980] 1 W.L.R. 219. See, J. Martin, [1980] Conv. 207.

[58] *ibid.* 226.

[59] See, *e.g. Binions v. Evans* [1972] Ch. 359, C.A.

Consider also the predicament of the purchaser in this case, who was not a party to the proceedings and, hence, the question of priorities as between him and Mrs Johnson did not call for judicial consideration. It has been suggested by Thompson that if, in this sort of case, the category of persons affected by the equity is limited to purchasers with actual or express notice, "a more equitable balance can be struck between competing interests".[60] This was, indeed, the tentative view reached by Browne-Wilkinson J. who opined[61] that "it may be that as a purchaser without express notice in an action for specific performance of the contract his rights will prevail over Mrs Johnson's".

The inchoate equity has also been held binding on the legal owner's personal representatives. In *Inwards v. Baker*,[62] a son wished to build a bungalow as his home. He was encouraged by his father to build on his father's land at a cost of some £300, of which the son provided £150 and the father the balance. The son went into occupation and lived in the bungalow thereafter, in the expectation and belief that he would be allowed to remain there for his lifetime or for so long as he wished. The father later died and, under his will, the land vested in trustees for the benefit of persons other than the son. The Court of Appeal held that the son's expenditure of his own money on his father's land in the expectation, induced and encouraged by his father, that he would be allowed to remain in occupation for as long as he desired, created an equity in the son's favour which could only be satisfied by allowing the son to remain in occupation of the bungalow for as long as he desired. In the course of his judgment, Lord Denning M.R. observed[63] that the son had a licence coupled with an equity such that any purchaser who took the land from the owner with notice of the son's interest would also be bound by the equity. This led to the conclusion that the trustees of the father's will (who were successors in title of the father) were also bound by this equity.

The decision in *Inwards* was applied in *Jones (A.E.) v. Jones (F.W.)*.[64] Here, the defendant's father bought a house near his own home for the defendant who left a job and council house and moved with his family into the house. The defendant gave his father sums amounting to one-quarter of the purchase price of the house. The defendant understood from his father that the house was his. When the father died, the house vested in the plaintiff, the defendant's step-mother and administratrix of his father's estate. The Court of Appeal held *inter alia* that the plaintiff was estopped from turning the defendant out of the house by the father's conduct which had led the defendant to leave his job and pay money to his father in the belief that the house would be his home for the rest of his life.

In *E. & L. Berg Homes Ltd v. Grey*,[65] it was conceded[66] that a change of ownership of the land between two associated companies (with common

---

[60] M.P. Thompson, [1983] Conv. 50 at p. 56.

[61] [1980] 1 W.L.R. 219 at 226, C.A.

[62] [1965] 2 Q.B. 29, C.A. See also, *Dillwyn v. Llewelyn* 4 De G.F. & J. 517; 45 E.R. 1285, where the court held that the claimant, a son, was entitled to call for a conveyance of the land from the trustee's of his father's will.

[63] *ibid.* 37.

[64] [1977] 1 W.L.R. 438, C.A. See also, *Dodsworth v. Dodsworth* (1973) 228 E.G. 115, C.A.

[65] (1979) 253 EG 473, C.A.

[66] *ibid.* 475.

directors) did not affect whatever estoppel rights had accrued against the legal owner. The same has been held in relation to a transfer of functions between different local authorities (*i.e.* city council to metropolitan county council, following local government reorganisation under the Local Government Act 1972).[67]

Where the land in question is registered, there is some authority for the proposition that an inchoate estoppel-equity is capable of constituting an overriding interest under section 70(1)(g) of the Land Registration Act 1925 when coupled with actual occupation of the land by the claimant.[68] In *National Provincial Bank Ltd v. Hastings Car Mart Ltd*,[69] Lord Denning M.R. addressed the question in the following terms[70]:

> "[Section 70(1)(g)] is a statutory application to registered land of the well-known rule protecting the rights of persons in occupation. It was stated by Wigram V.-C. in his judgment in *Jones v. Smith* (1841) 1 Hare 43 at 60: 'if a person purchases an estate which he knows to be in the occupation of another than the vendor, he is bound by all the *equities* which the party in such occupation may have in the land'. Likewise Mr Pemberton Leigh (afterwards Lord Kingsdown) in *Barnhart v. Greenshields* (1853) 9 Moore PCC 18 at 32 said: 'if there be a tenant in possession of land, a purchaser is bound by all the *equities* which the tenant could enforce against the vendor'. Those statements refer specifically to equities and are not confined to proprietary rights. Indeed, one can think of many cases where rights, not being proprietary rights, are protected by the section. An obvious example is the equity of a licensee arising from his expenditure on land."

Equally, there is some academic support for the proposition that an estoppel equity may be protected as a minor interest by the entry of a caution or notice on the register of title of the land affected.[71] In *Poster v. Slough Estates Ltd*,[72] however, Cross J.'s discussion[73] of the registration of equitable easements tacitly infers that an estoppel equity cannot be registered as a minor interest.

A further suggestion is to utilise the doctrine that equity will not permit a statute to be used as an instrument of fraud. Bailey has suggested that "if it can be established that it would be fraudulent as the word is used today for the transferee to seek to rely on his strict legal rights under the statute, a court would surely have the jurisdiction to hold the registered proprietor bound and, if necessary, order the rectification of the register whether or not it was originally

---

[67] *Salvation Army Trustee Co. Ltd v. West Yorkshire Metropolitan County Council* (1981) 41 P. & C.R. 179 at 193, 197.

[68] But see *National Provincial Bank Ltd v. Ainsworth* [1965] A.C. 1175 at 1238, H.L., *per* Lord Upjohn.

[69] [1964] 1 Ch. 665, C.A. See also, *Blacklocks v. J.B. Developments (Godalming) Ltd* [1982] 1 Ch. 183, where an equity of rectification accompanied by actual occupation of land was held to constitute an overriding interest within section 70(1)(g) of the Land Registration Act 1925. See further, D. G. Barnsley [1983] Conv. 361. Compare, *Canadian Imperial Bank of Commerce v. Bello* (1992) 64 P. & C.R. 48, 52, C.A., where Dillon L.J. had occasion to remark that a promissory estoppel would not be a sufficient interest in land to be an overriding interest within s.70(1)(g).

[70] *ibid.* 689.

[71] See, T. Bailey, [1983] Conv. 99 at pp. 102–105, M. Thompson, (1985) 44 C.L.J. 280.

[72] [1969] 1 Ch. 495.

[73] *ibid.* 507.

the latter's words or conduct that gave rise to the estoppel".[74] One example would be where "the transferee receives a continuing benefit from a reciprocal arrangement, under which his property was also to receive a certain burden".[75] In such a case, the transferee should be compelled to submit to the burden of the arrangement (by not acting inconsistently with the estoppel) so long as he receives the benefit.

It has also been suggested that the doctrine of notice may be applicable in the context of registered land.[76] The more orthodox view, however, is that there is no room for the doctrine of notice in the registered land system since every kind of interest (other than an overriding interest) must either be protected on the register or else be defeasible by a purchaser.[77]

According to Gray,[78] "the resolution of the present impasse is almost certainly to be found in the growing acceptance of constructive trust theory as supporting an *in personam* jurisdiction to restrain unconscionable conduct by third parties". On this basis, therefore, the inchoate equity would be binding "not on the basis of the notice doctrine or even because of the presence of an overriding interest" but "simply from his express or implied acceptance of a transfer of land on terms whereby he voluntarily subjected himself to the 'equity' of the estoppel and which terms he cannot now in conscience be heard to disavow".[79] One obvious advantage of such an approach is that the potential impact of the equity on any third party interest would be determined by the specific circumstances of the given case. In other words, the emphasis would shift to a determination of the question whether the third party's conduct was such as to justify the imposition of the equity against him. By way of illustration, reference may be made to the decision in *Lyus v. Prowsa Developments Ltd.*[80] Here, the plaintiffs had entered into a contract to buy a plot of registered land from a company which subsequently went into liquidation. Prior to the contract, the company's bank had obtained a legal charge on the land. The bank (as mortgagee) sold the land to a purchaser, subject to and with the benefit of the contract between the plaintiff and the company. The purchaser from the bank in turn sold on to another party, taking a covenant to perform the contract in favour of the plaintiff. Dillon J. held that the first purchaser was subject to a constructive trust to give effect to the original contract between the plaintiff and the company in liquidation. The second purchaser was similarly bound since it had purchased with notice of the contract. The rationale of the decision was that it would be a fraud on the part of the first purchaser to renege

---

[74] T. Bailey, [1983] Conv. 99 at p. 105.

[75] *ibid.* 105.

[76] See, P.T. Evans, [1989] Conv. 418 at p. 429, relying on the constructive trust case in *Lyus v. Prowsa Developments Ltd* [1982] 1 W.L.R. 1044, where the purchaser was bound having taken a conveyance of the property expressly subject to the interest of the constructive beneficiary. Compare, *The I.D.C. Group Ltd v. Clark* [1992] 1 EGLR 187; affirmed. (1992) 65 P. & C.R. 179, C.A., where no constructive trust was made out on the facts.

[77] Megarry & Wade, *The Law of Real Property*, (5th ed.) at p. 210.

[78] Gray, *Elements of Land Law*, (2nd ed.) at p. 367.

[79] *ibid.* 367–368.

[80] [1982] 1 W.L.R. 1044, approved by the Court of Appeal in *Ashburn Anstalt v. Arnold* [1989] Ch. 1, C.A. Compare, *The I.D.C. Group Ltd v. Clark* [1992] 1 EGLR 187; affirmed (1992) 65 P. & C.R. 179, C.A., where no special circumstances existed indicating that the transferee of the property undertook a new liability to give effect to the contractual provisions for the benefit of the estoppel claimant.

on the contract in favour of the plaintiff and for the second purchaser to rely upon the transfer of the land to it as confering upon it an absolute title freed from that contract. In *The I.D.C. Group Ltd v. Clark*,[81] Dillon J. put the matter succinctly[82]:

> "It is the conscience of the transferee which has to be affected and it has to be affected in a way which gives rise to an obligation to meet the legitimate expectations of the [claimant]".

It remains to be seen[83] to what extent constructive trust theory is utilised to bind inchoate estoppel rights against third parties.

(ii) The Equity in Its Crystallised Form

It is clear that, where the court decrees a proprietary interest of a recognised and established kind (*e.g.* by ordering a conveyance of the legal title or a grant of a life interest or right of way), the interest so created by the application of the estoppel doctrine will, according to its nature, be binding on third parties. Thus, "once the court has accepted the plea of estoppel, and decided how to 'satisfy the equity', it is reasonably clear whether the intention is simply to remove the personal prejudice of the sufferer, or to give him rights in the land which are at once capable of transfer and enforceable against third parties, in other words, to give him a real 'interest'".[84] Battersby, in an influential article,[85] suggests that the correct approach is to analyse the form of remedy awarded by the court in satisfaction of the inchoate equity. Thus, in relation to the grant of an easement in *Crabb v. Arun District Council*,[86] he states[87]:

> "The correct way for the defendants to implement the decision would be for them to execute a deed of grant in favour of the plaintiff, but until that was done the plaintiff had the benefit of the judgment and the order of the court is registrable under the Land Charges Act 1972. It may well be that, since the court declared that the plaintiff was entitled to an easement, he should be treated as already entitled to an equitable easement. If so, the interest would be registrable as a D(iii) land charge. If the title to the servient land were registered, the status of the easement, whether equitable by virtue of the court's declaration or legal after the execution of a deed of grant, would depend on whether such rights are overriding interests under the Land Registration Act."

At one extreme, the court, in the exercise of its discretionary jurisdiction, may do no more than is necessary to protect the occupation rights of the claimant by simply denying the legal owner's claim to possession. This was

---

[81] [1992] 1 EGLR 187; (affirmed) (1992) 65 P. & C. R. 179, C.A.
[82] *ibid.* 190.
[83] G. Battersby suggests that the *Lyus* principle can be applied in the context of unregistered as well as registered land, since "it depends on the overarching notion of a constructive trust", (1995) 58 M.L.R. 637 at p. 653, n. 80.
[84] A. Everton, (1976) 40 Conv. (N.S.) 209 at p. 220, n. 42.
[85] (1995) 58 M.L.R. 637.
[86] [1976] Ch. 179, C.A.
[87] *ibid.* 641.

considered to be the appropriate method of satisfying the equity in *Matharu v. Matharu*.[88] As a "possessory" remedy only, it does not involve the grant of any estate or interest in the land. As against third parties, therefore, it leaves the estoppel claimant in a precarious positon.[89] At the other end of the scale, the court may be persuaded to grant the estoppel claimant a full legal estate by ordering the landowner to convey the fee simple in satisfaction of the equity. This was the nature of the order made in *Dillwyn v. Lewellyn*[90] and the effect of the decision in *Re Basham (dec'd).*[91] Battersby argues[92] that such interests arising informally under the doctrine of proprietary estoppel fit satisfactorily into both the unregistered and registered systems of registration. He states[93]:

"... estoppel serves as a mechanism for the creation of the interest, a mechanism which, unlike the other methods of contract and grant, does not entail compliance with any formal requirements. However, once the interest has arisen, whether by court order or agreement between the parties satisfying the equity, the ordinary requirements of formality and registration become applicable. The court's order, or the parties' agreement, is registrable; if the order or agreement is to be implemented by the creation of the appropriate legal estate or interest, then the formal requirements for such creation (normally a deed) must be met and any registration requirements must also be complied with."

He takes as an example the case of *Pascoe v. Turner*,[94] where the Court of Appeal ordered the conveyance of the fee simple in the house in satisfaction of the claimant's estoppel equity. What would have been the position if the legal owner had sold the house to a third party prior to the court ruling? According to Battersby[95]:

"The defendant's inchoate rights have a sufficiently proprietary character (they may result in a proprietary interest) to be capable of binding a purchaser or other third party. In the case of unregistered land, the position will be governed by notice, but the defendant's continued presence in the plaintiff's house would amount to constructive notice. On the basis that the defenadnt's rights constitute an equity and not, as yet, a full equitable interest, it would seem that a purchaser of an equitable interest, *e.g.* an equitable mortgagee, would take free if without notice."

Battersby goes on to explain that, if the title were registered, the claimant's rights would constitute a minor interest requiring protection on the register but,

---

[88] (1994) 68 P. & C.R. 93, C.A. M. Welstead, [1995] Conv. 61. See also, *Duke of Beaufort v. Patrick* (1853) 17 Beav. 60; 51 E.R. 954.
[89] See the discussion in Chap. 5, pp. 82–84.
[90] (1862) 4 De G. F. & J. 517; 45 E.R. 1285. See also, *Pascoe v. Turner* [1979] 1 W.L.R. 431, C.A. For a full exposition of the range of remedies, see Chap. 5, pp. 82–99.
[91] [1986] 1 W.L.R. 1498.
[92] See, (1995) 58 M.L.R. 637.
[93] *ibid.* 652.
[94] [1979] 1 W.L.R. 431, C.A.
[95] *ibid.* 642.

since she is in actual occupation of the house, she has an overriding interest within section 70(1)(g) of the Land Registration Act 1925. Once the court makes its order in satisfaction of the equity, however, the position would alter. Now, the claimant's equity is replaced by a court order requiring the legal owner to execute a conveyance of the legal estate. Thus, Battersby states[96]:

> "If the land were regsitered, the plaintiff would execute a transfer in favour of the defendant and she would take steps to become the registered proprietor in his place. Prior to the execution of the conveyance, or the registration of the defendant as proprietor, the Court's judgment will operate in equity in favour of the defendant. What if the plaintiff at that stage were to sell his house? In the case of unregistered land, the Court's order is registrable under section 6 of the Land Charges Act 1972, and failure to register will render it void against a purchaser for value of an interest in the land. In the case of registered land, we have the familiar position that the defendant's rights constitute a minor interest, but her occupation of the house makes them an overriding interest."

Instead of awarding the claimant the fee simple, the court may satisfy the equity by granting a beneficial interest under a trust as in *Hussey v. Palmer.*[97] In *Inwards v. Baker,*[98] on the other hand, the Court of Appeal, although faced with a similar problem to that in *Dillwyn,* awarded the son a *de facto* life interest, presumably[99] operating outside the provisions of the Settled Land Act 1925.[1] By contrast, in *Dodsworth v. Dodsworth,*[2] the Court of Appeal held that the proper way to satisfy the equity was to declare that possession could only be obtained against the estoppel claimants if they were repaid their outlay on improvements they had made to the bungalow. According to Baughen,[3] this represents the correct approach when estoppel rights bind third parties: "the 'possessory' remedy granted in *Inwards v. Baker* sanctions the creation of a new form of property right standing outside the recognised categories of interests and estates in land. This runs contrary not only to section 4(1) of the Law of Property Act 1925 but also to the approach of the House of Lords in *National Provincial Bank v. Ainsworth* in denying proprietary effect to personal rights, even though these could be protected by equitable remedies in disputes between the original parties. It also blurs the distinction between contractual

---

[96] *ibid.* 643.
[97] [1972] 1 W.L.R. 1286 at 1291, C.A., *per* Lord Denning M.R. and Phillimore L.J.
[98] [1965] 2 Q.B. 29, C.A.
[99] In *Binions v. Evans* [1972] Ch. 359, C.A., Lord Denning M.R. suggested that the Settled Land Act 1925 had no application because the estate is not necessarily limited in trust for persons by way of succession in this type of case. Contrast, *Bannister v. Bannister* [1948] 2 All E.R. 133, C.A. and *Ungurian v. Lesnoff* [1990] Ch. 206 at 224–226, *per* Vinelott J. See, S. Moriarty, (1984) 100 L.Q.R. 376 at pp. 408–411.
[1] The fact that such a life interest may make the property settled land and give much more extensive rights than the parties contemplated was alluded to in *Dodsworth v. Dodsworth* (1973) 228 EG 115, C.A. See also, *Griffiths v. Williams* (1978) 248 EG 947, C.A., where the problem was avoided by the parties consenting to an order granting the claimant (a daughter) a lease determinable on her death at a nominal rent. This had the effect of giving her a right of occupation for life but without attracting the statutory powers under the Settled Land Act 1925.
[2] (1973) 228 EG 115, C.A.
[3] S. Baughen, (1994) 14 L.S. 147.

licence and estoppel rights which has become critical after the *dicta* in *Arnold v. Ashburn-Anstalt*".[4]

A similar difficulty arises in the context of a court-ordered occupational licence[5] which is granted to the claimant in satisfaction of the equity. In this connection, it now seems settled[6] that a contractual licence does not give rise to any estate or interest in land but merely creates personal rights between the contracting parties. A third party will be bound by such a licence only in exceptional circumstances where the court is prepared to impose a constructive trust on the ground that the third party's conscience is affected.[7] Assuming, therefore, that occupational licences are only personal under the general law, is an estoppel-based licence to be treated in a different way? One solution is to say that the court has no jurisdiction to declare licences created by estoppel as proprietary when similar rights created expressly have only personal effect.[8] This would then accord with the general principle that the court should not sanction the creation of new forms of property rights which remain unrecognised under the general law. Thus, in the context of unregistered land, a court-ordered occupational licence may be capable of binding a purchaser who has actual[9] (or constructive[10]) notice of the circumstances giving rise to the equity. In relation to registered land, constructive trust theory may bind the third party whose conscience is affected by the estoppel.

(D) Can the Equity Be Asserted By a Third Party?

This is an interesting question on which there is little authority. In *Fryer v. Brook*[11] Oliver L.J. suggested that an equity raised by a proprietary estoppel was merely a personal interest similar to the personal right of occupation created by a statutory tenancy. In *Jones (A.E.) v. Jones (A.F.)*,[12] Lord Denning M.R. concluded that the estoppel claimant had an equity of a possessory nature entitling him to remain in the house but that this would not extend to the claimant's wife.[13] On the other hand, in *E.R. Investments Ltd v. High*,[14] Lord Denning M.R. also had occasion to remark that the equity in that case could only be satisfied by allowing the claimant *and his successors in title* to have access over the yard so long as the block of flats had its foundations in his

---

[4] *ibid.* 153–154.
[5] See, *e.g. Greasley v. Cooke* [1980] 1 W.L.R. 1306, C.A., where the court declared that the claimant was entitled to occupy the house rent-free for so long as she wished to stay there. See also, *Maharaj v. Chand* [1986] A.C. 898, P.C., where the claimant (a *de facto* wife) was held as against the legal owner to have permission to reside permanently in the house on the basis that her children might be with her for as long as they needed a home.
[6] *Ashburn Anstalt v. Arnold* [1989] Ch. 1, C.A.
[7] *Ashburn Anstalt v. Arnold* [1989] Ch. 1, 25 at 27, C.A., *per* Fox L.J.
[8] G. Battersby, [1991] Conv. 36. See, *Maharaj v. Chand* [1986] A.C. 898, P.C., where Sir Robin Cooke noted that the occupational licence granted to the defendant was merely a personal right not amounting to a property interest diminishing the rights of the plaintiff's landlord and mortgagee: *ibid.* 112.
[9] See, *E.R. Ives Investments Ltd v. High* [1967] 2 Q.B. 379.
[10] See, *The Duke of Beaufort v. Patrick* (1853) 17 Beav. 60 at 78; 51 E.R. 954 at 961.
[11] [1984] L.S. Gaz. R. 2856, C.A.
[12] [1977] 1 W.L.R. 438, C.A.
[13] *ibid.* 443.
[14] [1967] 2 Q.B. 379, C.A.

land.[15] Gray[16] cites Australian caselaw[17] as clearly establishing the principle that the inchoate equity may be asserted by the claimant's successor in title.

As to the possible assignment of the benefit of an estoppel equity, the rules governing the annexation of the benefit of easements and restrictive covenants may indicate possible lines of development.[18]

(E) Revocation of the Equity

In what circumstances may the legal owner successfully re-apply for possession of the property, thereby revoking the claimant's court-ordered possessory licence? In *Williams v. Staite*,[19] the defendants (in a county court action in 1972) were held to have an equitable licence to occupy their cottage for life pursuant to a family arrangement made in 1960. The cottage, together with the adjoining cottage and paddock, was then sold to the plaintiff. The defendants created difficulties in relation to the plaintiff's occupation of the adjoining cottage and his use of the paddock, and (after two years) the plaintiff commenced an action for possession of the defendants' cottage. The Court of Appeal held that the defendants' established equitable licence to ocupy the cottage for life was not determined by their subsequent conduct. According to Lord Denning M.R., only in an extreme case might an equitable licence be revoked. Similarly, Goff L.J. concluded that excessive user or bad behaviour towards the legal owner could not bring the equity, once established by a decision binding on the legal owner, to an end or forfeit it. The appropriate remedy in such cases is an action for nuisance, trespass or an injunction restrainig the improper conduct. However, Goff L.J. also alluded[20] to the possibility that the equity may be in its nature for a limited period only or determinable upon a condition certain. In such a case, the court would need to see whether, in the events which had happened, the equity had determined or it had expired or been determined by the happening of the condition.

It has been suggested[21] that the correct approach in such cases is to consider the type of remedial order made by the court. If the order constitutes a final resolution of the dispute (*e.g.* by the grant of an estate in land), any future relationship between the parties relating to their former dispute should be governed by the incidents of that estate (whether freehold or leasehold). But where the court orders an occupational licence in favour of the applicant, the resolution of the parties' dispute may not be intended to be final. Thus, in *Hardwick v. Johnson*[22] Lord Denning M.R. awarded an estoppel licence to a deserted wife and her child to live in the house on payment of £7 per week. His Lordship went on to suggest that, had there been no grandchild and the wife had

---

[15] *ibid.* 395.

[16] Gray, *Elements of Land Law*, (2nd ed.) at p. 362.

[17] In particular, *Hamilton v. Geraghty* (1901) 1 S.R.N.S.W. (Eq.) 81 at 89 and *Cameron v. Murdoch* [1983] W.A.R. 321 at 360; (affirmed) (1986) 63 A.L.R. 575 at 595.

[18] See, F.R. Crane, (1967) 31 Conv. (NS) 332, 341. See also, *Jones (A.E.) v. Jones (F.W.)* [1977] 1 W.L.R. 438, C.A.

[19] [1979] 1 Ch. 291, C.A. See also, M.P. Thompson, [1986] Conv. 406 at pp. 412–414.

[20] *ibid.* 300.

[21] M.P. Thompson, [1986] Conv. 406 at p. 413.

[22] [1978] 1 W.L.R. 683, C.A. See also, *McGill v. S.* [1979] E.R. 283 at 293.

formed an association with another man in the house, the legal owner (the wife's mother in law) could have revoked her licence. But in the absence of any divorce (or judicial separation) and so long as she paid the £7 a week, the wife's licence could not be revoked, at least until some event occurred which would justify bringing it to an end.

8. ESTOPPEL AND COHABITEES

(A) Introduction

Although English courts have accepted that the principles underlying the law of proprietary estoppel may provide useful guidance in resolving property disputes between cohabitees,[1] it is evident that decisions in this field continue to be based predominantly on conventional principles requiring the establishment of an express or inferred common intention to support the imposition of a constructive trust. In *Stokes v. Anderson*,[2] for example, Nourse L.J. considered[3] that the two doctrines had not yet been assimilated and that the principles of *Gissing v. Gissing*[4] still applied.

In *Lloyds Bank plc v. Rosset*,[5] Lord Bridge[6] sought to clarify the basis upon which a non-owning cohabitee may acquire a beneficial interest in property which is in the sole legal ownership of his or her partner.[7] Essentially, two hurdles have to be overcome in order for a claimant to attract beneficial entitlement under a constructive trust. First, there must have been, at any time prior to the acquisition of the property (or exceptionally at some later date), an agreement, arrangement or understanding between the parties that the property was to be shared beneficially. Such an agreement or arrangement is based on evidence of express discussions between the parties, however imperfectly remembered and however imprecise their terms may have been.[8] Secondly, assuming that the necessary express common intention is established, the non-owning partner must also show that he or she has acted to his or her detriment or significantly altered his or her position in reliance on the agreement, arrangement, etc, in order to give rise to a constructive trust.

Alternatively, in the absence of any express discussions between the parties

---

[1] See, *e.g. Grant v. Edwards* [1986] Ch. 638 at 656, C.A., where Sir Nicholas Browne-Wilkinson V.-C. had occasion to remark that the principles underlying the law of proprietary estoppel were "closely akin" to those laid down for the establishment of a constructive trust: "In both, the claimant must to the knowledge of the legal owner have acted in the belief that the claimant has or will obtain an interest in the property. In both, the claimant must have acted to his or her detriment in reliance on such belief. In both, equity acts on the conscience of the legal owner to prevent him from acting in an unconscionable manner by defeating the common intention. The two principles have been developed separately without cross-fertilisation between them: but they rest on the same foundation and have on all other matters reached the same conclusions". See also, *Lloyds Bank plc v. Rosset* [1989] Ch. 350 at 387, C.A., *per* Nicholls L.J. and Chap. 1, pp. 10–16.
[2] [1991] 1 FLR 391, C.A.
[3] *ibid.* 399.
[4] [1971] A.C. 886, H.L.
[5] [1991] 1 A.C. 107, H.L.
[6] *ibid.* 132–133.
[7] For a good summary of what is required to support a constructive trust in this context, see, T. Lawson-Cruttenden and A. Odutola, [1995] Fam. Law 560.
[8] See, *e.g. Hammond v. Mitchell* [1991] 1 W.L.R. 1127.

giving rise to a common intention to share beneficially, the court is entitled to rely entirely on the conduct of the parties both as the basis from which to *infer* a common intention to share the property beneficially and as the conduct relied on to give rise to a constructive trust. In this latter case, however, it appears that only direct financial contributions to the purchase price of the property will suffice.[9] This has led one academic writer to comment that "a woman's place is often still in the home, but if she stays there, she will acquire no interest in it".[10]

It is evident from the foregoing that several points of similarity exist between constructive trust theory and proprietary estoppel doctrine.[11] First, the requirement of a common intention bears a close affinity to the pre-condition of a reasonable belief on the part of the estoppel claimant, encouraged or acquiesced in by the legal owner, that he or she has or will acquire an interest in the latter's property. Secondly, the requirement of detrimental reliance is common to both forms of doctrine.[12] Thirdly, both doctrines take account of the parties expectations (proceeding from the common intention or reasonable belief) in the award of a remedy. It has been suggested,[13] however, that, far from founding successful claims where constructive trust theory does not, proprietary estoppel doctrine may operate, in certain circumstances, to the claimant's disadvantage. This is because, unlike constructive trust cases where the courts are sometimes prepared to "invent" the requisite common intention,[14] estoppel doctrine insists upon a clear finding of assurance and reliance to found an equity in the claimant's favour. Despite this potential difficulty, estoppel doctrine can be viewed as a mechansim for enlarging the rights of claimants whose contribution to the quasi-matrimonial home consists solely of a non-financial, domestic contribution to the family's welfare over a number of years. Constructive trust theory currently denies such claimants equitable relief, and this is well-illustrated in the leading case of *Burns v. Burns*,[15] where a female cohabitee failed in her attempt to claim a beneficial share in the property since she had made no direct, or indirect, contributions to the purchase price of the house (which was in the male partner's sole name), despite the parties having lived together for 19 years and the claimant bearing their two children. Essentially, her claim rested on her bringing up the children and performing domestic duties during the period in question. In addition, she had used her earnings to contribute towards housekeeping expenses, and to buy fixtures and fittings and consumer durables (such as a washing machine) for the house. She

---

[9] But see the recent Court of Appeal decision in *Midland Bank plc v. Cooke* [1995] 4 All E.R. 562, C.A., where it was held that, where a partner in a matrimonial home without legal title had established an equitable interest through direct contribution, the court would assess (in the absence of express evidence of intention) the proportions the parties were to be assumed to have intended for their beneficial ownership by undertaking a survey of the whole course of dealing between the parties relevant to their ownership and occupation of the property and their sharing of its burdens and advantages and would take into consideration all conduct which threw light on the question what shares were intended. In particular, the court was not bound to deal with the matter on the strict basis of the trust resulting from the cash contributions to the purchase price.

[10] J. Eekelaar, [1987] Conv. 93.

[11] See further, Chap. 1, pp. 10–16.

[12] See *Grant v. Edwards* [1986] Chap. 638 at 665–657, *per* Sir Nicholas Browne-Wilkinson V.-C.

[13] S. Gardner, (1993) L.Q.R. 263 at p. 268.

[14] See *Grant v. Edwards* [1986] Ch. 638, C.A. and *Eves v. Eves* [1975] 1 W.L.R. 1338, C.A., (the so-called "excuse" cases).

[15] [1984] Ch. 317, C.A.

also decorated the interior of the house. None of these domestic activities was held sufficient to support a constructive trust.

The upshot of this (and other English decisions) is that English courts are not prepared to impute a common intention that a non-legal owner is to have a beneficial interest in property (solely owned by the other partner) merely from the fact that she had performed spousal services, in the absence of an express agreement/declaration regarding the beneficial interest in the property or, alternatively, direct financial contributions either to the purchase price or mortgage instalments.

There is a widely held view,[16] however, that, given the realities of contemporary family life, the property interests of parties who have been cohabiting together outside marriage should not turn on an elusive and often vain search for indication of a common intention in relation to the property to support a constructive trust. Indeed, much of the difficulty in this branch of the law arises from the reality that the parties in many *de facto* relationships never, in fact, turn their minds to the possibility of the breakdown of their relationship and consequential division of the property assets.

As an alternative to a claim based on a constructive (or resulting) trust, it may be possible to argue that the legal owner is estopped from denying the claimant's belief that he or she has or would be given a proprietary interest in the property. In fact, there are several English decisions in the context of property rights of unmarried couples where proprietary estoppel has been invoked to award the claimant an equity in the house. It is to these that we now turn.

(B) English Caselaw[17]

The leading case is *Pascoe v. Turner*,[18] where the legal owner was ordered to execute a conveyance of the house in favour of the female claimant in order to satisfy her estoppel equity. The plaintiff (a business man) and the defendant (a widow with an invalidity pension and a modest amount of capital) became acquainted in 1961. In 1963, she moved into the plaintiff's house as his housekeeper. The following year, they began to live together as man and wife. In 1965, the plaintiff purchased another house and the parties continued to live there in unmarried union. He gave her a housekeeping allowance but she used her own money to buy clothes. She collected some rents for him and was allowed to keep part of them to supplement the housekeeping allowance. In 1973, the plaintiff began an affair with another woman. The plaintiff left the house but reassured the defendant that the property was hers and everything in it. The defendant stayed on in the house and, in reliance upon the plaintiff's declaration that he had given her the house and its contents, she spent money (approximately £230) on redecorations, improvements and repairs. The

---

[16] See, *e.g.* S. Gardner, (1991) 54 M.L.R. 126 and (1993) 109 L.Q.R. 263; M.P. Thompson [1990] Conv. 314; D.J. Hayton, [1990] 106 L.Q.R. 87 at pp. 96–97; J. Eekelaar, [1987] Conv. 93.

[17] See, generally, S.J. Burridge, [1982] C.L.J. 290 at pp. 301–316.

[18] [1979] 1 W.L.R. 431, C.A. See, B. Sufrin, (1979) 42 M.L.R. 574. In *Thomas v. Thomas* [1956] N.Z.L.R. 785, a deserted wife was given the whole beneficial ownership of the matrimonial home which had been in joint names.

plaintiff knew that she was improving what she thought to be her property. No formal transfer of the house into the defendant's name was ever executed. In 1976, the plaintiff gave the defendant two months' notice to determine her licence to occupy the house.

The Court of Appeal had no difficulty in rejecting the plaintiff's action for possession. Although no constructive trust could be inferred from the circumstances,[19] the plaintiff's encouragement or acquiescence in the defendant improving the house in the belief that the property belonged to her gave rise to an estoppel and the "minimum equity"[20] to do justice to the defendant was to compel him to execute a conveyance of the property to the defendant. In effect, the Court ordered the plaintiff's imperfect gift to be perfected. It should be noted, however, that the form of relief granted was determined by a number of factors peculiar to the facts of the case.[21] The decision, it is submitted, must be treated as somewhat exceptional. As one academic writer has remarked[22]:

"It is difficult, reading the judgment, to resist the conclusion that in *Pascoe v. Turner* the Court of Appeal was acting like a judge of the Family Division dividing the family's assets after a divorce. She was a poor widow in her mid-fifties, he was comparatively wealthy and had other property, so why not let her have the house? . . . The obligation in regard to the equity raised by the estoppel could surely have been satisfied by a less drastic solution than transferring to the plaintiff a £16,000 house in fee simple in recompense for an expenditure of a few hundred pounds."

More usually, the court is likely to make some form of lesser order (*e.g.* a licence to occupy for life or monetary compensation). In *Greasley v. Cooke*,[23] for example, the female claimant was held entitled to occupy the house rent-free for the rest of her life. Here, the claimant had worked initially as a living-in maid to the legal owner, a widower with three sons and a daughter. From 1946, she cohabited in the house with one of his sons until his death in 1975. After the owner's death in 1948, she continued to look after the house and family and, in particular, cared for the daughter who (from 1947 until her death in 1975) was mentaly ill. She had received no payment for her services after the death of the owner in 1948 and had not asked for payment because she had been encouraged by members of the family to believe that that she could regard the property as her home for the rest of her life. The Court of Appeal, in acknowledging an equity in her favour, held that, once it was shown that she had relied on the assurances given to her, the burden of proving that she acted to her detriment in staying on to look after the house and family without payment did not rest on her.[24] The burden of proof rested on the owners to show that she had not acted to her detriment by staying on in the house. In the absence of such proof, it was to be presumed that she had acted to her detriment. It is to be observed also that,

---

[19] *ibid.* 435. The defendant's contribution to the acquisition of the house was insufficient to establish a trust.

[20] *ibid.* 438.

[21] See further Chap. 5, pp. 86–87.

[22] B. Sufrin, (1979) 42 M.L.R. 574 at pp. 577–578.

[23] [1980] 1 W.L.R. 1306, C.A.

[24] The county court judge had come to the opposite conclusion holding that the burden of proof that the claimant had acted to her detriment as a result of her belief rested on her.

unlike the claimant in *Pascoe*, she had not incurred any expenditure on the house.[25] Indeed, none of her acts giving rise to the estoppel-based equity were referable to the property. On this point, Lord Denning M.R. concluded[26]:

> "It so happens that in many of these cases of proprietary estoppel there has been expenditure of money. But that is not a necessary element... It is sufficient if the party, to whom the assurance is given, acts on the faith of it—in such circumstances that it would be unjust and inequitable for the party making the assurance to go back on it... Applying those principles here it can be seen that the assurances given by Kenneth and Hedley to Doris Cooke—leading her to believe that she would be allowed to stay in the house as long as she wished—raised an equity in her favour. There was no need for her to prove that she acted on the faith of those assurances. It is to be presumed that she did so. There is no need for her to prove that she acted to her detriment or to her prejudice. Suffice it that she stayed on in the house—looking after Kenneth and Clarice—when otherwise she might have left and got a job elsewhere."

By contrast, Dunn L.J. had no doubt that for proprietary estoppel to arise the person claiming must have incurred expenditure or otherwise have prejudiced himself or acted to his detriment[27] and subsequent caselaw has confirmed this orthodox view.[28] The decision in *Greasley* has been described as appearing to stretch the doctrine of proprietary estoppel to its utmost limits[29] not least because it seems do away with the necessity of showing expenditure or acting to one's detriment in order to found a proprietary estoppel. Moreover, it seems that the acts giving rise to the estoppel need bear no relation to the property concerned at all.

In *Coombes v. Smith*,[30] Mr Jonathan Parker Q.C. (sitting as a deputy judge of the High Court) had occasion to consider Lord Denning M.R.'s observations in *Greasley*. In *Coombes*, the plaintiff and defendant were both married to other partners when they became lovers. The defendant told the plaintiff that he wished them to live together and they discussed having a child. The defendant bought a house and, when the plaintiff became pregnant by the defendant, she left her husband and moved into the house, giving up her job two months before the birth of the child. The defendant did not move in with the plaintiff but visited her regularly, paid all bills including the mortgage instalments and gave the plaintiff an allowance for herself and the child. This arrangement continued when the defendant bought another house (nearer his work) into which the plaintiff moved with the child. The plaintiff redecorated the house several times, installed decorative beams and improved the garden. She twice asked the defendant if he would put the house into their joint names, but he refused, though during the course of their relationship, he assured her that he would

---

[25] See also, *Re Basham (dec'd)* [1986] 1 W.L.R. 1498.
[26] *ibid.* 1311–1312.
[27] *ibid.* 1313–1314.
[28] See, *Watts & Ready v. Storey* [1984] 134 New L.J. 631 and *Coombes v. Smith* [1986] 1 W.L.R. 808 at 818.
[29] R.E. Annand, [1981] Conv. 154. See also, G. Woodman, (1981) 44 M.L.R. 461.
[30] [1986] 1 W.L.R. 808. See also, *Re Basham, (dec'd)* [1986] 1 W.L.R. 1498 at 1506–1507, where Mr. Edward Nugee Q.C. applied the *Greasley* formula on the burden of proof.

always provide for her and that she would "always have a roof over her head". After 10 years the relationship broke down. The plaintiff claimed, on the basis *inter alia* of proprietary estoppel, that the property should be conveyed to her absolutely or, alternatively, that she was entitled to occupy it for life. Her claimed, however, was dismissed—two of the requisite elements[31] to give rise to an equity in her favour[32] were lacking, namely, a mistaken belief as to her legal rights and detriment.

On the evidence, the plaintiff had not held a mistaken belief that she would have the right to remain indefinitely against the defendant's wishes, since they had not discussed what was to happen if their relationship broke down. A belief that the defendant would always provide a roof over her head was not sufficient. In the words of the deputy judge[33]:

> "First, did the plaintiff hold a mistaken belief as to her legal rights? In the context of the facts of the instant case . . . the mistaken belief would have to be a belief on the part of the plaintiff that she had a legal right to occupy 33, Stanway Road which would entitle her to remain there notwithstanding that her relationship with the defendant had come to an end and that the defendant wished her to leave. In my judgment, no such mistaken belief has been established . . . a belief that the defendant would always provide her with a roof over her head is, to my mind, something quite different from a belief that she had a legal right to remain there against his wishes. Moreover, all the statements relied upon by the plaintiff were made by the defendant while his relationship with the plaintiff was continuing. There is no evidence before me of any discussion at all between the plaintiff and the defendant as to what should happen in the event of their relationship breaking down and of the defendant choosing to live with another woman".

The decision in *Pascoe v. Turner*,[34] referred to earlier, was distinguished on a number of grounds. First, there were in *Coombes* no words of gift. The defendant never said, as did the plaintiff in *Pascoe*, "The house is yours and everything in it", believing such a statement would clearly give rise to a mistake as to legal rights. Secondly, in *Pascoe* the court found that the plaintiff (as donor) stood by knowingly while the defendant improved the property thinking it was hers. No comparable finding was made in the *Coombes* decision. Thirdly, the representation relied on as the basis of proprietary estoppel in *Pascoe* was made after the relationship between the parties had finally come to an end (*i.e.* at a time when the defendant no longer had any expectation that she and the plaintiff would continue to live together in the property), whereas in *Coombes* the plaintiff continued to hold the expectation that the defendant would join her at the property.

---

[31] *i.e.* the five elements listed by Fry J. in *Willmott v. Barber* (1880) 15 Ch.D. 96 at 105–106, quoted by Scarman L.J. in *Crabb v. Arun District Council* [1976] Ch. 179 at 194–195, C.A. See further, Chap. 6, pp. 117–118.

[32] The plaintiff's action was dismissed on the defendant's undertaking to provide accommodation at the house for the plaintiff and the child until the child was 17.

[33] *ibid*. 818.

[34] [1979] 1 W.L.R. 431, C.A.

Quite apart from the lack of a mistaken belief in her legal rights, the plaintiff was also held not to have acted to her detriment in becoming pregnant, leaving her husband, looking after the house and child or in not looking for a job. It was argued, on behalf of the plaintiff, applying *Greasley v. Cooke*,[35] that once the plaintiff proves that she changed her position in reliance on the alleged assurances, the onus shifts to the defendant to prove the absence of detriment. This submission was rejected by the deputy judge as being based on a misreading of the judgments in *Greasley*. The statement of Lord Denning M.R. that "there is no need for [the plaintiff] to prove that she acted to her detriment or to her prejudice" was not to be read out of context. The statement was to be taken to mean that, where, following assurances made by the other party, the claimant has adopted a course of conduct which is prejudicial or otherwise detrimental to her, there is a rebuttable presumption that she adopted that course of conduct in reliance on the assurances. Such an interpretation is, indeed, consistent with earlier authority[36] and the judgment of Waller and Dunn L.JJ. in the *Greasley* case.

The question as to where the burden of proof should lie in such cases was further considered in *Wayling v. Jones*.[37] In this case, the plaintiff met the deceased in 1967 and they started to live together in a homosexual relationship in 1971 until the deceased's death in 1987. The plaintiff acted throughout this time as the deceased's companion and chauffeur and gave substantial help in running the deceased's business. In return for his services, the plaintiff received pocket-money, living and clothing expenses and the express promise that he would inherit the business. The deceased made several wills leaving a cafe and an hotel, the Glen-y-Mor Hotel, Aberystwyth, to the plaintiff. In 1985, this hotel was sold and subsequently the deceased bought the Royal Hotel, Barmouth, telling the plaintiff that it was bought for the plaintiff to run and to inherit after his death. The deceased had told the plaintiff that he would alter his will to substitute the Royal Hotel for the Glen-y-Mor hotel but this was never done. The plaintiff claimed that he was entitled to the proceeds of sale of the Royal Hotel (which was subsequently also sold) on the principle *inter alia* of proprietary estoppel. The Court of Appeal, upholding his claim, held that the plaintiff had relied on the promises made by the deceased to leave him the hotel under his will, to the plaintiff's detriment (*i.e.* by not asking for, or receiving, higher wages and continuing to serve the deceased until his death). Moreover, once the plaintiff had shown that the promises were made, and that the plaintiff's conduct was such that inducement could be inferred, the burden of proof shifted to the defendants (the executors of the deceased's will) to establish that the plaintiff did not rely on those promises. On the facts, the defendants had not discharged that burden (*i.e.* of showing that the plaintiff did not rely on the

---

[35] [1980] 1 W.L.R. 1306, C.A.

[36] In all previous cases of proprietary estoppel, some expenditure or detrimental action has been shown. For example, in *Pascoe v. Turner* [1979] 1 W.L.R. 431, C.A., the claimant spent £230 on improving the property and in *Crabb v. Arun District Council* [1976] Ch. 179, C.A., the plaintiff had sold part of his land in the belief that the defendant had granted him a right of access to the remaining part.

[37] (1995) 69 P. & C.R. 170, C.A. The case was actually decided in July 1993. See further, C.J. Davis, [1995] Conv. 409. See also, *Lim Teng Huan v. Ang Swee Chuan* [1992] 1 W.L.R. 113, P.C., where it was held that reliance might be established by an "inevitable" inference that could be drawn from the facts. See further, Chap. 3, pp. 44–47.

promises) and, accordingly, the plaintiff was held entitled to the proceeds of
sale of the hotel plus interest. Balcombe L.J., who gave the leading judgment of
the Court, relied on *Greasley* and *dicta* by Browne-Wilkinson V.-C. in *Grant v.
Edwards*[38] for the above proposition. It has been commented[39] that this
formulation may be unduly restrictive, having "similarities with the requirement for part performance that the acts done themselves have to indicate on a
balance of probabilities that they have been done in reliance on a contract".[40]

The five elements propounded by Fry J. in *Willmott v. Barber*,[41] requisite to
establish a proprietary estoppel claim, were successfully invoked in the recent
Court of Appeal decision in *Matharu v. Matharu*.[42] The facts may briefly be
summarised as follows. In 1968, the plaintiff bought a property which became
the matrimonial home of the defendant and the plaintiff's son, after their
marriage in 1971. During the course of the marriage, the defendant's husband
made extensive improvements to the property at his own expense. In 1988, the
marriage broke down, and in 1990 the defendant obtained an order excluding
the husband from the house. The husband died in 1991. Later that year, the
plaintiff emigrated to Canada but returned the following year. On his return, the
plaintiff demanded that the defendant vacate the house but she refused claiming
an equity based on proprietary estoppel. The majority[43] of the Court of Appeal,
applying *Willmott v. Barber*,[44] held that, in order to raise a proprietary estoppel,
the claimant needed to show five elements, namely:

(1)   that she had made a mistake as to her legal rights;
(2)   that she had expended money or done some act on that mistaken
belief;
(3)   the possessor of the legal right knew of the existence of his legal right
which was inconsistent with the equity;
(4)   the possessor of the legal right knew of the mistaken belief of the
person now claiming the equity; and
(5)   the possessor of the legal right encouraged the expenditure by the
person now claiming the equity either directly or by abstaining from
asserting his legal right.

On the facts, the defendant had satisfied each of those requirements and,
accordingly, the defendant's equity was held to defeat the plaintiff's claim for
possession. The defendant, however, was not awarded a beneficial interest in
the property but merely a licence for her to remain in the property for life or for
such shorter period as she wished.[45] The application of Fry J.'s five *probanda*
promulgated in *Willmott v. Barber*[46] may be considered somewhat surprising

[38] [1986] Ch. 638 at 657, C.A.
[39] C.J. Davis, [1995] Conv. 409 at pp. 411–412.
[40] *ibid.* 412.
[41] (1880) 15 Ch.D. 96 at 105–106.
[42] (1994) 68 P. & C.R. 93, C.A. See, M. Welstead, [1995] Conv. 61 and G. Battersby, (1995) 7
C.F.L.Q. 59–65.
[43] Roch and Hirst L.JJ., Dillon L.J. dissenting.
[44] (1880) 15 Ch.D. 96.
[45] For a discussion of the relief granted in this case, see further Chap. 5, pp. 82–84.
[46] (1880) 15 Ch.D. 96 at 105–106.

since it has been generally accepted that these rigid criteria are no longer of universal application.[47] Nevertheless, Roch L.J., who gave the majority judgment, proceeded to apply these criteria in a fairly liberal fashion. As Battersby has commented,[48] the court's approach "was to set out the five *probanda* and then attempt, artificially, to force the facts into the straitjacket created by Fry J." The better view, it is submitted, is that this was not a case of unilateral mistake (to which Fry J.'s formulation is relevant), but rather a case of common expectation in that both parties (the plaintiff and his son) shared an assumption that the latter and his family would be allowed to live in the property and, in reliance on that assumption, the son made considerable improvements to the house at his own expense with the knowledge of his father, the plaintiff. On this basis, it has been suggested[49] that the broader approach established by Oliver J. in *Taylor Fashions Ltd v. Liverpool Victoria Trustees Co Ltd*[50] should have been applied, rendering it unconscionable, as between the plaintiff and his son, for the former to obtain possession of the improved house.

It is unclear to what extent a claim by a cohabitee against the deceased's estate will fail if there are no specific assets which can be identified in relation to the alleged estoppel. In *Layton v. Martin*[51] the lack of specificity of the property was held to be fatal. Here, the plaintiff had met the deceased in 1967 and had become his mistress. She was 29 and unmarried. He was a married man, aged 50, whose wife was in poor health. By a letter, written in 1975, the deceased asked the plaintiff to come and live with him offering "what emotional security I can give, plus financial security during my life and financial security after my death". He implied and the plaintiff understood that the deceased would marry her after his wife died. She provided wifely services and was paid a salary plus an amount for housekeeping. In 1977, the deceased's wife died but he did not, in the event, marry the plaintiff. He made some provision for her in his wills, the last being in 1979 by way of a legacy of £15,000 with provisions relating to her continued residence with him until his death. Subsequently, the deceased cut the plaintiff out of his will and gave her a written notice of dismissal in 1980. They parted amicably and kept in touch until the deceased's death in 1982. In the following year, the plaintiff made a claim for financial provision based on the contents of the 1975 letter contending *inter alia* that, under the doctrine of proprietary estoppel, equity would subject the estate to such beneficial interest in her favour and would give effect to the representation on which she relied. Scott J. held, on this point, that the estoppel doctrine was wholly inappropriate since the deceased's representations did not relate to any specific assets. A mere promise of "financial security" did not suffice[52]. He said[53]:

---

[47] See, *e.g.* the judgment of Oliver J. in *Taylor Fashions Ltd v. Liverpool Victoria Trustees Co. Ltd* [1982] Q.B. 133; *Amalgamated Investment & Property Co Ltd v. Texas Commerce International Bank Ltd* [1982] Q.B. 84 and *Re Basham (dec'd)* [1986] 1 W.L.R. 1498. See further, Chap. 6, pp. 124–127 and Chap. 10.
[48] G. Battersby, (1995) 7 C.F.L.Q. 59 at p. 61.
[49] G. Battersby, (1995) 7 C.F.L.Q. 59 at p. 62.
[50] [1982] Q.B. 133. See further, Chap. 6, pp. 124–127 and Chap. 10.
[51] [1986] 2 FLR 227.
[52] It was intimated, however, that, if the plaintiff had continued to live with the deceased until his death, she would have been entitled to claim under the Inheritance (Provision for Family and Dependants) Act 1975: *ibid.* 240.
[53] *ibid.* 238–239.

"The proprietary estoppel line of cases are concerned with the question whether an owner of property can, by insisting on his strict legal rights therein, defeat an expectation of interest in that property, it being an expectation which he has raised by his conduct and which has been relied on by the claimant. The question does not arise otherwise than in connection with some asset in respect of which it has been represented, or is alleged to have been represented, that the claimant is to have some interest... The present case does not raise that question. A representation that 'financial security' would be provided by the deceased to the plaintiff, and on which I will assume she acted, is not a representation that she is to have some equitable or legal interest in any particular asset or assets."

A similar approach was canvassed in *Philip Lowe (Chinese Restaurant) Ltd v. Sau Man Lee*,[54] where May L.J. doubted whether any representation as to what would happen upon the legal owner's death (or what would be in his will) could be construed as one involving an intention that there should be a present acquisition of that future right by the representee. However, he found it unnecessary to decide the point.

By contrast, in *Re Basham (dec'd)*,[55] Mr Edward Nugee Q.C. (sitting as a High Court judge) held that the principle of proprietary estoppel was not limited to acts done in reliance on a belief relating to an existing right but extended to acts done in reliance on a belief that future rights would be granted. This meant that the estoppel doctrine could be raised in relation to the grant of rights over the deceased's residuary estate. In this case, the plaintiff was the deceased's step-daughter, who had acted to her detriment in reliance on her belief, encouraged by the deceased, that she would ultimately benefit by receiving his estate on his death.

A successful claim, based on proprietary estoppel, was made in *Maharaj v. Chand*,[56] where the parties were an unmarried couple. In 1968, the plaintiff began associating with the defendant, who had two children, and a child of the parties was born in 1970. In 1973, when the parties were living as man and wife, the plaintiff applied to the Fiji Housing Authority for land stating that he was married to the defendant and undertaking to use the land solely for the erection of a house for a residence for himself and his family. With the approval of the Native Land Trust Board, the plaintiff was granted a sublease of two lots. In reliance on the plaintiff's representation that it would be a permanent home for her and her children, the defendant gave up her flat and went to live with him in the house. She used her earnings for household requirements and looked after the family. The plaintiff left in 1980, giving the defendant permission to remain, but later sought vacant possession of the house against her. The Privy Council had no difficulty in holding that it would be inequitable, in the particular circumstances, for the plaintiff to evict the defendant. He was estopped from denying that she had his permission to reside permanently in the house.[57] The

---

[54] Unreported July 9, 1985, C.A., available on Lexis.
[55] [1986] 1 W.L.R. 1498. See, D. Hayton, [1987] C.L.J. 215 and J. Martin, [1987] Conv. 211.
[56] [1986] A.C. 898, P.C. See also, *Stevens v. Stevens*, unreported, March 3, 1989, C.A.
[57] The defendant's equity, being a purely personal right not amounting to a property interest, was held not to amount to a dealing with the land for the purposes of s.12 of the Native Land Trust Act,

court, however, emphasised that it was "the particular combination of facts which has led to the estoppel in the present case"[58] and added the caveat that it was "far from saying that whenever a union between an unmarried couple comes to an end, one who is the sole owner in law and equity of the property hitherto their home should not be able to obtain an order for possession against the other".[59] Thus, an estoppel claim failed in *Windeler v. Whitehall*.[60] In this case, the plaintiff went to live with the defendant and became his mistress. The plaintiff looked after his house and entertained for him (the plaintiff being a successful theatrical agent). In 1979, the defendant sold his house and bought a larger one. The plaintiff made no contribution to the purchase—indeed, she had no money of her own, never worked or earned money and was supported by the defendant. She supervised some minor building works caried out on the new house. In June of that year, the defendant made a will leaving the plaintiff his residuary estate. By 1980, however, the relationship was deteriorating and in 1984 it ended. The plaintiff accepted some money from the defendant and removed her belongings from the house. Her contention that she had acquired a proprietary interest in the house based on proprietary estoppel was firmly rejected for a number of reasons. First, it had not been pleaded. Secondly, there was no evidence that the defendant had ever promised to leave his property to the plaintiff if she continued to live with him. Thirdly, there was no evidence that the plaintiff believed that whatever happened she would inherit the house and that the defendant had encouraged her in that belief. Finally, even if she had been encouraged to believe she would inherit the property if she continued to live with him until he died, she herself had destroyed the contingency on which her claim depended.

(C) Alternative Approaches?[61]

In Commonwealth jurisdictions, the courts have taken a more robust approach to the question of the acquisition of property rights by cohabitees and moved away from the juristic confines of the express or inferred common intention, which currently forms the basis of constructive trust doctrine under English law. In New Zealand, for example, the courts have invoked the principle of estoppel as forming the basis for conferring beneficial entitlement on a non-owning cohabitee. In Canada, the doctrine of unjust enrichment provides the juristic basis for awarding a share in the property. In Australia, the principle of unconscionability now governs the position. It may well be that these alternative approaches will pave the way forward for the English courts, in the absence of specific legislation[62] recognising both financial and non-financial

---

and so was not defeated by that section.

[58] *ibid.* 908.

[59] *ibid.* 908.

[60] [1990] 2 FLR 505. See also, *Thomas v. Fuller-Brown* [1988] 1 FLR 237, C.A., where it was re-affirmed that the mere fact that A has expended money or labour on B's property did not entitle A to an interest in the property, in the absence of either an express agreement or of a common intention to be inferred from the conduct of the parties or of any question of estoppel.

[61] See, S. Gardner, (1993) 109 L.Q.R. 263; R. Pearce & J. Stevens, *The Law of Trusts and Equitable Obligations*, (Butterworths, 1995), pp. 648–654.

[62] See, *e.g.* the New South Wales De Facto Relationships Act 1984; Property Law (Amendment) Act 1987; South Australian Family Relationships Act 1975 and the Australian Territory Domestic

contributions as conferring an equity in quasi-matrimonial property. In particular, it is submitted that English law should more readily reflect the reasonable expectations of the parties in stable *de facto* relationships. This, in turn, should lead to the recognition of domestic and spousal services as giving rise to equitable claims in quasi-marital relationships. Such a hypothesis, it is submitted, is in line with judicial developments in New Zealand, Canada and Australia and also statutory intervention in several Australian states,[63] vesting large powers in the courts to declare interests in property after a *de facto* relationship has broken down.

(i) Estoppel Doctrine

In New Zealand, the leading case is *Gillies v. Keogh*,[64] where the Court of Appeal of Wellington identified a general equitable principle asserting the unfairness of resiling from underlying assumptions that have been acted upon. According to Cooke P., the court should have regard to the reasonable expectations of the respective parties (*i.e.* adopting an objective test approach) giving particular weight to a variety of factors. First, the degree of sacrifice by the claimant, which corresponds to the need to show detrimental conduct. The degree of sacrifice is related to the length of the parties' union and the term "sacrifice", in this context, falls to be measured not just in terms of financial contributions but also foregone opportunities in life. This is seen to be highly relevant, especially in cases involving longer relationships, in assessing the parties' reasonable expectations. Secondly, the value of the contributions of the claimant compared to the value of the benefits received. Thus, it is recognised that contributions to household expenses, or to maintenance, repairs or additions, may amount to no more than fair payment for board and lodging and the advantages of a home for the time being. For this reason, something more is commonly needed to justify beneficial entitlement. Thirdly, any property arrangements the parties may have made themselves. Thus, a claimant will not succeed if the conduct of the parties and the circumstances of the case show that a reasonable person in the claimant's position would not expect a benefit or that, throughout the relationship, the other party had positively declined to acquiesce in any property sharing or other right.

According to Richardson J. in *Gillies*, a two-part test can be applied to *de facto* union property claims, namely:

> (1) has there been a direct or indirect contribution by the claimant in respect of the property in circumstances such that it should be inferred that the claimant should have understood that the efforts would naturally result in an interest in the property? and, (2) do the settled principles of estoppel preclude the legal owner from denying the existence of an equitable interest in the property?

In this context, the doctrine of estoppel requires (1) the creation or encouragment of a belief or expectation; (2) a reliance by the other party, and (3) detriment as a result of the reliance.

Relationships Act 1994.
[63] See, n. 62.
[64] [1989] 2 N.Z.L.R. 327, Court of Appeal of Wellington.

It is noteworthy, in this context, that Lord Diplock in *Gissing v. Gissing*[65] emphasised that[66]:

"A resulting, implied or constructive trust ... is created by a transaction between the trustee and the [beneficiary] in connection with the acquisition by the trustee of a legal estate in land, whenever the trustee has so conducted himself that it would be inequitable to allow him to deny to the [beneficiary] a beneficial interest in the land acquired. And he will be held so to have conducted himself if by his words or conduct he has induced the [beneficiary] to act to his own detriment in the reasonable belief that by so acting he was acquiring a beneficial interest in the land."

Thus, according to Lord Diplock, such implied, resulting or constructive trust gives effect to the inferences as to the intentions of the parties to a transaction which a *reasonable man* (or woman) would draw from their words or conduct and not to any *subjective* intention or absence of intention which was not made manifest at the time of the transaction itself.[67] Lord Diplock's formulation was applied in *Austin v. Keele*,[68] where Lord Oliver of Aylmerton (delivering the judgment of the Privy Council) concluded that, in essence, the doctrine of *Gissing* was an application of proprietary estoppel. This formulation also highlights the reasonable expectation and objective test approach promulgated by the New Zealand courts. It is submitted, therefore, that the doctrine of estoppel depends not on the actual intention of the representor but on the effect of his or her conduct or statements on a reasonable person in the position of the claimant.[69]

In *Gillies*, Richardson J., when assessing the requisite elements of encouragement (of a belief or expectation), reliance on that encouragement and detriment, considered that domestic services might be as significant as (or more significant) than any financial contributions. In the course of his judgment, he observed[70]:

"In many cases, if not in the ordinary case, [domestic services] are likely to have been induced by reasonable expectations of security of the family environment and of sharing the family assets on which the *de facto* relationship is based. And, when it comes to the nature and quantification of the relief to be provided, there is no presumption that a direct contribution of a monetary nature to particular property is of greater value to the relationship than any other contribution to the relationship and its property base".

On the facts of *Gillies* itself, however, the female partner (who purchased the house in her sole name) had made it quite clear to the male partner throughout

---

[65] [1971] A.C. 886, H.L.
[66] *ibid.* 905.
[67] *ibid.* 906.
[68] [1987] A.L.J.R. 605 at 609–610, P.C.
[69] See further, D.J. Hayton, [1990] Conv. 370 and R. Ferguson, (1993) 109 L.Q.R. 114.
[70] [1989] 2 N.Z.L.R. 327 at 346.

their relationship that she asserted the house was hers alone and, accordingly, he was held to have acquired no beneficial interest in it.

The *Gillies* case has not been without its judicial critics. In *Bryson v. Bryant*,[71] a childless couple, after sixty years of marriage, died within a few months of each other, the wife predeceasing the husband. The matrimonial home was in the sole name of the husband. By his will, he left the property to a charity, after a life interest to his wife. A dispute arose between the charity and the sole beneficiary in the wife's estate, her brother, who claimed that she was entitled to an equal share as an equitable tenant in common. The New South Wales Court of Appeal (by a majority of two to one)[72] held that the charity took all. Sheller J.A. considered that, if the husband had predeceased the wife, the result of the case might not have been the same, but that the order of deaths being otherwise there was nothing unconscionable in his estate retaining the property. Referring to *Gillies*, he concluded that the wife had no reasonable expectation that her estate would have an interest in the property if she predeceased her husband. In a judgment to the same effect, Samuels A.J.A. opined[73] that, if the claim succeeded, "it would seem to follow that in any marriage of the conventional pattern ... the wife would become entitled to any property acquired by the husband merely because she had carried out her role as homemaker".

This implicit rejection of *Gillies* as invovling the judicial creation of a quasi-matrimonial property regime has not, however, deterred the New Zealand courts who have continued to apply the "reasonable expectations" test with considerable success.[74] It is evident, however, that awards have been moderate and less than would be expected in matrimonial property cases.[75] This may, indeed, be appropriate bearing in mind that a *de facto* union will not always fall to be treated as the full equivalent of marriage. In *Phillips v. Phillips*,[76] Cooke P. observed[77] that, in particular circumstances, there may be no reason why reasonable expectations could not lead to treating a *de facto* union for property sharing purposes as on a par with marriage (*e.g.* where there is a long relationship and the claimant's contributions are particularly meritorious). However, in his view, a strong case, would be required to justify the court in going so far:

"The truth remains that a *de facto* union is fundamentally different in the eyes of society and law from a legal marriage. In a legal marriage [statute] creates a very strong presumption of equal sharing of the matrimonial home and chattels, with a less strong presumption of equal sharing of other matrimonial property. The Courts have no warrant to impose a similar

---

[71] (1992) 29 N.S.W.L.R. 188, New South Wales Court of Appeal.
[72] Sheller J.A. and Samuels A.J.A., Kirby P. dissenting.
[73] *ibid.* 231.
[74] See the judgment of Cooke P. in *Phillips v. Phillips* [1993] 3 N.Z.L.R. 159 at 170, for a review of some of the New Zealand High Court decisions. Cooke P. concluded that "the reasonable expectations test appears to be working reasonably well, furnishing the judges with an approach adequate to enable justice to be done in the very varied circumstances of *de facto* union cases":*ibid.* 170.
[75] See the remarks of Doogue J. in *D. v. A* (1992) 9 F.R.N.Z. 43.
[76] (1993) 3 N.Z.L.R. 159.
[77] *ibid.* 171.

regime on so-called stable *de facto* relationships which prove eventually unstable."[78]

Thus, on the facts in *Phillips* itself, the intermittency of the relationship and the claimant's unwillingness at times to commit herself to legal matrimony militated against her claim to an equal share in the property.[79]

(ii) Unjust Enrichment Doctrine

In Canada, the courts have adopted the concept of unjust enrichment as the basis for "remedying the injustice that occurs when one person makes a substantial contribution to the property of another without compensation".[80] An early example of this approach is to be found in *Re Spears and Levy*.[81] Here, a man and woman lived together believing themselves to be married. In fact, their ceremony of marriage was invalid due to a former marriage of the woman which both parties wrongly believed to have been previously dissolved. The marriage ceremony included the formula "with all my wordly goods I thee endow". On several occasions, the man expressed his belief that, if he died intestate, his property would go to the woman. The man died intestate and the woman claimed from his estate remuneration for her services during the supposed marriage. The Supreme Court of Nova Scotia held that the expectation of the man and woman arising from the marriage ceremony and from the subsequent statements was that she should receive from the estate the widow's share on intestacy. The heirs would be unjustly enriched if that expectation were defeated and, accordingly, were bound by a constrcutive trust to pay the woman the amount she would have received as widow. In this case, the deceased's estate had benefited from the woman's original capital outlay and also her services as a wife and in the administration of the deceased's business as a drilling and excavating contractor.[82] MacKeigan C.J.N.S. said[83]:

"The word 'endow' is used in its traditional sense of 'to furnish with a dower or dowry' . . . In making this pledge or promise the husband assured his wife of her rights in his estate created by the assumption of married status. He thus promised that on his death she would receive such dower in land and such other share of his estate as the law requires. That share in modern times is not less than the statutory minimum on intestacy . . . The covenant to 'endow' was part of a holy pact that in intention and conscience bound Mr and Mrs Spears. He intended and expected, then and throughout his life, that the status which they thought they had asssumed would protect her . . . I place no special stress on the endowment pledge;

---

[78] *ibid.* 171.
[79] The strength of the parties' relationship as a key factor in determining entitlement has been recognised by S. Gardner, (1993) 109 L.Q.R. 263 at p. 279 *et seq.*
[80] *Peter v. Beblow* (1993) 101 D.L.R. (4th) 621 at 642–643, *per* McLachlin J.
[81] (1975) 52 D.L.R. (3d) 146, Nova Scotia Supreme Court.
[82] She looked after their trailer home, cutting grass, painting and doing other chores. Except for a two-year period whilst she was working part-time as a tailoress, she acted as bookkeeper and office manager of his small business, looking after payrolls and other records, answering the telephone, taking orders, issuing invoices, and arranging for purchase of supplies and repairs of equipment: *ibid.* 149.
[83] *ibid.* 152.

Mr Spears probably did not know what it meant. There can be no doubt, however, that both of them thought they were married and that both expected she would have a widow's rights on his death. They lived faithfully together over 20 years. The tacit promise or assurance to her implicit in the ceremony was confirmed by their life together. Indeed, he expressly confirmed during his lifetime and just before his death that she was being looked after . . . These equities, adhering to him when he died, should be honoured by his estate. His heirs, in my opinion, hold his proprety under a constructive trust."

In this case, therefore, the constructive trust, "that versatile handmaiden of equity",[84] was invoked to prevent unjust enrichment of the heirs to the deceased's estate "to ensure they do not get what they have no right to get".[85]

The leading Canadian authorities are now *Pettkus v. Becker*,[86] *Sorochan v. Sorochan*[87] and *Peter v. Beblow*.[88] In the *Sorochan* case,[89] the three requirements to be satisfied before an unjust enrichment could be said to exist were stated as being (1) an enrichment; (2) a corresponding deprivation and (3) the absence of juristic reason for the enrichment. On this basis, the performance of normal spousal services has been held sufficient to constitute a benefit and, therefore, an enrichment.[90] In *Pettkus*,[91] Dickson J., who has been a leading protagonist of this approach, expressed his reasoning in the following terms[92]:

"As for the third requirement, I hold that where one person in a relationship tantamount to spousal prejudices herself in the reasonable expectation of receiving an interest in property and the other person in the relationship freely accepts benefits conferred by the first person in circumstances where he knows or ought to have known of that reasonable expectation, it would be unjust to allow the recipient of the benefit to retain it."

The test put forward here is, once again, an objective one. It is evident that the parties entering a common law relationship will rarely have considered the question of compensation of benefits. It seems logical, therefore, to view the situation objectively and to make the inference that, in the absence of evidence establishing a contrary intention, the parties expected to share jointly in the assets created in the quasi-matrimonial relationship upon its breakdown. According to Dickson J., in the absence of contrary indication, spousal services are given with the expectation of something in return and should be received as

---

[84] *ibid*. 154, *per* MacKeigan C.J.N.S.

[85] *ibid*. 154, *per* MacKeigan C.J.N.S.

[86] (1980) 117 D.L.R. (3d) 257.

[87] (1986) 29 D.L.R. (4th) 1. See also, *Rathwell v. Rathwell* (1978) 83 D.L.R. (3d) 289.

[88] (1993) 101 D.L.R. (4th) 621.

[89] Here, the parties had lived together in unmarried union for 42 years, jointly working a farm. The Supreme Court of Canada held that the male partner had been enriched because he derived a benefit from the claimant's many years of labour in the home and on the farm which he would otherwise have had to pay for out of his own resources.

[90] See, *Everson v. Rich* (1988) 53 D.L.R. (4th) 470 at 474.

[91] In this case, the Supreme Court of Canada held that the female claimant, who had lived with her male partner for 14 years working on a honey farm which he owned, was entitled to a half-share in the property by way of a constructive trust.

[92] (1980) 117 D.L.R. (3d) 257 at 274.

such, so that, in terms of the third requirement, there is no juristic right to retain the benefit without compensation. The point is well-illustrated in a recent decision of the Supreme Court of Canada in *Peter v. Beblow*.[93] Here, the parties commenced cohabiting in 1973, when the appellant, together with her four children, moved into the respondent's home. The parties continued to live together in a *de facto* relationship for over 12 years, separating in 1985. The appellant acted as a stepmother to the respondent's two children while they remained in the home until 1977, as well as caring for her own children, the last of whom left in 1980. During the 12 years of cohabitation, the appellant did housework and also engaged in numerous projects which improved the respondent's property. Both the appellant and the respondent contributed to the general household bills. The Supreme Court of Canada[94] had no difficulty in holding that the three elements needed to establish a claim of unjust enrichment were made out. The appellant's housekeeping and child care services constituted a benefit to the respondent, in that he received household services without paying compensation, which in turn enhanced his ability to pay off his mortgage and purchase other assets (*i.e.* a van and a houseboat). These services also constituted a corresponding deprivation to the appellant in that she had provided the services without compensation. Thirdly, there was no juristic reason for the enrichment. There was no obligation on a common law spouse to perform work and services for her partner and there was no suggestion that the appellant's services constituted a gift.

At this point, it may be convenient to consider two potential objections to this approach. First, it may be argued that the appellant's services should not give rise to an unjust enrichment claim since her services were voluntarily given to the respondent in her role as *de facto* wife and stepmother. Secondly, it may be contended that equity should not recognise such services because they arise from natural love and affection and not by virtue of any intention to acquire proprietary rights in the respondent's home. It is true to say that much of our current (English) judicial thinking in this area is based on these two inter-related suppositions.[95] In terms of an unjust enrichment claim, such arguments raise obvious policy considerations relevant to determining the third requirement for such a claim, namely, whether there is an absence of juristic reason for the unjust enrichment. As a matter of public policy, therefore, should home-making and child care services be viewed as giving rise to equitable claims in a quasi-matrimonial relationship? In the *Beblow* case, McLachlin J gave an emphatic affirmative answer to this question in the following terms[96]:

"The notion that household and child care services are not worthy of recognition by the court fails to recognize the fact that these services are of great value, not only to the family, but to the other spouse ... The notion,

---

[93] (1993) 101 D.L.R. (4th) 621.

[94] *Per* McLachlin J., with La Forest, Sopinka and Iacobucci JJ. concurring. The other leading judgment of the Court was given by Cory J., largely to the same effect, with L'Heureux-Dube and Gonthier JJ. concurring.

[95] See, *e.g.* the remarks of Browne-Wilkinson V.-C. in *Grant v. Edwards* [1986] Ch. 638 at 657.

[96] *ibid.* 647–648. The learned judge referred to the observation made by Lord Simon that "the cock-bird can feather his nest precisely because he is not required to spend most of his time sitting on it": Holdsworth Lecture, "With All My Wordly Goods", (University of Birmingham, March 20, 1995, at p. 32).

moreover, is a pernicious one that systematically devalues the contributions which women tend to make to the family economy. It has contributed
to the phenomenon of feminization of poverty . . . "

There is, it is submitted, much logic in assimilating domestic services with
other forms of contribution in the family context.[97] Thus, according to Cory J.,[98]
who gave the other leading judgment in *Beblow*, it was not unreasonable for the
party providing the domestic labour required to create a home to expect to share
in the property when the relationship came to an end. The learned judge
observed[99]:

> "Women no longer are expected to work exclusively in the home. It must
> be recognized that when they do so, women forgo outside employment to
> provide domestic services and child care. The granting of relief in the form
> of a personal judgment or a property interest to the provider of domestic
> services should adequately reflect the fact that the income earning capacity
> and the ability to acquire assets by one party has been enhanced by the
> unpaid domestic services of the other".

Here again, the reasoning of the learned judge is evident, namely, that, where
a person provides spousal services to another, those services should be taken as
having been given with the expectation of compensation unless there is
evidence to the contrary. In the *Beblow* case, having regard to the duration of the
relationship (*i.e.* 12 years) and the appellant's significant contribution to the
home and property, she would reasonably (looking at the matter objectively)
have had an expectation of sharing the wealth she helped to create.

As to the nature of the remedy appropriate to satisfy the appellant's equity,
the Supreme Court in *Beblow* was faced with two choices, namely, an award of
money on the basis of the value of the services rendered by the appellant (*i.e.* a
quantum meruit) or the grant of title to the respondent's house based on a
constructive trust. According to McLachlin J., for a constructive trust to arise,
monetary damages must be inadequate and the claimant must establish a direct
link between the services rendered and the property in which the trust is
claimed.[1] In the instant case, a monetary judgment was considered inadequate
because the respondent had few assets (other than his van and a houseboat) and
no income except from a war veteran's allowance. The sufficiency of a direct
connection between the services rendered and the property to support a
constructive trust was also held to be made out on the facts. The appellant had

---

[97] See, *e.g.* Welstead, [1987] Denning L.J. 151.
[98] L'Heureux-Dube and Gonthier JJ. concurring.
[99] *ibid.* 633–634.
[1] Compare the judgment of Cory J., who concluded that, in a family relationship, the services and
contributions by one of the parties need not be clearly and directly linked with specific property in
order for a constructive trust to be imposed. As long as there was no compensation paid for the
services, then it could be *inferred* that their provision permitted the other party to acquire lands or
to improve them: *ibid.* 637–638. See also, *Sorochan v. Sorochan* (1986) 29 D.L.R. (4th) 1, where
it was held that it was not necessary that there be a connection between the deprivation and the
actual *acquisition* of the property. The connection had to be substantial and direct (*i.e.* a clear
proprietary relationship) but the connection could take the form of preservation or maintenance of,
or improvement to the property.

shown that there was a positive proprietary benefit conferred by her domestic services upon the respondent's property. The property was looked after and maintained as a result of the appellant's efforts, which also permitted the respondent to pay off the mortgage. In quantifying the trust, McLachlin J. adopted a "value survived" approach representing the amount by which the respondent's property had been improved (as opposed to a "value received" approach which merely looked to the value of the services which the appellant had rendered).[2] On this basis, the appellant was awarded the respondent's house which represented a fair approximation of the value of the appellant's efforts as reflected in the family assets.

The principle of unjust enrichment was also alluded to by Toohey J. in *Baumgartner v. Baumgartner*,[3] a decision of the High Court of Australia, who sought to assimilate the two concepts of unjust enrichment and unconscionable conduct[4] and concluded that these two approaches would inevitably produce the same result. In his view, the object of a constructive trust is "to redress a position which otherwise leaves untouched a situation of unconscionable conduct or unjust enrichment".[5]

The Canadian approach is, of course, very different from that adopted by the English courts. It is evident from cases such as *Burns v. Burns*[6] and *Lloyds Bank plc v. Rosset*[7] that an English cohabitee, in the absence of an express common intention, will fail if her contribution is non-financial and not directly related to the acquisition of the house.[8] In other words, her contribution to the welfare of the family by performing domestic duties of the household and bringing up the children are treated as insufficient to raise an *inference* of a common intention under constructive trust theory. It may be, however, (as we have seen earlier), that this purely "spousal" form of contribution may be enough to provide the necessary detriment to support an estoppel-based equity in the claimant provided the other requisite elements of assurance and reliance are also made out. In *Pascoe v. Turner*,[9] the female claimant had spent her own monies (approximately £230) on decorations, improvements and repairs to her male partner's property. In *Greasley v. Cooke*,[10] on the other hand, the female claimant had looked after the legal owner's house and family and, in particular, cared for his daughter who was mentally ill. It is to be observed that, unlike the claimant in *Pascoe*, she had not incurred any expenditure on the house and

---

[2] Compare the judgment of Cory J., who suggested that either the "value survived" approach or the "value received" approach may be utilised to quantify the value of the constructive trust.

[3] (1988) 62 A.L.J.R. 29, High Court of Australia.

[4] See below, pp. 168–169.

[5] *ibid.* 36. The judgment of Barker J. in *Fitness v. Berridge* (1986) 4 N.Z.L.R. 243 at 251, is to the same effect. See further, D.J. Hayton, [1990] Conv. 370 at p. 385–387 and J.L. Dewar, (1984) 60 Can. Bar Rev. 265.

[6] [1984] Ch. 317, C.A.

[7] [1991] 1 A.C. 107, H.L.

[8] As to whether indirect financial contributions (which relieve the legal owner from paying the mortgage instalments which he would otherwise have had to pay) may still give rise to a beneficial interest in property under *resulting trust* principles, see, M. Pawlowski, (1995) Lit. 14/8, 311–317.

[9] [1979] 1 W.L.R. 431, C.A. In *Matharu v. Matharu* (1994) 60 P & C.R. 93, C.A., the claimant's husband made substantial improvements to his father's house at his own expense.

[10] [1980] 1 W.L.R. 1306, C.A. Compare, however, *Coombes v. Smith* [1986] 1 W.L.R. 808, where the female claimant was held not to have acted to her detriment in becoming pregnant, leaving her husband, looking after the house and child or not looking for another job.

none of her acts giving rise to the estoppel-based equity were referable to the property. Similarly, in *Maharaj v. Chand*,[11] involving an unmarried couple, the defendant gave up her flat to live with the plaintiff and used her earnings for household requirements and looked after the family. Again, in *Re Basham (dec'd)*,[12] the plaintiff had provided unpaid services in looking after her step-father's house. This was held to be sufficient detriment to support an equity on the basis of proprietary estoppel.

The recognition of domestic and spousal services as giving rise to equitable entitlement in the estoppel context is also mirrored in the judicial acceptance of such forms of contribution as supporting a constructive trust based on *express* common intention. In this connection, it is evident that very little detriment is required to support a constructive trust where the claimant relies on express discussions between the parties giving rise to a common intention to share beneficially. In the words of Sir Nicholas Browne-Wilkinson V.-C. in *Grant v. Edwards*[13]:

> "... once it has been shown that there was a common intention that the claimant should have an interest in the house, any act done by her to her detriment relating to the joint lives of the parties is, in my judgment, sufficient to qualify. The acts do not have to be inherently referable to the house."

The case of *Hammond v. Mitchell*[14] is a good example. Here, the claimant was able to point to an express understanding that she should have a beneficial interest in a bungalow owned by her male partner. Waite J. held that, in reliance on this understanding, the claimant had acted to her potential detriment in allowing her rights as occupier to be subordinated to those of the bank mortgagee and by supporting her male partner in his speculative business ventures. By contrast, the claimant was held to have acquired no beneficial interest in a Spanish house also owned by her male partner since, in relation to this property, in the absence of express discussions, there was no evidence to justify the imputation of a constructive trust. With regard to the Spanish house, her activities were held to fall "a long way short of justifying any inference of intended proprietary interest".[15]

One of the interesting features of the Canadian approach is that it openly recognises the female claimant's contribution to the welfare of the family (in terms of domestic and child care services) as *per se* giving rise to the conferment of a benefit (with corresponding deprivation) and, hence, a reasonable expectation of compensation in the absence of any juristic reason for the enrichment. The English courts, on the other hand, have denied giving judicial recognition to such spousal services, save in circumstances where the female claimant can point to either an express assurance by the legal owner that

---

[11] [1986] A.C. 898, P.C.
[12] [1986] 1 W.L.R. 1498.
[13] [1986] Ch. 638 at 657, C.A., endorsed by Nicholls L.J. in *Lloyds Bank plc v. Rosset* [1989] Ch. 350 at 381, C.A. But see, *Midland Bank plc v. Dobson* [1986] 1 FLR 171 at 176–177, *per* Fox L.J.; *Ungurian v. Lesnoff* [1990] 2 FLR 299, C.A.
[14] [1991] 1 W.L.R. 1127. See further, L. Carke and R. Edmunds, [1992] Fam. Law 523; P. Clarke, [1992] Fam. Law 72.
[15] *ibid.* 1138.

she has or will acquire an interest in the property (*i.e.* estoppel doctrine) or, alternatively, an express common intention to share beneficially (*i.e.* constructive trust theory).[16] This, it is submitted, is the fundamental difference between the two jurisdictions. Under Canadian law, the situation is viewed objectively and, in the absence of evidence establishing a contrary intention, an inference is drawn that the parties *expected* to share in the assets created in the quasi-matrimonial relationship. It is unnecessary to establish promises or assurances to compensate the claimant for the services provided. In *Beblow*, for example, the inference was that the appellant would reasonably have had an expectation of sharing the wealth she helped to create by maintaining and preserving the home and, more importantly, through the provision of domestic services. Her work around the house and in caring for the children saved the respondent the expense of hiring a housekeeper and someone to care for their children. As a result, he was able to use the money which he had saved to purchase other property and to pay off the mortgage on his property.

The reasons for the restrained approach of the English courts have already been noted earlier. It may be impossible to say whether or not the claimant would have done the acts relied on as a detriment even if she thought she had no interest in the house. Conduct such as setting-up house together, having a baby, making payments to general housekeeping expenses (which are not strictly necessary to enable the mortgage to be repaid) and looking after the family are all treated as potentially referable to the mutual love and affection of the parties and not specifically referable to the claimant's belief that she has an interest in the property.[17] Such reasoning, however, overlooks the inherently valuable nature of spousal and domestic services both to the family but, more importantly, to the other partner whose earning capacity and ability to acquire assets may be greatly enhanced as a result.

The English approach is typified by the following remarks of Fox L.J., in the constructive trust context, in *Burns v. Burns*[18]:

"... the mere fact that the parties live together and do the ordinary domestic tasks is, in my view, no indication at all that they thereby intended to alter the existing property rights of either of them... The undertaking of such work is, I think, ... the sort of things which are done for the benefit of the family without altering the title to property".

An assertion that spousal and domestic services can alter property rights is seen, essentially, as reverting to the idea of the "family asset", which has been

---

[16] But see the recent Court of Appeal decision in *Midland Bank plc v. Cooke* [1995] 4 All E.R. 562, where it was held that, where a partner has successfully established an equitable interest through direct contribution, it was open to the court to undertake a survey of the whole course of dealing between the parties relevant to their ownership and occupation of the property and their sharing of its burdens and advantages in determining their beneficial ownership. Such survey will take into account "all conduct which throws light on the question what shares were intended": *ibid.* 574, *per* Waite L.J. On this basis, the court took into account the wife's contribution to household bills, bringing up three children of the family, undertaking liability in respect of a second mortgage, and maintenance and improvement of the house, in awarding her a half-share therein, which was purchased in the husband's sole name.

[17] See, in particular, the observations of Sir Nicholas Browne-Wilkinson V.-C. in *Grant v. Edwards* [1986] Ch. 638 at 657, C.A.

[18] [1984] Ch. 317 at 331, C.A. See also, May L.J., at 345.

consistently rejected by the English courts including the House of Lords in *Pettit v. Pettit*[19] and *Gissing v. Gissing*.[20] It is also apparent that the English judiciary are mindful of the fact that the wide powers conferred by the Matrimonial Causes Act 1973, in relation to the property of married persons, do not apply to unmarried couples. Hence, the court's reluctance to take on board a broader-based jurisdiction to re-allocate property rights of *de facto* partners in the absence of specific statutory intervention.[21]

(iii) Unconscionable Conduct

In the leading case of *Baumgartner v. Baumgartner*,[22] the High Court of Australia adopted the principle that, in appropriate circumstances, equity will impose a constructive trust to prevent the unconscionable conduct of the legal owner in refusing to recognise the existence of the claimant's equitable interest in property. In that case, the parties had, for some time, lived together in unmarried union, pooling their earnings for the purposes of their relationship, including the acquisition of land, the building of a house and the purchase of furniture. When they separated, the male partner claimed the house was his exclusive property. The High Court of Australia held that his exclusive claim to the house amounted to unconscionable conduct that attracted the intervention of equity and the imposition of a constructive trust representing the beneficial interests of the parties in the proportions 55 per cent to the male partner and 45 per cent to the female partner, subject to various allowances being made to the male partner to cover specific entitlements due to him in respect of the house and furniture.

In the earlier case of *Muchinski v. Dodds*,[23] Deane J. (with whom Mason J. agreed) formulated the principle in the following terms[24]:

> "The content of the principle is that, in such a case, equity will not permit that other party to assert or retain the benefit of the relevant property to the extent that it would be unconscionable for him to do so."

Essentially, in this context, the constructive trust serves as a remedy which equity imposes, regardless of actual or presumed agreement or intention, to preclude the retention or assertion of beneficial ownership of property to the extent that such retention or assertion would be contrary to equitable principle.[25] The joint judgment of Mason C.J., Wilson and Deane JJ. in *Baumgartner* also recognises that the remedy will be available regardless of actual or presumed agreement or intention, but also implicitly rejects the notion that a constructive trust will be imposed in accordance with the notions of justice and fairness *simpliciter* (*i.e.* Lord Denning M.R.'s new model

---

[19] [1970] A.C. 777, H.L.

[20] [1971] A.C. 886, H.L.

[21] See, *e.g.* the remarks of May L.J. in *Burns v. Burns* [1984] Ch. 317 at 333, C.A.: "In my view, as Parliament has not legislated for the unmarried couple as it has for those who have been married, the courts should be slow to attempt in effect to legislate themselves".

[22] (1988) 62 A.L.J.R. 29, High Court of Australia.

[23] (1985) 160 C.L.R. 583.

[24] *ibid.* 620.

[25] *ibid.* 614.

constructive trust formulated in *Eves v. Eves*[26] and *Hussey v. Palmer*).[27] On this basis, therefore, the *Baumgartner* case was one in which[28]:

> " ... the parties have pooled their earnings for the purposes of their joint relationship, one of the purposes of that relationship being to secure accommodation for themselves and their child. Their contributions, financial and otherwise, to the acquisition of the land, the building of the house, the purchase of furniture and the making of their home, were on the basis of, and for the purposes of, that joint relationship. In this situation the appellant's assertion, after the relationship had failed, that the Leumeah property, which was financed in part through the pooled funds, is his sole property, is his property beneficially to the exclusion of any interest at all on the part of the respondent, amounts to unconscionable conduct which attracts the intervention of equity and the imposition of a constructive trust ... "

It is, perhaps, not surpising that cases decided after *Baumgartner* have sought to confine the juristic parameters of the unconscionability doctrine. Thus, in *Arthur v. Public Trustee*,[29] the Court of Appeal of the Northern Territory held that the male partner's assertion of sole legal title was not unconscionable where the female claimant had made no monetary contribution to the acquisition of the property. By contrast, in *Hibberson v. George*,[30] the majority of the New South Wales Court of Appeal concluded that it would be unconscionable for the legal owner to deny the claimant a beneficial interest in view of the fact that she spent most of her earnings on the home and the family. The absence of a pooling arrangement was held (by the majority, Mahoney J.A. dissenting) not to be fatal to the claimant's case. The emphasis placed by the post-*Baumgartner* decisions on financial contributions has led one academic writer to comment that "disappointingly, the brave new world of unconscionability appears to be leading back to the family property law of 20 years ago ... the more imaginative features of *Baumgartner v. Baumgartner* are in danger of being overlooked".[31]

Whilst the principle of unconscionability is now viewed by the Australiam courts as providing an overall theoretical basis for both constructive trust and proprietray estoppel doctrine,[32] it is evident that the decision in *Baumgartner*, although discarding the artificial concept of common intention, is limited to cases involving direct financial contributions to the acquisition of property. Unfortunately, therefore, it provides little assistance to the claimant whose contribution to the family comprises purely domestic and spousal services. Indeed, it is likely that the same result would have been achieved applying conventional (English) principles of the resulting trust (based on direct

---

[26] [1975] 1 W.L.R. 1338 at 1341, C.A.
[27] [1972] 1 W.L.R. 1286 at 1290, C.A.
[28] (1988) 62 A.L.J.R. 29 at 34, *per* Mason C.J., Wilson and Deane JJ.
[29] (1988) 90 FLR 203.
[30] (1988) 12 Fam L.R. 725. See also, *Lipman v. Lipman* (1989) 13 Fam. L.R. 1; *Woodward v. Johnson* (1991) 14 Fam. L.R. 828.
[31] M. Bryan, (1990) 106 L.Q.R. 25 at p. 27. See also, generally, D.J. Hayton, [1988] Conv. 259 and S. Gardner, (1993) 109 L.Q.R. 263 at pp. 274–278.
[32] See, *Waltons Stores (Interstate) Ltd v. Maher* (1988) 62 A.L.J.R. 110, High Court of Australia.

financial contributions) and the constructive trust (based on a common intention inferred from the parties' conduct in pooling their earnings).

(iv) Monetary Award Arising From Unjust Enrichment

In Canada, there is judicial support for the proposition that the remedy for unjust enrichment may take the form of a pure monetary award of compensation. In *Peter v. Beblow*,[33] the Supreme Court of Canada referred to the possibility of granting a monetary award (*i.e.* a *quantum meruit*) as a means of remedying unjust enrichment on the basis of the value of services rendered by the claimant during the period of the *de facto* union. In that case, it was considered that a monetary judgment would be inadequate in view of the fact that the respondent had few assets and only a moderate income. In the course of his judgment, Cory J.[34] alluded to the situations where an award of a monetary sum may be the most appropriate remedy. First, where the rights of *bona fide* third parties would be affected as a result of the granting of a constructive trust remedy. Secondly, where the relationship between the parties was of short duration or where there were no assets surviving its dissolution. In the absence of third party rights, the choice between a monetary award and a constructive trust would be entirely discretionary and should be exercised flexibly.

In *Everson v. Rich*,[35] the Court of Appeal of Saskatchewan, accepting the notion that the performance of spousal services was sufficient to constitute a benefit and thus an enrichment, held that there was no juristic right to retain that benefit without compensation in the absence of any contrary indications. In this case, the appellant's claim for a constructive trust failed because of an insufficient nexus between the provision of the appellant's services and the respondent's acquisition of property. However, she was entitled to the alternative remedy in the form of monetary damages. These damages (assessed at $10,000) fell to be calculated, not by reference to the market price of domestic services, but by a proportion of the increase in value of the legal owner's property.[36] However, the benefits the appellant received from the relationship fell to be taken into account. These consisted largely of support during the relevant period at a higher standard of living than she (and her daughter) would have enjoyed on their own.

In *Sorochan v. Sorochan*,[37] the Supreme Court of Canada awarded the claimant a proprietary remedy (one third share of the farm in question) under a constructive trust but also a monetary award ($20,000 to be reduced to $15,000 if paid within six months) to remedy the unjust enrichment.

The approach of awarding equitable (monetary) compensation, which was also approved by Cooke P. in the New Zealand Court of Appeal in *Gillies v. Keogh*,[38] further illustrates the inherent flexibility of the unjust enrichment doctrine adopted by the Canadian courts. It is in marked contrast to the English

---

[33] (1993) 101 D.L.R. (4th) 621.
[34] *ibid.* 640.
[35] (1988) 53 D.L.R. (4th) 470.
[36] This is the method of assessment of compensation adopted in several of the estoppel cases. See, Chap. 5, pp. 91–95.
[37] (1986) 29 D.L.R. (4th) 1.
[38] [1989] 2 N.Z.L.R. 327 at 332, *per* Cooke P.

position, since the constructive trust is seen as not the only means by which restitution can be effected.

(D) The Future?

In *Phillips v. Phillips*,[39] Cooke P. had occasion to observe that[40]:

> "... the Commonwealth jurisdictions have all been travelling, albeit at different speeds and using differently named conceptual vehicles, towards open recognition of the principle that the history of a *de facto* union and the conduct of the parties may give rise to reasonable expectations of property interests to which equity will give effect ... "

Accepting the premise that social attitudes in England readily lead to expectations, by those within stable and enduring *de facto* relationships, that family assets are ordinarily shared and not the exclusive property of one or other of the parties (unless there is a clear indication to the contrary), there is, it is submitted, a strong argument that English courts should adopt a more liberal approach to the conferment of beneficial entitlement based upon notions of estoppel or unjust enrichment. The New Zealand courts have already recognised domestic and spousal services as significant (if not more significant) than financial contributions in assessing the requisite elements of assurance, reliance and detriment for the purposes of establishing an estoppel-based equity. The importance of the *Gillies* decision lies in the judicial recognition that the performance of domestic and spousal services may lead to reasonable expectations of beneficial entitlement, particularly where there has been a long-standing relationship and the claimant's contribution has been substantial over a number of years.[41] The Canadian cases have gone further in accepting the importance of non-financial contributions as justifying the imposition of a constructive trust or, alternatively, a monetary award of compensation based on the value of the services rendered by the claimant or on a proportion of the increase in value of the property.

It is apparent that the female claimant in *Burns*[42] would have faired better in establishing an equity adopting either of these two approaches. It will be recalled that, in this case, the parties had lived together since 1961 for 19 years, Mrs Burns bearing her male partner's two children. She remained at home to look after the children and to perform domestic duties and was thus unable to

---

[39] (1993) 3 N.Z.L.R. 159, New Zealand Court of Appeal.
[40] *ibid.* 167–168.
[41] Compare the approach taken in *Attorney-General of Hong Kong v. Humphreys Estate (Queen's Gardens) Ltd* [1987] A.C. 114 at 124–125, P.C., where the Privy Council refused to uphold an estoppel claim in favour of the claimant who had "acted in the confident and not unreasonable hope" that an agreement in principle would be carried into effect and not withdrawn. See further, Chap. 2, pp. 24–25.
[42] Compare the recent Court of Appeal decision in *Midland Bank plc v. Cooke* [1995] 4 All E.R. 562, C.A., ante, p. 148, n. 9, where the wife's direct contribution to the purchase price comprised her notional half-share in a wedding gift of £1,100 from the husband's parents (*i.e.* £550). Once an equitable interest was shown through direct contribution, the Court of Appeal held it was entitled to survey the whole course of dealing between the parties in determining the wife's ultimate share in the property, including her contribution to household bills and "maintenance and improvement contribution": *ibid.* 576, *per* Waite L.J.

earn until 1975 when she started work as a driving instructor. She used her earnings to pay the rates and the telephone bills and to buy fixtures, fittings and certain domestic chattels for the house. She also decorated the interior of the house. It is, perhaps, significant, that the plaintiff had made a statutory declaration of change of name (to Mrs Burns), that her passport was in the name of Mrs Burns and the parties' friends and acquaintances believed the parties to be married. The degree of "sacrifice", measured in terms of foregone opportunities in life and the length of the parties' union, can, on any view, be considered as substantial. The value of her contribution in terms of spousal and domestic services may also be taken to have outweighed the value of the benefits she received, in terms of money, whilst the relationship continued. Although her male partner had encouraged her to develop her own abilities and to build up a successful driving instruction business, this produced only a modest income which did not materialise until the latter part of the relationship. There was no suggestion in the evidence that her male partner had positively declined to acquiesce in any property sharing or other right. On a *Gillies* analysis, therefore, it is certainly arguable that Mrs Burns's claim would have met with success. Her claim becomes even stronger when one approaches the case from the Canadian standpoint of unjust enrichment. Clearly, her contribution in the form of spousal and domestic services would qualify as a benefit to her male partner (in the absence of compensation), and hence an enrichment with a corresponding deprivation. There was no juristic reason for the enrichment in the sense that there was no obligation on her to perform work and services for her partner and there was no suggestion that her services constituted a gift. What is crucial, under the Canadian approach, is that her services, viewed objectively, would be taken as having been given with the expectation of compensation unless there was evidence to the contrary. It is this "presumptive inference" which distinguishes the Canadian cases from the New Zealand approach.

Assuming the pre-requisites to a restitutionary claim had been made out, the court would then be faced with the choice of a monetary award or, alternatively, the grant of a share in the house based on a constructive trust. On the facts in *Burns*, it is likely that the requisite causal link between the services rendered and the property in which the trust was claimed would not be made out. Unlike the *Beblow* case, it would be difficult to show that Mr Burns's contribution towards the welfare of the family had facilitated her male partner, who was financially independent, to acquire other assets or to repay the mortgage. In these circumstances, a monetary award would have been appropriate, taking into account the benefits Mrs Burns received from the relationship. This, it will be recalled, was the form of relief granted by the Court of Appeal of Saskatchewan in *Everson v. Rich*.[43]

For the sake of completeness, it may be mentioned that the unconscionability doctrine, as propounded by the Autralian courts, would afford no basis for claim for the *Burns* type of claimant, in the absence of any financial contributions towards the acquisition of the house.

In *Gillies*,[44] Cooke P. suggested that the requirement of reasonable

---

[43] (1988) 53 D.L.R. (4th) 470, Court of Appeal of Saskatchewan. See below, p. 170.
[44] [1989] 2 N.Z.L.R. 327 at 330, 333.

expectation lay at the heart of the related doctrines of constructive trust, proprietary estoppel, unjust enrichment and unconscionability and that, at the end of the day, all the cases came to the same thing. It is submitted, however, that, despite their similarities, the doctrines retain distinct features. Under the English constructive trust, it is necessary to show an express or inferred common intention from the parties' conduct. The notion of "reasonable expectation", on the other hand, is based primarily on an objective test of what a reasonable person would have expected to receive in the given circumstances of the case, albeit that it also takes into account any property arrangements the parties may have made themselves in rejecting an estoppel-based claim. The Canadian notion of "unjust enrichment", whilst considering the parties reasonable expectations, also requires an examination of the parties' actual intention in so far as this may afford a juristic reason for the enrichment. The Australian doctrine of unconscionability involves the imposition of a constructive trust regardless of actual or presumed agreement or intention. There are differences also in the extent to which estoppel and constructive trust "equities" may be said to bind third parties. It is considered[45] that, under English constructive trust doctrine, the claimant's equitable right has retrospective effect capable of taking priority over creditors and purchasers of the legal estate. This is not generally the case where an inchoate estoppel-based equity is involved. On the other hand, the Australian constructive trust (imposed on the grounds of unconscionability) is treated as having either retrospective or prospective effect, depending on the exercise of the court's discretion.[46] Other distinctions have already been noted. For example, it has been shown that the Canadian approach benefits from a flexible approach as to the choice of remedy to be awarded to the spousal claimant. This may take the form of an equitable interest in the property by virtue of the imposition of a constructive trust or, alternatively, a restitutionary award of compensation. By contrast, the English constructive trust affords no option other than a retrospective equitable interest in the property.

It is submitted that a general principle which asserts the injustice of resiling from underlying assumptions and expectations that have been acted upon has much to recommend it in preference to the current "judicial quest for that fugitive or phantom common intention".[47] This, however, is not to admit an award *whenever* one party has benefitted from the contributions (financial or non-financial) of the other party. In the words of Richardson J. in *Gillies v. Keogh*[48]:

"If one party has insisted throughout that a particular item of property in that party's name is his (or hers) to the exclusion of the other, he (or she) cannot be said to have encouraged the other to a belief or expectation that it would be shared, nor that the other party relied on that even though the

---

[45] See, *e.g.* D. Hayton, [1990] Conv. 370 and P. Ferguson, (1993) 109 L.Q.R. 114. See further, Chap. 7 and Chap. 1, pp. 10–16.

[46] See, *e.g. Muschinski v. Dodds* (1985) 160 C.L.R. 583 at 615, *per* Deane J.

[47] *Pettkus v. Becker* (1980) 117 D.L.R. (3d) 257 at 269, *per* Dickson J.

[48] [1989] 2 N.Z.L.R. 327 at 347.

performance of spousal services and financial contributions constituted a detriment."[49]

Although Richardson J.'s observations were made in the context of estoppel doctrine, it is apparent that the same conclusion will apply when applying principles of unjust enrichment and unconscionability. Thus, a person who confers a benefit on another is not entitled to restitution unless it is justified by the circumstances under which it takes place.[50] Moreover, it will not be unconscionable for the legal owner to retain the benefit in the absence of any juristic reason for its return (*i.e.* because the conferment of the benefit was by way of gift or contract).

Whatever judicial route is taken to resolve property disputes arising upon the breakdown of *de facto* relationships, it is important that our law accurately reflects current social attitudes in the area of family relations. In the face of continued judicial reluctance in England to adopt a broader based philosophy to the resolution of such disputes (whether it be in the form of estoppel, unjust enrichment or unconscionability), there is growing force in the argument that a statutory code[51] should be enacted in this country which would provide a clear set of principles (based on considerations of policy) for allocating property interests between unmarried couples. Pending such legislation, in view of Lord Bridge's conclusions in *Lloyds Bank plc v. Rosset*,[52] it seems unlikely that a broader based "unjust enrichment" model (on remedial constructive trust lines) will find judicial acceptance in this country in the foreseeable future. There may still be room,[53] however, for the development of estoppel doctrine along the lines of the New Zealand experience.

The Law Commission is currently examining whether, on the breakdown of non-marital cohabitation, some way can be found to make an adjustment between the parties because of any economic advantage derived by one party from the relationship or any economic disadvantage suffered by the other party.[54] It remains to be seen whether this will eventually lead to the enactment of legislation in this country giving the courts power to declare interests in property after an ummarried union has broken down, based on financial and non-financial contributions (including contributions made in the capacity of homemaker or parent).

---

[49] See, *e.g.* the precedent of a deed preventing a cohabitant acquiring a share in the beneficial interest in a property, appearing in New L.J. Practitioner, October 21, 1994.

[50] *Gillies v. Keogh* [1989] 2 N.Z.L.R. 327 at 347, *per* Richardson J.

[51] Along the lines of the New South Wales De Facto Relationships Act 1984 (and Property Law (Amendment) Act 1987) or the South Australian Family Relationships Act 1975. See further, K. Everett and M. Pawlowski, [1995] Fam. Law 417, where it is suggested that the provisions of s.15 and Sched. 1 to the Children Act 1989 may provide some comfort to the English cohabitee.

[52] [1991] 1 A.C. 107 at 132–133, H.L.

[53] See the remarks of Nourse L.J. in *Stokes v. Anderson* [1991] 1 FLR 391 at 399, C.A.: "It is possible that the House of Lords will one day decide to solve the problems presented by these cases, either by assimilating the principles of *Gissing v. Gissing* and those of proprietary estoppel, or even by following the recent trend in other Commonwealth jurisdictions towards more generalised principles of unconscionability and unjust enrichment". See also, P.T. Evans, [1989] Conv. 418, who argues for the resurgence of a remedial constructive trust in English law.

[54] The Centre for Socio-Legal Studies, Oxford, was commissioned to undertake a study of what happens in practice on the break-up of non-marital home sharing. A consultation paper is expected in late 1996: Law Com. 30th Annual Report 1995, Law Com. No. 239, paras 6.7–6.12. See also, Scottish Law Com. Report on Family Law, (1992) Scot. Law Com. No. 135, Part XVI and M.P. Thompson [1996] Conv. 154.

9. ESTOPPEL AND ADVERSE POSSESSION

(A) Introduction

In this Chapter, we examine the question as to whether an estoppel-based right can give rise to a possessory title under the provisions of the Limitation Act 1980. The matter has been the subject of some judicial discussion.

The point arose in the Irish case of *Cullen v. Cullen*,[1] where the facts were as follows. The plaintiff had built up a successful business at Enniscorthy and Adamstown, County Wexford. He lived with his family in his premises at Adamstown where he carried on the business of a licensed grocer and merchant. There was also a small farm attached to the business. The eldest son, Sean, left school in 1945 and joined his father in the business, and the second son, Martin, did likewise in 1946. A younger son, Patrick, worked in the business from 1954. From about 1945 onwards, a series of family quarrels began between the father on one side and the mother and sons on the other. In 1952, the plaintiff first accused his wife and children of robbing him. In 1954, Sean left the house and set up in business on his own. In the same year, Martin, who had previously left the house after a quarrel, returned at the request of his father to take over the complete running of the business, save that the plaintiff reserved the right to sign cheques drawn in connection therewith. About 1956, the plaintiff began making difficulties about signing cheques and, ultimately, it was agreed that Martin would hand over the management of the business to his father in January 1958. Martin then received £3,500 from his father and bought himself a farm. He continued to reside in the family home. The plaintiff became erratic in some of his business affairs and, in 1959, his wife caused him to be examined by doctors, including a mental specialist, who diagnosed a paranoid illness. An attempt was made to remove the plaintiff to a mental hospital but he escaped to Dublin. When in Dublin, the plaintiff sent word to his wife by messenger that he was transferring the property at Adamstown to her, and that she should carry on the business in her own name. In return for this, he required a signed statement from his wife and sons that he was sane and the withdrawal of any arrest which might have been made in connection with the attempt to commit him to a mental hospital. Early in 1959, the plaintiff's wife won a portable house in a competition. She gave this house to her son, Martin. He offered it to his father who refused it. Martin then began to prepare a site for it on his own lands. When the plaintiff went to Dublin, his wife thought it would be suitable to have the house erected on the lands at Adamstown, and she sought her husband's

[1] [1962] I.R. 268.

permission to do so. He replied by messenger that he was making the place over to her and she could erect the house where she liked. As a result, Martin erected the house on the lands at Adamstown rather than on his own lands. In September 1959, the plaintiff sent letters to Martin and Patrick requiring them to leave the house and give up any connection with the management of the farm or business. In 1960, the plaintiff commenced an action against his sons claiming, *inter alia*, an injunction to restrain them from interfering in the business and from trespassing on the property at Adamstown. By way of counterclaim, Martin claimed that he was entitled to the house and the site on which it stood.

Kenny J., in a lengthy judgment, refused to grant an injunction and held that, although Martin could not require the plaintiff to execute a conveyance of the site of his house, nevertheless, the plaintiff was estopped by his conduct from asserting his title to it. More particularly, it was suggested *obiter* by Kenny J. that, after 12 years, Martin could bring a successful application, based on limitation, to be registered as the owner of the site. He said[2]:

> " ... neither the plaintiff nor any person claiming through him can now successfully assert a title to the lands on which the house is built by any proceedings and, at the end of the twelve-year period from the date when the erection of the bungalow commenced, Martin will be able to bring a successful application under section 52 of the Registration of Title Act, 1891, for his registration as owner".

In several of the English cases, the estoppel-based equity has been satisfied by simply denying the legal owner's claim to possession of the property.[3] In these cases, the claimant is given protection from possession but without obtaining any proprietary interest in the land. His right of occupation is personal to him—he cannot sell, mortgage or lease his privilege and, if he leaves the property, his "equity" terminates. As Maudsley has observed,[4] "he owns nothing new, but his status becomes one of irremovability". The barring of the legal owner's right to possession thus raises the issue of a potential claim of possessory title on the part of the claimant since it is, at least, arguable that he is in occupation adversely to the legal owner and the latter is unable to assert title to the property to bring that occupation to an end. But is the occupancy of such a nature as to constitute adverse possession? In *Cobb v. Lane*,[5] for example, a case involving a family arrangement whereby a house was bought in the name of an elder sister who allowed her brother to live in it, the Court of Appeal held that the brother was a mere licensee, and not a tenant at will, in order to escape the provisions of the Limitation Act 1939. Denning L.J. said[6]:

> "It is said that he was a tenant at will, that under the Limitation Act, 1939, s.9(1), his tenancy is deemed to be determined at the end of the first year, that he has been there for twelve years since, and so the property is his absolutely. It seems to me that the answer to that argument is that he was

---

[2] *ibid*. 292.
[3] See, Chap. 5, pp. 82–84.
[4] R.H. Maudsley, (1965) 81 L.Q.R. 183 at p. 184.
[5] [1952] 1 All E.R. 1199, C.A.
[6] *ibid*. 1202.

not a tenant at will at all, but only a licensee. The question in all these cases is one of intention: Did the circumstances and the conduct of the parties show that all that was intended was that the occupier should have a personal privilege with no interest in the land? It seems to me that the judge has so found. The defendant had only a personal privilege with no interest in the land, which he could assign or sub-let, and he could not part with possession to another. He was only a licensee, and he cannot pray in aid the provisions of the Limitation Act 1939."

(B) Difficulties in Applying the Doctrine

There are obvious difficulties in applying the doctrine of adverse possession to estoppel cases. In the first place, possession for the purpose of limitation does not usually result in acquisition of title to land unless it is "adverse"[7] to the legal owner. In other words, the claimant's occupation of the land must be actionable by the owner as a trespass. It is evident, therefore, that, where the occupation is referable to a licence granted by the legal owner, the period of limitation cannot run. In *BP Properties Ltd v. Buckler*,[8] for example, the landlord obtained a possession order against the defendant but subsequently allowed her to remain in occupation of the house rent-free for the rest of her life. The Court of Appeal held that, although this licence was unilateral, nevertheless, her possession of the house was no longer adverse and time had ceased to run in her favour under the Limitation Act 1939. The principle is that possession is not adverse if it can be referred to a lawful title. However, once the legal owner seeks to revoke the licence, it is arguable that the possession then becomes adverse and the licensee is a trespasser. In an estoppel case, therefore, until the legal owner attempts to go back upon the basic assumption which underlay the parties' transaction, the estoppel claimant has a right of occupation with permission of the legal owner which will thus negative any adverse possession.

What, however, is the position once the legal owner departs from his assurance and retracts the claimant's licence? At this point, it is arguable that the claimant's possession is adverse since his licence has been replaced by an inchoate estoppel equity. To put it another way, the claimant's occupation is now "referable to that 'inchoate equity' and not to any lawful right"[9] and, if the occupation persists for more than 12 years before any action is taken by the legal owner to recover possession, it may well give rise to a possessory title. Even if the legal owner brings an action to evict promptly, his claim for possession may be unsuccessful resulting in an award in favour of the claimant appropriate to satisfy the equity. This award may take the form of granting the claimant a proprietary interest in the land (*e.g.* the grant of the fee simple or beneficial share in the property) or, alternatively, simply a licence to occupy for life. In the latter case, the claimant's occupation is referable to the court's order

---

[7] See, Sched. 1, para. 8, Limitation Act 1980.
[8] [1987] 2 EGLR 168, C.A.
[9] M. Welstead, [1991] Conv. 280 at 283, who also refers to *Hyde v. Pearce* [1982] 1 All E.R. 1029, C.A., where it was held that there could be no adverse possession when the person seeking to rely on that possession occupied the property by virtue of an equitable interest arising under a contract of sale.

and it has been suggested[10] that "such possession can hardly be viewed as adverse unless the concept of judicially imposed adverse possession is accepted". It may be, however, that a distinction needs to be drawn, in this context, between the satisfaction of the equity by means of an irrevocable occupational licence[11] (*i.e.* a positive remedy) and the simple denial of the legal owner's claim to possession[12] (*i.e.* a negative remedy). In the latter case, the court's order may be viewed simply as a confirmation of the estoppel claimant's status of irremovability triggered by the inchoate equity resulting from the legal owner's unconscionable assertion of his strict legal rights. If the view of Kenny J. in *Cullen* is correct, it seems to place the legal owner in an odd situation since "he has a trespasser on his land acquiring title under the Statute of Limitations and, yet, there appears to be nothing effective he can do to prevent this. Equity denies him the remedy necessary to remove the trespasser from possession of his land and thereby to prevent time running against him".[13] It has already been mentioned elsewhere that, save in exceptional cicumstances, the estoppel claimant's equity, once satisfied in terms of a court order, is irrevocable.[14] Even subsequent misconduct on the part of the estoppel claimant affords little opportunity for the legal owner to re-apply for possession of the property. The appropriate remedy in such cases is an action for nuisance, trespass or an injunction restraining the improper conduct.[15] Given that the legal owner cannot bring a successful action to recover possession after the court hearing, it is doubtful whether, following the court order, time can continue to run for the purposes of adverse possession. It has been held,[16] however, that adverse possession may continue despite the fact that the legal owner has only a *restricted* right to recover possession. It remains to be seen whether adverse possession can run if the legal owner has, effectively, no right of action to evict the claimant save in exceptional circumstances.

Another difficulty alluded to by Welstead[17] lies in the fact that the estoppel claimant, if he is to successfully claim adverse possession, must show the requisite intention to possess the land. The authorities on adverse possession do

---

[10] M. Wesltead, [1991] Conv. 280 at p. 284.

[11] See, *e.g. Inwards v. Baker* [1965] 2 Q.B. 29, C.A.; *Greasley v. Cooke* [1980] 1 W.L.R. 1306, C.A.; *Maharaj v. Chand* [1986] A.C. 898, P.C.

[12] See, *e.g. Matharu v. Matharu* (1994) 68 P. & C.R. 93, C.A.; *Jones (A.E.) v. Jones (F.W.)* [1977] 1 W.L.R. 438, C.A.; *Hopgood v. Brown* [1955] 1 W.L.R. 213, C.A.

[13] J.C.W. Wylie, *Irish Land Law*, (1975), p. 809.

[14] See, *Williams v. Staite* [1979] 1 Ch. 291, C.A., discussed in Chap. 5, pp. 74–75, and Chap. 7, pp. 145–146.

[15] See, *Williams v. Staite* [1979] 1 Ch. 291 at 300, C.A., *per* Goff L.J., who also alluded to the possibility that the equity may be in its nature for a limited period only or determinable upon a certain condition. In such a case, the court would need to see whether, in the events which had happened, the equity had determined or it had expired or been determined by the happening of the condition. See further, M. Thompson, [1986] Conv. 406 at pp. 412–414.

[16] See, *Moses v. Lovegrove* [1952] 2 Q.B. 533, C.A., where it was held that the test of adverse possession, for the purposes of s.10(1) of the Limitation Act 1939, was not the existence of an absolute unqualified right to recover possession on the part of the owner of the land. Possession for the purposes of the Limitation Act 1939 was nonetheless adverse because Parliament (*e.g.*, under the Rent Acts) had put certain serious qualifications upon the right of a person whose land was in adverse possession to enter and recover possession of that property. See further, *Bridges v. Mees* [1957] Ch. 475, where Harman J. held that a purchaser under a contract of sale could be in adverse possession of the land despite the fact that the bare trustee of the legal title could not bring an effective action to recover possession of it. See also, *Re Cussons* [1904] 73 L.J. Ch. 296 at 298.

[17] M. Wesltead, [1991] Conv. 280 at 285–286.

not make it clear whether the adverse possessor must establish an intention merely to possess the land[18] or whether he must also prove an intention to exclude the legal owner.[19] If the latter view is correct, it seems doubtful whether an estoppel claimant could establish the necessary intention since:

> "the representee who has an 'inchoate equity' clearly has no intention to exclude the legal owner other than for the period covered by the engendered assumption. He may have been led to believe that he has been granted a right for his lifetime or for some shorter period of time but this is not inconsistent with an acknowledgment of the permanent nature of the legal owner's dormant title during that period. Similarly, a representee whose 'inchoate equity' has been satisfied by the grant of an occupational licence does not intend to deny the nature of the landowner's title."[20]

Welstead concludes by saying[21]:

> "It is the aim of the Limitation Act to end long dormant claims and ensure that persons with good causes of actions should pursue them with reasonable diligence. It would seem to defeat this aim to allow the Act to be used as an additional remedy by those whose "inchoate equity" has already been satisfied under the doctrine of proprietary estoppel. On the other hand the policy behind the Limitation Act also urges that, where there is a long-term occupation by someone other than the legal owner, it may be advantageous that factual possession of the land and legal title should ultimately become synonymous. It is arguable that long-term estoppel licences fall within this policy."

(B) Can a Party Be Estopped From Relying on a Claim of Adverse Possession?

It has been held that where, in a *bona fide* compromise agreement, an occupier of land acknowledges that his occupation of the land has not been adverse to the legal owner, he is estopped from relying on a claim for adverse possession in any subsequent proceedings against the same party. The point arose in *Colchester Borough Council v. Smith.*[22] In this case, for over 12 years prior to November 1983, a Mr Tillson occupied certain land adversely to the freehold owner, the Colchester Borough Council. In correspondence starting in November 1982, the Council sought to regularise Mr Tillson's occupation by granting him a licence for a fee, but Mr Tillson's solicitors initially maintained that he had acquired the freehold title by adverse possession. After threats

---

[18] See, *e.g. Ocean Estates Ltd v. Norman Pinder* [1969] 2 A.C. 19, P.C.
[19] See, *e.g. Littledale v. Liverpool College* [1900] 1 Ch. 19, C.A. and *Powell v. McFarlane* (1979) 38 P. & C.R. 452. The competing authorities are discussed by M. Dockray, [1982] Conv. 256, 345, [1983] Conv. 398, and [1985] Conv. 272. See also, M.J. Goodman, (1970) 33 M.L.R. 281; P. Jackson, (1980) 96 L.Q.R. 333.
[20] M. Welstead, [1991] Conv. 280 at p. 286.
[21] M. Wesltead, [1991] Conv. 280 at pp. 286–287.
[22] [1992] Ch. 421, C.A.

by the council to institute proceedings for possession, an agreement was concluded for a lease of the land by the council to Mr Tillson, in which the latter acknowledged the council's title to the land and stated that he had not gained any right, title or interest to or in it by adverse possession. In subsequent proceedings, the council sought a declaration that it was the freehold owner of the land and that Mr Tillson had no estate or interest except as a tenant under the agreement. It was argued on behalf of Mr Tillson that the council's title, having been extinguished by his adverse occupation of the land for more than 12 years, was impossible to be revived. The Court of Appeal, however, rejected this argument, holding that Mr Tillson was estopped from going behind the agreement and asserting a freehld title by adverse possession.

10. TOWARDS AN UNDERLYING CONCEPT?

(A) English Caselaw

The modern English trend is to move away from a strict adherence to Fry J.'s five *probanda* established in *Willmott v. Barber*[1] and to apply a broader formulation based on the notion of unconscionability.[2]

This trend was begun by Oliver J. in *Taylor Fashions Ltd v. Liverpool Victoria Trustees Co Ltd*,[3] where he drew a clear distinction between common expectation and unilateral mistake cases and suggested that, whilst the five *Willmott* criteria may be relevant to a unilateral mistake case, not all would necessarily be appropriate to a common expectation case.[4] He also suggested that all the *probanda* may still have to be satisfied if the defendant has simply stood by without protest (*i.e.* silently acquiesced) while his rights have been infringed but, in cases of active encouragement, then it may be immaterial whether the legal owner knew of his own legal rights and that the claimant was acting in the mistaken belief that they will not be enforced against him. In cases where all the five criteria set out in *Willmott* were not relevant, Oliver J. was able to identify from the authorities "a much wider equitable jurisdiction to interfere in cases where the assertion of strict legal rights is found by the court to be unconscionable.[5] Instead of seeking to fit the circumstances "within the confines of some preconceived formula serving as a universal yardstick for every form of unconscionable behaviour",[6] he suggested a much broader approach "which is directed rather at ascertaining whether, in particular individual circumstances, it would be unconscionable for a party to be permitted to deny that which, knowingly or unknowingly, he has allowed or encouraged another to asssume to his detriment".[7] On this basis, therefore, knowledge of the true position by the legal owner is treated as merely one of the relevant factors (or even a determining factor in some cases) in the overall inquiry.

Oliver J. referred to a number of earlier authorities in support of this broader

---

[1] (1880) 15 Ch. D. 96.
[2] See generally, M. Lunney, *Towards a Unified Estoppel—The Long and Winding Road*, [1992] Conv. 239 at pp. 247–251 and P.D. Finn, Chap. 4, *Equitable Estoppel*, in P.D. Finn, *Essays in Equity*, (Sydney, 1985).
[3] [1982] Q.B. 133.
[4] See further, Chap. 6, pp. 124–127.
[5] *ibid.* 147.
[6] *ibid.* 152.
[7] *ibid.* 151–152. This broad test of unconscionability would do away with the necessity of "forcing those incumbrances into a Procrustean bed constructed from some unalterable criteria": *ibid.* 154.

based jurisdiction. In *Inwards v. Baker*,[8] a common expectation case, the underlying principle was stated very broadly both by Lord Denning M.R. and by Danckwerts L.J. Lord Denning M.R. said[9]:

> "All that is necessary is that the licensee should , at the request or with the encouragement of the landlord, have spent the money in the expectation of being allowed to stay there. If so, the court will not allow that expectation to be defeated where it would be inequitable so to do."

And Danckwerts L.J. said[10]:

> "It seems to me that this is one of the cases of an equity created by estoppel, or equitable estoppel, as it is sometimes called, by which the person who has made the expenditure is induced by the expectation of obtaining protection, and equity protects him so that an injustice may not be perpetrated."

Similarly, in *E.R. Ives Investment Ltd v. High*,[11] Lord Denning M.R. reiterated the broad principle that the court would not allow an expectation to be defeated "when it would be inequitable so to do".[12] Again, in *Crabb v. Arun District Council*,[13] both Lord Denning M.R. and Scarman L.J. emphasised the flexibility of the proprietary estoppel doctrine. Although Scarman L.J. ultimately adopted and applied the five *Willmott* criteria, it is noteworthy that he described these as "a valuable guide"[14] and emphasised that the court "cannot find an equity established unless it is prepared to go as far as to say that it would be unconscionable and unjust to allow [the legal owners] to set up their undoubted rights against the claim being made by the plaintiff".[15] Moreover, he reformulated what Fry J. in *Willmott v. Barber*[16] called "fraud" in this context into a modern requirement that the plaintiff should "establish as a fact that the defendant, by setting up his right, is taking advanatge of him in a way which is unconscionable, inequitable or unjust".[17] This, however, does not necessarily signify that the defendant's conduct is in any way morally reprehensible.[18]

In *Shaw v. Applegate*,[19] Buckley L.J. took the opportunity to interpret Fry J.'s *probanda* in *Willmott* as meaning that "where a man has got a legal right ... acquiescence on [his] part will not deprive [him] of that legal right unless it is of such a nature and in such circumstances that it would really be dishonest or

---

[8] [1965] 2 Q.B. 29, C.A.

[9] *ibid.* 37.

[10] *ibid.* 38.

[11] [1967] 2 Q.B. 379, C.A. See also, *Ward v. Kirkland* [1967] Ch. 194 at 235, where Ungoed-Thomas J. said: "The foundation of [the equity] ... in all these instances, is the recognition by the court that it would be unconscionable in the circumstances for a legal owner fully to exercise his legal rights".

[12] *ibid.* 394–395.

[13] [1976] Ch. 179, C.A.

[14] *ibid.* 194.

[15] *ibid.* 195.

[16] (1880) 15 Ch.D. 96.

[17] *ibid.* 195.

[18] *Salvation Army Trustee Co. Ltd v. West Yorkshire Metropolitan County Council* (1981) 41 P. & C.R. 179 at 198, *per* Woolf J.

[19] [1977] 1 W.L.R. 970, C.A.

unconscionable of [him] to set up that right after what has occurred".[20] He went on to observe that it may be "open to doubt"[21] whether, in order to reach that state of affairs, it was really necessary to comply strictly with all five *Willmott* criteria. In his view, it was not essential to find all the five *probanda* strictly applicable and satisfied in any particular case. The real test, according to Buckley L.J.[22] was:

> " ... whether upon the facts of the particular case the situation has become such that it would be dishonest or unconscionable for the plaintiff, or the person having the right sought to be enforced, to continue to seek to enforce it".

Goff L.J. also expressed doubts whether it was necessary in all cases to establish the five tests laid down by Fry J. and agreed that the test was whether, in the circumstances, it had become unconscionable for the plaintiff to rely upon his legal right.[23] In *Moorgate Mercantile Co Ltd v. Twitchings*,[24] Lord Denning M.R. had occasion to observe that[25]:

> "[Estoppel] is a principle of justice and equity. It comes to this: when a man, by his words or conduct, has led another to believe in a particular state of affairs, he will not be allowed to go back on it when it would be unjust or inequitable for him to do so."

The broad approach taken by Oliver J. in *Taylor Fashions* was adopted by Robert Goff J. in *Amalgamated Investment & Property Co Ltd v. Texas Commerce International Bank Ltd*,[26] who also emphasised the flexible nature of the estoppel doctrine and rejected rigid over-categorisation. In that case, a company had guaranteed a loan to be given by a bank. The loan was, in fact, made by a subsidiary of the bank. The company had encouraged the bank to believe that the guarantee was effective to cover the subsidiary's loan. It was held, on the facts, that it would be unconscionable for the company to take advantage of the bank's mistaken belief as to the validity of the guarantee and, accordingly, the company was estopped from denying that the guarantee applied to the subsidiary's loan. In Goff J.'s view, the doctrines of acquiescence and encouragement were aspects of a much wider jurisdiction to interefere in cases where the assertion of strict legal rights was found by the court to be unconscionable. In the same case, Lord Denning M.R. (in the Court of Appeal) perceived all forms of estoppel (*i.e.* proprietary estoppel, estoppel by representation of fact, estoppel by acquiescence and promissory estoppel) as merging into one general principle shorn of limitations, namely[27]:

---

[20] *ibid.* 977–978.
[21] *ibid.* 978. See also the observations of Sir Raymond Evershed M.R. in *Electrolux Ltd v. Electrix Ltd* (1954) R.P.C. 23 at 33.
[22] *ibid.* 978.
[23] *ibid.* 980.
[24] [1976] Q.B. 225, C.A.
[25] *ibid.* 241.
[26] [1982] Q.B. 84, C.A., 103–104, and Lord Denning M.R. at 122. The decision at first instance was given by Goff J.
[27] *ibid.* 122.

"When the parties to a transaction proceed on the basis of an underlying assumption—either of fact or law—whether due to misrepresentation or mistake makes no difference—on which they have conducted the dealings between them—neither of them will be allowed to go back on that assumption when it would be unfair or unjust to allow him to do so. If one of them does seek to go back on it, the courts will give the other such remedy as the equity of the case demands".

More recently, the Privy Council in *Attorney-General of Hong Kong v. Humphreys Estate (Queen's Gardens) Ltd*[28] referred with approval to a general test, indicated by Scarman L.J. in *Crabb v. Arun District Council*,[29] that equity will interfere if "it would be unconscionable and unjust to allow the defendants to set up their undoubted rights against the claim being made by the plaintiff". Their Lordships also approved the judgment of Oliver J. in *Taylor Fashions*, reiterated in the Court of Appeal in *Habib Bank Ltd v. Habib Bank AG Zurich*,[30] and also the above-cited passage from the judgment of Lord Denning M.R. in the *Amalgamated Investment* case. Significantly, however, the Privy Council held that all three elements of estoppel (*i.e.* assurance, reliance and detriment) had to be satisfied. While the Hong Kong government had acted to its detriment, the other two essential elements were not present—the creation or encouragement of a belief or expectation by the company and a reliance on that by the government. The case was not approached as a question of "unfairness" or unconscionability in the round.

A good illustration of the application of the broader approach is to be found in *Lim Teng Huan v. Ang Swee Chuan*,[31] a decision of the Privy Council on appeal from the Court of Appeal of Brunei Darussalam. Here, the plaintiff and defendant jointly purchased land which was transferred into their fathers' names. In 1982, the defendant decided to build a house on the land for himself. At his own expense, preparatory works were carried out and construction commenced. In March 1985, when the house had been partially built, the parties entered into a written agreement whereby the plaintiff acknowledged that the construction was with his consent and agreed to exchange his undivided share in the land for unspecified land expected to be allotted to the defendant by the government. The house was completed and the defendant went into occupation, fencing nearly all of the land. Both fathers then died and the plaintiff, as administrator of his father's estate, brought an action against the defendant claiming *inter alia* a declaration that he was the owner of a one-half undivided share of the land. The Privy Council held that it would be unconscionable for the plaintiff to renege on the assumption that the defendant would have a sole beneficial interest in the house and land on paying compensation to the plaintiff for relinquishing his half-share and, accordingly, he was estopped from denying the defendant's title to the whole of the land. In applying *Taylor Fashions*, the Privy Council reiterated that, in order to found a proprietary estoppel, it was not essential that the representor should have been guilty of unconscionable

---

[28] [1987] 2 W.L.R. 343, P.C.
[29] [1976] Ch. 179 at 195, C.A.
[30] [1981] 1 W.L.R. 1265 at 1285, C.A. See also, *Hammersmith and Fulham London Borough Council v. Top Shop Centres Ltd* [1990] Ch. 237 at 253–254, *per* Warner J.
[31] [1992] 1 W.L.R. 113, P.C.

conduct in permitting the representee to assume that he could act as he did—it was enough if, in all the circumstances, it was unconscionable for the representor to *go back on the assumption* which he permitted the representee to make.

Another example of the application of the unconscionbale doctrine in the estoppel context is to be found in the unreported case of *Appleby v. Cowley*,[32] where the plaintiff, the current head of a set of barristers' chambers, claimed that the defendants, a former head of chambers and a family company associated with him, held the chambers on trust for the present members of the set. The plaintiff claimed, in the alternative, that the members' expectation and expenditure on the building (*i.e.* on constructing an extension and renovating the roof and exterior walls) resulted in an equity based on proprietary estoppel. Sir Robert Megarry V.-C. held that (1) such fiduciary relationship as existed between the parties was insufficient to establish the obligations of trusteeship and (2) the assertion of legal rights would not in any way be unconscionable. In the course of his judgment, he said:

> "As the law has developed, it may be that in cases in which a claim based on proprietary estoppel is made, the real question comes down simply to whether or not the assertion of strict legal rights would be unconscionable, without any detailed conditions or criteria being specified. In the present case, would it be unconscionable for the company to take the benefit of these remedial works to its building?"

In answering this question, the Vice-Chancellor intimated that there might be circumstances in which taking the benefit of the building works would be unfair. For example, if soon after the works had been done, the company had evicted all the members of chambers, or had required them to make payments equal to the full rental value of the chambers, then the company could well be said to be reaping the fruits of the expenditure unfairly. However, that was not what had happened in the instant case. On the contrary, the plaintiff had received "sufficient satisfaction" for his expenditure.

In *Swallow Securities Ltd v. Isenberg*,[33] the question in issue was whether the occupier of a flat (the appellant) was a person whom the landlords were estopped by their conduct from ejecting. An arrangement had been made between the protected tenant of the flat and the appellant whereby the latter was installed in occupation without the knowledge of the landlords. The tenant subsequently left to join her husband in the USA. The appellant caused substantial refurbishment works to be carried out to the flat at her own expense, which works were known to the resident porter but not known at that time to the managing agents or the landlords. The Court of Appeal, in rejecting the submission that the landlords were estopped from asserting a right to eject the appellant, held that, although the porter was aware of the works, there was nothing to put him on inquiry that they were being carried out on behalf of the appellant rather than on the order of the person who was still assumed to be the tenant. Moreover, there was no evidence of any action on the part of the landlords, their servants or agents, inducing an expectation on the part of the

---

[32] *The Times*, April 14, 1982; [1982] C.L.Y. 1150, available on Lexis.
[33] [1985] 1 EGLR 132, C.A.

appellant that she had rights more extensive than she actually had, which would make it unconscionable for the landlords to dispossess the appellant. Cumming-Bruce L.J., giving judgment for the Court, alluded to the formulation by Fry J. of the requirement of five *probanda* as being guidelines only "which will probably prove to be necessary and essential guidelines, to assist the court to decide the question whether it is unconscionable for the plaintiffs to assert their legal rights by taking an advantage of the defendant".[34] The concept of "taking an advantage of the defendant" arose because it was an essential ingredient of the equity that "the conduct of the plaintiff in whom the legal right is vested must have been such as to induce in the defendant an expectation that the defendant's rights are different from and more extensive than the defendant's strict legal rights".[35]

The broader-based jurisdiction initiated by Oliver J. in *Taylor Fashions* has also been alluded to by Mr Edward Nugee Q.C. (sitting as a High Court judge) in *Re Basham (dec'd)*.[36] In this case, the plaintiff's mother married the deceased in 1936 when the plaintiff was 15 years old. She lived with them until her marriage in 1941. She continued to help them to run their business and was never paid but understood that she would inherit the deceased's property when he died. In 1947, the plaintiff's husband was considering moving to a job with a tied cottage but the deceased was opposed to that, saying that he was willing to help them get another suitable house. Shortly afterwards, the deceased purchased a tenanted cottage with money provided largely by the plaintiff's mother. She died in 1976 and the deceased moved into the cottage which had become vacant. Shortly afterwards there was a boundary dispute between the deceased and his neighbour and the plaintiff took advice from her own solicitors, the deceased having told her that it was for her benefit because the house was hers. The plaintiff and her family lived near the deceased and, although the plaintiff's husband did not get on well with the deceased, he provided food for him, kept the garden in order and helped the plaintiff with work about the house. The plaintiff bought carpets for it and laid them herself and regularly prepared meals for the deceased. She was told by him that she would lose nothing by doing those acts for him. A few days before his death, the deceased indicated that he wanted to make a will leaving money to the plaintiff's son and that she was to have the house. The deceased, however, died intestate, and the plaintiff claimed that she was absolutely entitled to the house and to the deceased's furniture and other property. Mr Edward Nugee Q.C. had no hesitation in upholding the plaintiff's claim. Since the plaintiff had established that she had acted to her detriment in reliance on her belief, encouraged by the deceased, that she would ultimately benefit by receiving the deceased's property on his death, she was absolutely entitled to the deceased's residuary estate, including the house. The equity was not limited to acts done in reliance on a belief relating to an existing right but extended to acts done in reliance on a belief that future rights would be granted. In reaching his conclusion, the learned judge accepted the "broadening process"[37] initiated by

---

[34] *ibid.* 134.

[35] *ibid.* 134.

[36] [1986] 1 W.L.R. 1498. See, J. Martin, [1987] Conv. 211.

[37] *ibid.* 1508. At page 1510, he concluded: "But as Oliver J. indicated in the *Taylor Fashions* case equitable doctrines cannot be confined within a straitjacket by the labels which have become

Oliver J. in *Taylor Fashions* and suggested that the principle of proprietary estoppel, at least where the belief is that the representee is going to be given a right in the future, was properly to be regarded as giving rise to a species of constructive trust, this being "the concept employed by a court of equity to prevent a person from relying on his legal rights where it would be unconscionable for him to do so".[38] On this basis, the rights to which proprietary estoppel gives rise (and the machinery by which effect is given to them) are similar in many respects to those involved in cases of secret trusts, mutual wills and the acquisition of co-ownership interests in the matrimonial or quasi-matrimonial home. According to Mr Edward Nugee Q.C.[39]:

"In cases of proprietary estoppel the factor which gives rise to the equitable obligation is A's alteration of his position on the faith of a similar understanding. A third situation in which the court imposes a constructive trust is where A and B set up house together in a property which is in the name of B alone, and A establishes a common intention between A and B, acted on by A to his (or more usually her) detriment, that A should have a beneficial interest in the property ... Here too, if the two elements of common understanding or intention and detrimental acts on the part of A are established, they give rise to an equitable obligation enforceable against B which is in the nature of a constructive trust. A common theme can be discerned in each of these classes of case; and although different situations may give rise to differences of detail in the manner in which the court will give effect to the equity which arises in favour of A, one would expect the general principles applicable in the different situations to be the same unless there is a sound reason to the contrary".

In the instant case, the evidence clearly established that (1) the plaintiff had a belief (at all material times) that she was going to receive both the cottage and the remainder of the deceased's property on his death; (2) this belief was encouraged by the deceased; (3) the plaintiff acted to her detriment; and (4) the plaintiff's acts were done in reliance on or as a result of her belief that she would become entitled to the deceased's property on his death.

The notion that the doctrine of proprietary estoppel is a species of constructive trust was also alluded to by Nourse L.J., giving the judgment of the Court of Appeal in *Sen v. Headley*[40] a case involving a death-bed gift of land. In the course of his judgment, Nourse L.J. intimated that, where the doctrine gives the claimant a right to call for a conveyance of the land (as in the leading case of *Dillwyn v. Llewelyn*),[41] it could be said that the right is the consequence of an implied or constructive trust which arises once all the requirements of the doctrine have been satisfied.

Despite the modern trend towards a broader-based philosophy underlying

---

attached to them. It is clear that the doctrine which bears the label 'proprietary estoppel' is not limited to cases like *Willmott v. Barber* where A believes that he already has the interest which he asks the court to confirm, but extends to cases in which A believes that he will obtain an interest in the future."

[38] *ibid.* 1504.
[39] *ibid.* 1504.
[40] [1991] Ch. 425, C.A.
[41] (1862) 4 De G.F. & J. 517; 45 E.R. 1285.

proprietary estoppel doctrine, it is evident that the principle of unconscionability has not been universally applied in the English caselaw. Indeed, there is a noticeable concern that a wider-based principle may lead to uncertainty in the law and a "charter for idiosyncratic concepts of justice and fairness".[42] Thus, in *Haslemere Estates Ltd v. Baker*,[43] Sir Rober Megarry V.-C. expressed concern over "some far-reaching contentions which would raise a proprietary estoppel whenever justice and good conscience require it"[44] and concluded that: "I do not think that the subject is as wide and as indefinite as that".[45] In the earlier case of *Western Fish Products Ltd v. Penwith D.C.*,[46] Megaw L.J., giving the judgment of the Court of Appeal, observed[47] that "the system of equity has become a very precise one" and that "the creation of new rights and remedies is a matter for Parliament, not the judges". In his view, the cases had put clear limits to the application of the proprietary estoppel doctrine. In *Philip Lowe (Chinese Restaurant) Ltd v. Sau Man Lee*,[48] May L.J. considered it "essential" to remember that in this type of dispute "the courts do not have a general power to do what they think is fair and reasonable in all the circumstances." Again, in *Watts & Ready v. Storey*,[49] Slade L.J. considered that proprietary estoppel claims should be treated "with a degree of caution" since the estoppel principle may have the "drastic effect of conferring on one person a permanent, irrevocable interest in the land of another, even though he has given no consideration for such acquisition, by way of contractual arrangement, and no legally effective gift of it has been made in his favour". A note of caution was also expressed by Ormrod L.J. in *E. & L. Berg Homes Ltd v. Grey*[50]:

> " ... I think it is important that this court should not do or say anything which creates the impression that people are liable to be penalised for not enforcing their strict legal rights. It is a very unfortunate state of affairs when people feel obliged to take steps which they do not wish to take, in order to preserve their legal rights and prevent the other party acquiring rights against them. So the court in using its equitable jurisdiction must, in my judgment, approach these cases with extreme care".

In his view, it was "vital" that the courts recognise and apply the limits of the estoppel doctrine as set out in the first place by Lord Kingsdown in *Ramsden v. Dyson*[51] and later by Fry J. in *Willmott v. Barber*. It was not to be invoked "as a general jurisdiction in equity to relieve hardship resulting from the application of the ordinary law". One striking example of the Court of Appeal's strict adherence to the Fry J. *probanda* is to be found in the recent Court of Appeal decision in *Matharu v. Matharu*,[52] which has already been discussed else-

---

[42] *Legione v. Hateley* (1983) 152 C.L.R. 406 at 431, *per* Mason and Deane JJ., High Court of Australia.
[43] [1982] 1 W.L.R. 1109.
[44] *ibid.* 1119.
[45] *ibid.* 1119.
[46] [1981] 2 All E.R. 204, C.A.
[47] *ibid.* 218.
[48] Unreported, July 9, 1985, C.A., available on Lexis.
[49] [1984] 134 New L.J. 631, C.A., available on Lexis.
[50] (1979) 253 EG 473 at 479, C.A.
[51] (1866) L.R. 1 H.L. 129 at 170, H.L.
[52] (1994) 68 P. & C.R. 93, C.A.

where.[53] Another illustration is to be found in the earlier case of *Coombes v. Smith*,[54] a decision of Mr Jonathan Parker Q.C. (sitting as a deputy High Court judge), who applied Fry J.'s five tests with full rigour to the facts before him. This has been viewed by many commentators[55] as a retrograde step in the development of proprietary estoppel, not least because it produces "hard" cases where the courts have either strained the facts artificially within the confines of the five *probanda* so as to give the claimant an equity or, alternatively, dismissed the estoppel claim on the ground that all five tests (regardless of applicability) were not fully satisfied.

(B) Commonwealth Authorities

In Commonwealth jurisdictions, there has been a strong move away from the confines of Fry J.'s *probanda* in *Willmott v. Barber* towards a more generalised theory of unconscionability.

(i) New Zealand

In *Stratulatos v. Stratulatos*,[56] the defendant was the registered proprietor of a property in Ellice Street, Wellington. Her son, Spiros, married the plaintiff and the couple lived briefly with the defendant for a month before embarking on a trip overseas. On their return, they moved back into Ellice Street and, shortly thereafter, the defendant moved into another property. The plaintiff and Spiros then began a programme of renovation and, in the course of several years, expended more than $22,000 plus labour and costs on the Ellice Street property. In addition, they paid the rate demands and insurance premiums and (before his marriage to the plaintiff) Spiros also paid the mortgage instalments. Sub-sequently, Spiros died intestate and the plaintiff continued to reside in the property on her own. A dispute arose between the plaintiff and the defendant concerning their respective interests in the property. The High Court of Wellington held that Spiros and the plaintiff had expended considerable sums of money and effort on renovating and upgrading the property (and enhancing its capital and rental value) in the belief that they had the right to permanent occupation of the house pending the defendant's death, which belief the defendant had encouraged. Accordingly, the grounds of proprietary estoppel were made out. In the course of his judgment, McGechan J. said[57]:

> "The classical doctrine in recent years has become considerably more flexible. There has been a tendency to move away from strict adherence to the five *probanda*, each being regarded as essential, towards a more general approach based simply upon "unconscionability". A trend to that effect had developed in England ... That liberalising trend was picked up and applied in New Zealand ... "

---

[53] See, Chap. 6, p. 115.
[54] [1986] 1 W.L.R. 808.
[55] See, *e.g.*, Welstead, [1995] Conv. 61 and G. Battersby, [1995] 7 C.F.L.Q. 59. See further, Chap. 6, p. 115.
[56] [1988] 2 N.Z.L.R. 424, High Court of Wellington.
[57] *ibid*. 435.

In this case, McGechan J. did not ignore the classical five *probanda* but simply treated them as indicators (as opposed to prerequisites) providing some guidance towards a modern and more generalised test of unconscionability. There are a number of earlier New Zealand cases which also illustrate this "liberalising" trend. Thus, in *Andrews v. Colonial Mutual Life Assurance Society Ltd*,[58] Barker J. had occasion to observe[59] that "recent cases in England have demonstrated a flexible approach which does not rely so heavily on the . . . five *probanda*". He proceeded to apply Fry J.'s five criteria liberally to the facts of the case, commenting that "strict adherence to the five *probanda* is not necessary" and that "it would be unconscionable for a party to be permitted to deny that which knowingly or unkowingly he has allowed another to assume to his detriment rather than inquiring whether the circumstances can be fitted into some preconceived formula".[60] Similarly, in *Wham-O MFG Co v. Lincoln Industries Ltd*,[61] Davison C.J., giving the judgment of the Court of Appeal of Wellington, after a *verbatim* quotation of the five *probanda*, observed[62]:

> "However, of recent years there has been a trend away from the strict application of those five *probanda* to a more flexible test based on 'unconscionability'."

Reference may also be made to *Westland Savings Bank v. Hancock*,[63] in which Tipping J., after an extensive review of the English and New Zealand authorities, approached the matter as involving the question whether:

> " . . . there is anything acting on the conscience of the party sought to be estopped which should as a matter of fair dealing prevent him from asserting his strict legal rights".

Here, the Westland Savings Bank, in response to Mr and Mrs Hancock's loan application, made a written loan offer which specified the interest rate to be "current rate which for the time being is 6.75% per annum". The Hancocks duly executed a form of mortgage tendered by the bank. Unbeknown to the parties, the mortgage contained a provision restricting the bank's right to increase the interest rate to intervals of not less than three years. In response to a further loan application, the bank made a second loan offer which specified the interest rate to be "current rate at which for the time being is 9% per annum".

A variation of the existing mortgage was executed by the Hancocks to secure the second advance. In the 11 years following execution of the mortgage, the bank notified the Hancocks of increases in the interest rate both under the original and the varied mortgage on nine separate occasions, each of which was within three years of the preceding increase. The Hancocks paid to the bank interest at the increased rates from time to time without any protest. In 1985, the

---

[58] [1982] 2 N.Z.L.R. 556, High Court of Auckland.
[59] *ibid*. 568.
[60] *ibid*. 570.
[61] [1984] 1 N.Z.L.R. 641, Court of Appeal of Wellington.
[62] *ibid*. 671.
[63] [1987] 2 N.Z.L.R. 21, High Court of Christchurch.

parties became aware of the restriction in the mortgage on the bank's right to increase the interest rate. The bank issued proceedings claiming rectification of the mortgage to embody the interest rate terms stated in the bank's two loan offers and a declaration that it was entitled to charge interest at its current rate from time to time on the ground that the Hancocks were estopped from denying the bank's right to do so. In this case, the Hancocks had unknowingly encouraged the bank to assume that, contrary to the strict terms of the mortgage, it had the right to increase the interest rate to its current rate from time to time without restriction. The mortgage was, in fact, rectified, but had it not been, the Hancocks would have been estopped from recovering overpaid interest on past instalments under the mortgage because they had said nothing during the years when there had been numerous increases in the interest rate under the mortgage. It was argued, on behalf of the Hancocks, that no estoppel could arise in the absence of actual knowledge of their contractual position—in a case of mere passivity (as here) the five *probanda* in *Willmott v. Barber* should continue to be strictly applied. Tipping J., however, rejected this narrow proposition holding that the question came down to "whether in the particular circumstances it would be inequitable for a party to be allowed to deny that what he knowingly *or unknowingly* [emphasis added] has allowed or encouraged the other party to assume to his detriment".[64] Accepting that there must be some test or principle to be applied "so that those who have to consider the matter in advance of a decision by the court can have a reasonable prospect of forecasting what the result will be", Tipping J. proceeded to adopt the formulation of the estoppel doctrine set out by the Privy Council in *Attorney-General of Hong Kong v. Humphreys Estate (Queen's Gardens)*.[65] Thus, on the facts, the Hancocks had, albeit unknowingly, encouraged the bank to assume that, contrary to the strict terms of the mortgage (which were also unknown to the bank) the bank had the right to increase the interest rate without restriction. The bank acted to its detriment because, in the belief that it was entitled to increase the interest rate as it did, it structured its whole operation accordingly. The Hancocks had also contributed to the creation of a belief on the part of the bank that it had the right to increase the interest rate as it did. The fact that the bank already held that belief did not prevent the conduct of the Hancocks from reinforcing that belief as it applied to themselves. The bank also relied on that belief by adopting towards the Hancocks a stance different as to their interest rate from what it would have been if the rate could only have been adjusted three yearly. In all the circusmtances, therefore, Tipping J. held that it would be inequitable for the Hancocks to be permitted to deny the contractual validity of the bank's actions regarding their interest rate.

The trend away from the strict application of Fry J.'s *probanda* to a more flexible test of unconscionability has also been noted by the Court of Appeal of Wellington in the celebrated case of *Gillies v. Keogh*[66] and the Court of Appeal of New South Wales in *Austotel Property Ltd v. Franklins Selfserve Property Ltd.*[67]

---

[64] *ibid.* 36.
[65] [1987] 2 W.L.R. 343 at 349, P.C.
[66] [1989] 2 N.Z.L.R. 327. See further, Chap. 8, pp. 158–160.
[67] [1989] 16 N.S.W.L.R. 582.

(ii) Australia

A leading case is *Beaton v. McDivitt*.[68] Here, the McDivitts, fearing that the zoning of their 25 acre property would be changed in such a way as to increase their rates, made a proposal to Beaton that he would come on to part of the land and work it rent free and that when sub-division took place, Beaton would be given the fee simple title to the part he occupied. Beaton entered onto part of the land, worked it and, with the help of McDivitt, built a rock hut which was used as a dwelling. Neither the contemplated rezoning or subdivision of the land ever took place. Beaton subsequently sought to enforce the arrangement. At first instance, Young J. held *inter alia* that proprietary estoppel was a special type of equity employed only in situations where the ordinary legal rights between the parties produced a situation which was unconscionable. In the instant case, however, he held that the doctrine had no application where, in the circumstances, the relationship between the parties was one of contract based on a finding that consideration therefor arose from a detriment suffered upon a promise already made. On appeal, his decision was reversed. The majority[69] of the Court of Appeal concluded that for a contract to be enforceable at law consideration must be found in the form of a price in return for the exchange of the relevant promise or a *quid pro quo*. McHugh J.A. took the opportunity to reiterate that the jurisprudential basis of the proprietary estoppel doctrine was not contractual but based on the principle that equity will not allow a person to insist upon his strict rights when it would be unconscionable for him to do so.[70]

In the later case of *Waltons Stores (Interstate) Ltd v. Maher*,[71] a case involving promissory estoppel, the judgments of a majority of the High Court of Australia held that equitable estoppel yields a remedy in order to prevent unconscionable conduct on the part of the party who, having made a promise to another who acts on it to his detriment, seeks to resile from the promise. Thus, Mason C.J. and Wilson J. in a joint judgment had occasion to observe that[72]:

> "One may discern in the cases a common thread which links them together, namely, the principle that equity will come to the relief of a plaintiff who has acted to his detriment on the basis of a basic assumption in relation to which the other party to the transaction has 'played such a part in the adoption of the assumption that it would be unfair or unjust if he were left to ignore it' ... equity comes to the relief of such a plaintiff on the footing that it would be unconscionable conduct on the part of the other party to ignore the assumption."

More recently, in *Commonwealth of Australia v. Verwayen*,[73] Mason C.J. had the opportunity to further consider the nature of the estoppel doctrine. In his

---

[68] [1985] 13 N.S.W.L.R. 134, (Young J.); [1987] 13 N.S.W.L.R. 162, Court of Appeal of New South Wales.

[69] Kirby P., Mahoney J.A. (and McHugh J.A. dissenting).

[70] *ibid.* 182.

[71] [1988] 62 A.L.J.R. 110, High Court of Australia. See further, A. Duthie, (1988) 104 L.Q.R. 362. See also, *Foran v. Wight* (1989) 168 C.L.R. 385, 411, 434, *per* Mason C.J. and Deane J., respectively, High Court of Australia.

[72] *ibid.* 116. See also, Brennan J. at 123–124.

[73] (1990) 95 A.L.R. 321, High Court of Australia.

view, all categories of estoppel (*i.e.* promissory estoppel, proprietary estoppel and estoppel by acquiescence) are intended to serve the same fundamental purpose, namely, "protection against the detriment which would flow from a party's change of position if the assumption (or expectation) that led to it were deserted".[74] In conformity with this fundamental purpose, the modern cases, according to Mason C.J., point inexorably towards the emergence of one overarching doctrine of estoppel rather than a series of independent rules, citing as examples, *inter alia* the English decisions in *Taylor Fashions Ltd v. Liverpool Victoria Trustees Co Ltd*,[75] *Amalgamated Investment Property Co Ltd v. Texas Bank Ltd*[76] and *Attorney-General (Hong Kong) v. Humphreys Estate (Queen's Gardens) Ltd.*[77] This overarching doctrine, which both attracts the jurisdiction of a court of equity and shapes the remedy to be given, is unconscionable conduct on the part of the person bound by the equity. But a limiting factor, according to Mason C.J., is that estoppel will permit a court to do only that what is required *in order to avoid detriment* to the party who has relied on the assumption induced by the party estopped, *and no more*. On this basis, the court will go no further than is necessary to prevent unconscionable conduct. Whilst in some cases this may mean that the party estopped will be held to his assurance (even if this involves the effective enforcement of a voluntary promise), in other cases a different (lesser) form of relief will be appropriate to satisfy the minimum equity to do justice to the claimant. What is significant here is the rejection of the notion that the purpose of the estoppel rules is simply to make good the relevant assurance. On the contrary, the court must look at all the circumstances in each case to decide in what way the equity can be satisfied. Thus[78]:

> "The result is that it should be accepted that there is but one doctrine of estoppel, which provides that a court of common law or equity may do what is required, but no more, to prevent a person who has relied upon an assumption as to a present, past or future state of affairs (including a legal state of affairs), which assumption the party estopped has induced him to hold, from suffering detriment in reliance upon the assumption as a result of the denial of its correctness."

An important feature of this analysis is that there must be a "proportionality" between the remedy and the detriment which is its purpose to avoid: "It would be wholly inequitable and unjust to insist upon a disproportionate making good of the relevant assumption".[79] The judgment of Brennan J. also recognises that the estoppel doctrine is not designed to enforce the assurance in every case. The vital question in each case is: "What is the minimum equity needed to avoid the relevant detriment?".[80]

---

[74] *ibid.* 330.
[75] [1982] Q.B. 133.
[76] [1982] Q.B. 84.
[77] [1987] A.C. 114, P.C.
[78] *ibid.* 333, *per* Mason C.J.
[79] *ibid.* 333.
[80] *ibid.* 345. See also, the judgments of Deane J., Dawson J. and McHugh J.

(C) Conclusion

The jurisdiction to grant relief in proprietary estoppel cases is based on the inequity that would result from the strict assertion of legal rights. Many of the English cases talk in terms of the conduct necessary to "raise the equity".[81] It is possible that the English doctrine of proprietary estoppel may ultimately develop into a simple proposition that a person who has induced another into an expectation should have to provide a remedy if it would be unconscionable to deny it.[82] English law, however, is still some way from accepting such a universal principle which may have far reaching implications for the contractual principle of consideration. The doctrine, in its widest form, also threatens to encroach upon other traditional principles of law. As a potential mechanism for creating informal rights in property,[83] it is seen[84] as being inconsistent with the doctrine of formalities, which requires that rights and interests in land may, generally speaking, only be created by writing or by means of a deed.[85] The doctrine also conflicts with the principle that gratuitous promises are unenforceable and that services rendered voluntarily are not the subject of compensation. Such potential conflicts with well-established legal principles explain the reluctance of the English judiciary to expand the doctrine of proprietary estoppel into a wider notion of "unconscientious dealing" in relation to property. As the editors of *Cheshire, Fifoot and Furmston's Law of Contract*[86] point out,[87] the "possible lines of development have been charted if the courts are bold enough to take them".

It is apparent that current English law, though accepting a much broader understanding of proprietary estoppel,[88] is likely to retain the Fry J. *probanda* as being useful guidelines in determining whether or not an estoppel equity has been made out. To this extent, the Fry J. formualtion is to be welcomed as providing a basis from which the court can make its assessment of the facts. Far from providing a rigid set of criteria, however, the five tests merely assist the court in answering the essential question, namely, whether the defendant's assertion of his strict legal rights would, in all the circumstances, be unconscionable. It should be remembered that the requirements in *Willmott v. Barber*[89] were laid down in the context of a case where the claimant was acting under a mistake as to his existing rights. This should be distinguished from cases where the claimant founds his claim upon an expectation encouraged or created by the legal owner. In this latter case, the Fry J. criteria have even less

---

[81] *Ramsden v. Dyson* (1866) L.R. 1 H.L. 129, H.L., *per* Lord Kingsdown.

[82] See generally, M. Halliwell, (1994) 14 Legal Studies 15.

[83] See generally, M. Howard and J. Hill, (1995) 15 Legal Studies, 356 at pp. 365–368.

[84] See, *e.g. Watts & Ready v. Storey* [1984] 134 New L.J. 631, C.A., where Slade L.J. observed: "In a case where the doctrine of proprietary estoppel operates, it may have the drastic effect of conferring on one person a permanent, irrevocable interest in the land of another, even though he has given no consideration for such acquisition, by way of contractual arrangement, and no legally effective gift of it has been made in his favour".

[85] See, ss. 52 and 53 of the Law of Property Act 1925 and s. 2 of the Law of Property (Miscellaneous Provisions) Act 1989, replacing s.40 of the Law of Property Act 1925 in respect of contracts entered into after September 27, 1989.

[86] 7th N.Z. ed., (1988).

[87] *ibid.* 123.

[88] See, generally, P.T. Evans, [1988] Conv. 346.

[89] (1880) 15 Ch. D. 96.

significance, the courts tending to resort to a more straightforward inquiry of the existence of a requisite assurance, reliance and detriment to support an estoppel claim. In all cases, however, "unconscionability is the essence of the doctrine".[90]

In terms of the requirement of detriment, it is apparent that the English courts are moving steadily towards a concept of "change of position".[91] In *Greasley v. Cooke*,[92] Lord Denning M.R. considered[93] it sufficient "if the party, to whom the assurance is given, acts on the faith of it—in such circumstances that it would be unjust and inequitable for the party making the assurance to go back on it". According to Grey,[94] this "movement towards a doctrine of 'acting' on the faith of an assurance is symptomatic of the more general contemporary tendency to re-state the several elements of proprietary estoppel in terms of a composite formula of unconscionability".

However, one obvious consequence of adopting a broader-based doctrine of unconscionability is that estoppel cases will be longer with ever wider and deeper analyses of the facts. Without doubt, the inquiry into whether it would be "unjust and inequitable for the party making the assurance to go back on it" is likely to be complex and protracted giving rise to a sophisticated assessment of all the circumstances in the given case. As was stated by Dunn L.J. in *Watts & Ready v. Storey*,[95] in each case it is a question of "fact or degree" as to whether an equity has been made out. An obvious criticism of any wide remedial discretion is uncertainty. It must be possible to predict with some degree of accuracy whether or not an estoppel claim is likely to meet with success and, if so, the choice of remedy adopted by the court to satisfy the equity. An obvious danger is that "the process of robust over-simplification may lead, if followed far enough, to palm-tree justice".[96]

---

[90] *Bennett v. Bennett*, unreported, May 18, 1990, C.A., *per* Slade L.J., available on Lexis.

[91] See, Chap. 4., p. 57.

[92] [1980] 1 W.L.R. 1306, C.A.

[93] *ibid.* 1311.

[94] Gray, *Elements of Land Law*, (2nd ed), p. 338.

[95] [1984] 134 New L.J. 631, available on Lexis.

[96] See, Spencer Bower and Turner, *The Law Relating to Estoppel by Representation*, (3rd ed., 1977), Chap. 12 at p.309, citing Harman J. in *Campbell Discount Ltd v. Bridge* [1961] 1 Q.B. 445 at 459, C.A., who said: "Equitable principles are I think perhaps rather too often bandied about in common law courts as though the Chancellor still had only the length of his own foot to measure when coming to a conclusion. Ever since the time of Lord Eldon the system of equity for good or evil has been a very precise one, and equitable jurisdiction is exercised only on well known principles."

Appendix—Selection of Forms

The forms set out below (which are by no means intended to be exhaustive) are provided to assist the practitioner in the drafting of pleadings associated with proprietary estoppel claims. They should be treated merely as examples and not as standard precedents. The reader is referred to *Atkin's Court Forms*, (2nd ed., 1992 Issue), Vol. 18 at pp. 357–359, for a further selection of useful forms in this area.

Contents

Form 1: *Statement of Claim: Imperfect gift of house—plaintiff seeking order that defendant execute transfer of fee simple in her name. See, Pascoe v. Turner [1979] 1 W.L.R. 431, C.A.*

IN THE HIGH COURT OF JUSTICE   199.. A. No....

CHANCERY DIVISION

BETWEEN:

A.B.	Plaintiff
and	
C.D.	Defendant

STATEMENT OF CLAIM

1. The Plaintiff and the Defendant, formerly and at all material times until the events mentioned in paragraph 4 hereof, although unmarried lived together as husband and wife.

2. In or about   19 , at a time when the parties were living together in rented furnished accommodation, the Defendant purchased the freehold of the premises situate at and known as
   (hereinafter called "the property") for the sum of £   . On
                    19 , he was duly registered at H.M. Land Registry as the sole registered proprietor thereof with title absolute.

3. On   19   , at the invitation of the Defendant, the Plaintiff moved into the property with the Defendant. The property comprises a three-bedroomed semi-detached house, a garage and small garden.

4. In or about   19   , the Defendant left the property leaving the Plaintiff in occupation thereof.

5. Prior to his leaving the property, the Defendant told the Plaintiff on several occasions that the property was hers including all the furniture therein. In particular, he orally informed the Plaintiff that he had executed a transfer of the property and its contents in her favour.

PARTICULARS OF STATEMENT

[Set out particulars of statement]

6. In reliance upon the Defendant's said statement, the Plaintiff to the Defendant's knowledge and encouragement spent considerable sums of money in repairs to and improvements on the property.

PARTICULARS OF EXPENDITURE

[Set out items of expenditure]

7. In fact, unknown to the Plaintiff until shortly before the commencement of

the issue of the writ herein, the Defendant never executed a transfer of the property in the Plaintiff's favour and title thereto remains vested in the Defendant.

8. On or about   19   , the Defendant wrote to the Plaintiff denying that she has any legal right or interest in the property and demanding that she vacate the same forthwith.

AND THE PLAINTIFF CLAIMS:

(1) A Declaration that the property is vested in fee simple in the Plaintiff;

(2) A Declaration that the Plaintiff is the owner of all the furniture situate in the property;

(3) An Order that the Defendant do execute a transfer of the fee simple in the property to the Plaintiff;

(4) Such further or other relief to which the Plaintiff may in the circumstances be entitled;

(5) Costs.

Dated this   day of   19   .

Form 2: *Statement of Claim: Extension to house—plaintiff claiming beneficial interest based on resulting/constructive trust and, alternatively, lien or charge based on proprietary estoppel. See, Hussey v. Palmer [1972] 1 W.L.R. 1286, C.A.*

IN THE HIGH COURT OF JUSTICE   199.. A. No....

CHANCERY DIVISION

BETWEEN:

A.B.   Plaintiff

and

C.D.   Defendant

STATEMENT OF CLAIM

1.   The Defendant is the freehold owner of the house situate at and known as (hereinafter called "the house"). The Plaintiff is the mother of the Defendant.

2.   In or about   19   , the Plaintiff, upon the invitation of the Defendant and his wife, moved into the house occupying a small bedroom on the upper floor thereof rent free.

3.   In or about   19   , the Plaintiff agreed with the Defendant that she would pay for the construction of an extension to the ground floor of the house on the understanding that, when constructed, she would be entitled to use it as a living room for herself exclusively, in addition to occupying the existing dining room in the house as a bedroom, rent free for the rest of her life.

4.   Pursuant to the said agreement, the Plaintiff paid the sum of £   for the construction of the said extension, which was duly completed in or about   19   .

5.   Despite completion of the said extension, the Defendant has insisted that the Plaintiff continue to occupy the small bedroom on the upper floor of the house paying therefor the weekly rent of £   . The Defendant has stated to the Plaintiff that she would not be welcome to occupy the said extension which, at all material times, has been used as a sitting room for the Defendant and his wife exclusively.

6.   On   19   , the Plaintiff moved out of the house as a result of the Defendant's increasingly hostile attitude towards her.

7.   The Plaintiff contends that, by virtue of the said expenditure referred to in paragraph 4 hereof, the Plaintiff became entitled to a beneficial interest in the house or the net proceeds of sale thereof equal to the proportion which her said expenditure bore to the value of the house immediately after completion of the said extension and that the Defendant became entitled to

the remainder of the beneficial interest in the house or the net proceeds of sale thereof and that the Defendant holds the house upon trust to sell the same and to hold the net proceeds of sale and the net rents and profits until sale upon trust for the Plaintiff and the Defendant in the said shares.

8. Alternatively, the Plaintiff contends that she expended the said sum in the expectation or belief that she would have an interest in the house, and the Defendant knew or ought to have known that she was incurring the said expenditure in that belief or expectation. In the premises, the Plaintiff contends that she is entitled to an equitable lien or charge on the house for the amount of her said expenditure.

AND THE PLAINTIFF CLAIMS:

(1)   A Declaration in the terms of the Plaintiff's contention set out in paragraph 7 hereof;

(2)   Alternatively to (1) above, a Declaration in the terms of the Plaintiff's contention set out in paragraph 8 hereof;

(3)   An Order for sale of the house;

(4)   Further or other relief;

(5)   Costs.

Dated this   day of   19   .

Form 3: *Particulars of Claim: Construction of driveway on defendant's land—plaintiff claiming entitlement to strip of land by virtue of proprietary estoppel. See, Clayton v. Singh, April 12 1984, unreported, C.A., available on Lexis.*

IN THE   COUNTY COURT   Case No......

BETWEEN:

A.B.   Plaintiff

and

C.D.   Defendant

PARTICULARS OF CLAIM

1. The Plaintiff is the freehold owner of the land and premises situate at and known as   (hereinafter referred to as "the Plaintiff's premises"). The Defendant is the freehold owner of the adjoining premises situate at and known as   (hereinafter referred to as "the Defendant's premises").

2. By an oral agreement made in or about   19   between the Plaintiff and the Defendant, the Defendant agreed to grant to the Plaintiff a small strip of land lying at the rear of the Defendant's premises of a sufficient width to enable a driveway to be constructed giving access to the rear of the Plaintiff's premises from the main road and the Plaintiff agreed to construct a wall along the new rear boundary of the Defendant's premises.

3. In pursuance of the said agreement, the Plaintiff constructed the said wall and cleared the said strip of land by removing large quantities of rubble therefrom and made up the same as a driveway.

4. The Plaintiff thereafter constructed a garage for use in connection with the said driveway and he constructed a gateway at the entrance thereto at the main road.

5. The Plaintiff used the said strip of land as a driveway and subsequently in or about   19   concreted the surface thereof and, at all material times, used and occupied the same as part and parcel of his own property.

6. The Plaintiff contends that he has acquired a permanent interest in the said strip of land by virtue of a proprietary estoppel binding on the Defendant by the Plaintiff's said works and expenditure incurred thereon, carried out in the belief that he was the owner thereof and by the act of the Defendant authorising such works and expenditure and by his knowledge that the Plaintiff was carrying out such works and incurring such expenditure in such belief as aforesaid.

7. In the premises, the Defendant holds the said strip of land on trust to give effect to the parties agreement referred to in paragraph 2 hereof.

8. On   19   , the Plaintiff wrote to the Defendant requesting that he formally acknowledge that the said strip of land belongs to the Plaintiff, but the Defendant has failed or refused to do so.

AND THE PLAINTIFF CLAIMS:

(1) A Declaration that the Plaintiff is entitled to the said strip of land absolutely by virtue of the said agreement or interest acquired by proprietary estoppel;

(2) A Declaration that the Defendant holds the said strip of land on trust to give effect to the said agreement or interest acquired by proprietary estoppel;

(3) An Order directing the Defendant to transfer the said strip of land to the Plaintiff absolutely;

(4) Further or other relief;

(5) Costs.

Dated this   day of   19   .

Form 4: Defence and Counterclaim to action for possession alleging licence for life based on proprietary estoppel. See, Rogers v. Eller and Another, May 20, 1986, unreported, C.A., available on Lexis.

IN THE   COUNTY COURT   Case No......

BETWEEN:

A.B.   Plaintiff

and

C.D.   Defendant

DEFENCE AND COUNTERCLAIM

DEFENCE

1. The Defendant admits that on or about   19   the said property was purchased by the Plaintiff and registered in his sole name but denies that he is entitled to possession of the same as alleged or at all.

2. By reason of the matters set out below, the Defendant contends that the Plaintiff is estopped and precluded from claiming possession of the said property against the Defendant.

3. In or about the time of the transfer of the said property to the Plaintiff, he assured the Defendant that, if at any time in her lifetime he left the said property, it would be hers or that, if he married and stayed in the said property, there would be enough money for her to purchase alternative accommodation.

4. On divers occasions thereafter, the Plaintiff assured the Defendant that she need never worry as she would always have a roof over her head.

5. Alternatively, the Plaintiff knowingly allowed or encouraged the Defendant to assume that she would always enjoy a right to reside in the said property.

6. In reliance on the Plaintiff's express assurances or, alternatively, upon the assumption of the Defendant allowed or encouraged by the Plaintiff, the Defendant acted to her detriment by expending money on the said property and carrying out substantial improvement works to the same over a period of many years.

PARTICULARS OF EXPENDITURE AND IMPROVEMENTS

[Set out particulars in full]

7. In or about 199 , the Plaintiff left the said property leaving the Defendant in sole occupation thereof.

COUNTERCLAIM

8. The Defendant repeats paragraphs 1 to 7 of her Defence.

9. In the premises, the Defendant contends that she is entitled to reside in the said property for her life upon such terms as the Court thinks fit.

AND THE PLAINTIFF CLAIMS:

(1) A Declaration that the Defendant is entitled to occupy the said property as an equitable licensee for life;

(2) An Order that the Defendant be permitted and is entitled to reside in the said property for her life upon such terms as the Court may, in its absolute discretion, think fit;

(3) Further or other relief;

Dated this   day of   19   .

Form 5: *Defence and Counterclaim denying mere licence to occupy and claiming equitable licence for life based on proprietary estoppel. See Stevens v. Stevens, March 3, 1989, unreported, C.A. and Bennett v. Bennett, May 18, 1990, unreported, C.A., available on Lexis.*

IN THE   COUNTY COURT   Case No......

BETWEEN:

A.B.   Plaintiff

and

C.D.   Defendant

DEFENCE AND COUNTERCLAIM

DEFENCE

1. The Defendant denies that the Plaintiff orally granted to the Defendant a revocable licence to occupy the said property without payment as alleged in paragraph 1 of the Particulars of Claim and that the same was duly terminated by the Plaintiff's letter, dated   19   , and that the Plaintiff is entitled to possession. The Defendant avers that, by reason of the matters hereinafter referred to, she has acquired an interest in the said property.

2. The Defendant avers that in or about   19   , in consideration of the Defendant taking over responsibility for the liabilities and outgoings in respect of the said property and in order to provide the Defendant and her said children with accommodation and a secure capital asset, the Plaintiff orally agreed and declared that the said property should be a permanent home for the Defendant and her said children for so long as the Defendant so wished.

3. Since about   19   , in accordance with and in reliance upon the Plaintiff's said oral agreement and declaration, the Defendant has occupied the said property together with her said children and has acted to her detriment to the knowledge of the Plaintiff by refraining from seeking alternative permanent accommodation, paying the outgoings and liabilities in respect of the said property and by carrying out substantial repairs and improvements thereat at her own expense.

PARTICULARS OF DETRIMENT

[Set out full particulars of detriment]

4. By reason of the matters aforesaid, the Plaintiff is estopped from denying that the Defendant has the right to possession and occupation of the said

property for so long as she desires to use the same as a home for herself and her said children.

COUNTERCLAIM

5.   The Defendant repeats paragraphs 1 to 4 of her Defence and Counterclaims for a Declaration as to her interest in the said property.

AND THE PLAINTIFF CLAIMS:

(1)   A Declaration that the Defendant has a licence to occupy the said property for the rest of her life;

(2)   An Order that the Defendant be permitted and is entitled to occupy the said property for the rest of her life upon such terms as the Court thinks fit.

Dated this   day of   19   .

Form 6: Order declaring that defendant has licence for life upon terms as to the payment of outgoings etc. See, Stevens v. Stevens, March 3, 1989, unreported, C.A., available on Lexis.

IN THE HIGH COURT OF JUSTICE   199.. A. No....

Chancery Division

BETWEEN:

A.B.	Plaintiff
and	
C.D.	Defendant

DEFENCE

Order that Defendant has a right to remain in possession and occupation of the property known as   for as long as she desires to use the premises as her home, upon terms that:

(a)   she indemnifies the Plaintiff in respect of all usual outgoings;

(b)   she maintains the property in a reasonable state of repair and redecoration; and

(c)   the Defendant is not entitled to call upon the Plaintiff in respect of costs of any repairs or decorative works.

Form 7: Defence to claim for transfer of fee simple based on proprietary estoppel: (See Form 1).

IN THE HIGH COURT OF JUSTICE   199.. A. No....

Chancery Division

BETWEEN:

A.B.   Plaintiff

and

C.D.   Defendant

DEFENCE

1. The Defendant admits paragraphs 1 to 4 of the Statement of Claim.

2. In regard to the statements alleged in paragraph 5 of the Statement of Claim, the Defendant denies that he ever made any such statements to the Plaintiff. The Defendant avers that he orally informed the Plaintiff that she could remain in the property temporarily only until such time as it was once again required by the Defendant for his own occupation. At no time did the Defendant suggest to the Plaintiff that the property (or its contents) had been transferred to her, as alleged or at all.

3. As to paragraph 6 of the Statement of Claim, the Defendant denies that he had any knowledge of the fact of the expenditure alleged to have been incurred by the Plaintiff at the time the same is alleged or at all prior to   19   , when, for the first time, he became aware that the Plaintiff was raising her present claims.

4. Further or in the alternative, the nature and extent of the alleged expenditure by the Plaintiff (as to which the Defendant puts the Plaintiff to strict proof) is such that she would have incurred the same if she had a mere licence to remain in occupation of the property until the same was required for occupation by the Defendant.

5. In the premises, the Defendant denies that the Plaintiff is entitled to the relief prayed for or to any relief.

Dated this   day of   19   .

INDEX